Teena Kamen

Teaching Assistant's Handbook Level 3

Supporting Teaching and Learning in Schools

HODDER EDUCATION
AN HACHETTE UK COMPANY

Orders: please contact Bookpoint Ltd, 130 Milton Park, Abingdon, Oxon OX14 4SB. Telephone: (44) 01235 827720. Fax: (44) 01235 400454. Lines are open from 9.00–5.00, Monday to Saturday, with a 24 hour message answering service. You can also order through our website www.hoddereducation.co.uk

If you have any comments to make about this, or any of our other titles,
please send them to educationenquiries@hodder.co.uk

British Library Cataloguing in Publication Data
A catalogue record for this title is available from the British Library

ISBN: 9781444121322

First Edition Published 2011
Impression number   10 9 8 7 6 5 4 3
Year   2013 2012

Hachette UK's policy is to use papers that are natural, renewable and recyclable products and made from wood grown in sustainable forests. The logging and manufacturing processes are expected to conform to the environmental regulations of the country of origin.

Cover photo © 2010 Monkey Business Images Ltd/Stockbroker/Photolibrary
Typeset by Pantek Arts Ltd, Maidstone, Kent
Printed in Dubai for Hodder Education, An Hachette UK Company,
338 Euston Road, London NW1 3BH

Contents

1. Supporting child and young person development

This chapter relates to QCF unit:

CYP Core 3.1 Understand child and young person development

Observing children's development

Accurate observations and assessments are essential to effective educational practice. Careful observations enable you and the teacher to make objective assessments relating to each pupil's: behaviour patterns; learning styles; levels of development; existing skills; curriculum strengths and weaknesses; current learning needs and learning achievements. Assessment of this information can help highlight and celebrate pupils' strengths as well as identify any gaps in their learning. This information can form the basis for the ongoing planning of appropriate learning activities; it may also be a useful starting point for future learning goals or objectives.

The purpose of observation

There are many reasons why it is important to observe pupils. For example:

- To understand the wide range of skills in all areas of their development.
- To know and understand the sequences of development.
- To use this knowledge to link theory with your own practice in the school.
- To assess development and existing skills or behaviour.
- To plan activities appropriate to individual learning needs.

You will usually be observing activities which are part of the pupil's usual routine. You can observe pupils' development, learning and behaviour in a variety of situations. For example, you might observe the following situations:

- A child talking with another child or adult.
- An adult working with a small group of children or young people.
- A child or a small group of children playing indoors or outdoors, or participating in a small or large group discussion, for example circle time.
- An adult reading/telling a story to a child or group of children.
- A child or group of children participating in a creative, literacy, mathematics or science activity, such as doing painting, writing, numeracy work or carrying out an experiment.

Issues to think through

Portfolio building
- what to include?
- how to use your portfolio

Why observe?
- developing quality practice

What to observe?
- the importance of quality observation
- meeting the requirements of the course
- recognising a suitable opportunity to observe

Pass it on?
- whom to pass it on to?
- what to pass on?
- when to pass it on?

Making assessments
- background information
- aims
- areas of development
- recommendations
- personal learning
- bibliography

Where to observe?
- working in a variety of settings

Methods of recording observations
- choosing a suitable method
- advantages and disadvantages of each method
- record keeping

How to observe?
- planning
- preparation
- aims
- front sheet
- observing
- evaluations
- presenting work
- getting work assessed

Figure 1.1: *Thinking about observing* by Jackie Harding and Liz Meldon-Smith

 **Activity!**

Write a short account explaining the importance and purpose of observing and assessing pupils' development.

The basic principles of child observation

Some important points have already been mentioned with regard to observing children's development, learning and behaviour. You also need to consider the following:

1. **Confidentiality** must be kept at all times. You must have the senior practitioner's and/or the parents' permission before making formal observations of children. (See details below.)
2. **Be objective**. You should not jump to premature conclusions. Only record what you actually see or hear not what you think or feel. For example, the statement 'The child cried ' is objective, but to say 'The child is sad' is subjective, as you do not know what the child is feeling; children can cry for a variety of reasons, for example to draw attention to themselves or to show discomfort.
3. **Remember equal opportunities**. Consider children's cultural backgrounds, for example children may be very competent at communicating in their community language, but

may have more difficulty in expressing themselves in English; this does not mean they are behind in their language development. Consider how any special needs may affect children's development, learning and/or behaviour.

4. **Be positive!** Focus on the children's strengths not just on any learning or behavioural difficulties they may have. Look at what children can do in terms of their development and/or learning and use this as the foundation for providing future activities.

5. **Use a holistic approach**. Remember to look at the 'whole' child. You need to look at all areas of children's development in relation to the particular aspect of development or learning you are focusing on.

6. **Consider the children's feelings**. Depending on the children's ages, needs and abilities, you should discuss the observation with the children to be observed and respond appropriately to their views.

7. **Minimise distractions**. Observe children without intruding or causing unnecessary stress. Try to keep your distance where possible, but be close enough to hear the children's language. Try not to interact with the children (unless it is a participant observation – see below), but if they do address you be polite and respond positively, for example explain to the children simply what you are doing and keep your answers short.

8. **Practise!** The best way to develop your skills at observing children's development, learning and behaviour is to do observations on a regular basis.

Confidentiality

The teacher and your college tutor/assessor will give you guidelines for the methods most appropriate to your role in your particular school. Your observations and assessments must be in line with the school's policy for record keeping and relevant to the routines and activities of the pupils you work with. You must follow the school's policy regarding confidentiality at all times and be able to implement data protection procedures as appropriate to your role and responsibilities. (See sections on confidentiality matters in Chapter 3 and maintaining pupil records in Chapter 10.)

The school should obtain permission from the parents or carers of the pupils being observed, for example a letter requesting permission to do regular observations and assessments could be sent out for the parents to sign giving their consent. If you are a student, before doing any tasks for your assessment involving observations of children you MUST negotiate with the class teacher when it will be possible for you to carry out your observations and have written permission to do so.

In practice

Jamie is working as a teaching assistant with pupils aged 6 to 7 years. During a learning activity, Jamie observes that one of the pupils is very quiet and withdrawn, which is unusual behaviour for this particular child. What would you do in this situation? Who would you report your concerns to?

Observation methods

When observing pupils you need to use an appropriate method of observation as directed by the teacher. When assisting the teacher in observing and reporting on a pupil's development ensure that you consider all relevant aspects of development, for example: Social; Physical; Intellectual; Communication; Emotional. These can easily be remembered using the mnemonic **SPICE**.

You may observe an individual pupil or group of pupils on several occasions on different days of the week and at different times of the day. Use developmental charts for the pupil's age group to identify areas of development where the pupil is making progress, as well as those where the pupil is underachieving. For example, a pupil with limited speech may still be developing positive social relationships with other children by using non-verbal communication during play activities.

Observations and assessments should cover all relevant aspects of development including: physical skills; language and communication skills and social and emotional behaviour during different activities. You may be able to assist the teacher to compile a portfolio of relevant information about each pupil. A portfolio could include: observations; examples of the children's work and checklists of the children's progress. Assessment of this information can help highlight and celebrate the pupil's strengths as well as identify any gaps in their learning. This information can form the basis for the ongoing planning of appropriate learning activities and be a useful starting point for future learning goals/objectives. (Information about formative and summative assessments is in Chapter 10.)

 **Activity!**

Find out what your school's policies are regarding pupil observations and assessments, confidentiality and record keeping and data protection procedures.
Keep this information in mind when doing your own observations of pupils.

Recording observations and assessments

You should record your observations and assessments using an agreed format. This might be a: written descriptive account; structured profile (with specified headings for each section) or a pre-coded system of recording. Once you have recorded your observation of the pupil (or group of pupils), you need to make an assessment of this information in relation to:

- The aims of the observation, for example why you were doing this observation.
- What you observed about the pupil's development, learning and/or behaviour in this particular activity.
- How this compares to the expected level of development for a pupil of this age.
- Any factors which may have affected the pupil's ability to learn and/or behave, such as the immediate environment, significant events, illness, pupil's cultural background or special needs.

Your assessment may include charts, diagrams and other representations of the data you collected from your observation (see examples of observation charts opposite). Your college tutor or assessor should give you guidelines on how to present your observations. Otherwise you might find the suggested format on page 6 useful:

Tick chart: *Group observations of children at snack/meal time*

Self-help skills	Children's names			
	Shafik	Sukhvinder	Ruth	Tom
goes to the toilet				
washes hands				
dries hands				
chooses own snack/meal				
uses fingers				
uses spoon				
uses fork				
uses knife				
holds cup with 2 hands				
holds cup with 1 hand				

KEY: ✓ = competent at skill.   \ = attempts skill/needs adult direction.   ✗ = no attempt/requires assistance.

Pie chart: *Time sample observation of child's play activities*

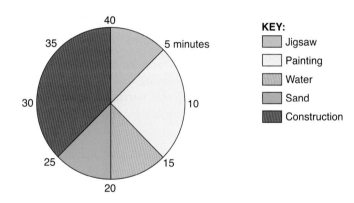

KEY:
- Jigsaw
- Painting
- Water
- Sand
- Construction

Bar graph: *Time sample observation of child's social play*

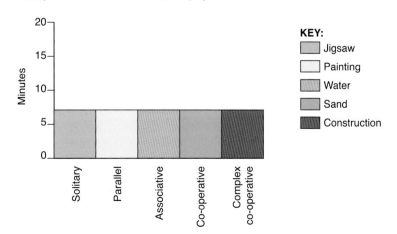

KEY:
- Jigsaw
- Painting
- Water
- Sand
- Construction

Figure 1.2: *Observation charts*

Suggested format for recording observations

Number/title of observation:
Date of observation:
Method: e.g. naturalistic, structured, snapshot, longitudinal, time sample, event sample, participant, non-participant, target child, trail or movement, checklist, coded observation or diary.
Start time:
Finish time:
Number of pupils/staff:
Permission for observation: e.g. teacher
Type of setting and age range: e.g. primary school, secondary school, special school.
Immediate context/background information: including the activity and its location.
Description of pupil(s): including age(s) in years and months.
Aims: why are you doing this particular observation?
Observation: the actual observation, e.g. free description, pie chart, bar graph or tick chart.
Assessment: include the following: ● Did you achieve your aims? ● Comparison of the pupil's development with the expected development of a pupil of this age, looking at all aspects of the pupil's development but with particular emphasis on the focus area (e.g. physical, social and emotional, or communication and intellectual skills) ● References to support your comments.
Personal learning: what you gained from doing this observation, e.g. what you have learned about this aspect of development and using this particular method of observing pupils, e.g. was this the most appropriate method of observation for this type of activity?
Recommendations: ● On how to encourage/ extend the pupil's development, learning and/or behaviour in the focus area, e.g. suggestions for activities to develop the pupil's literacy or numeracy skills. ● For any aspect of the pupil's development, learning and/or behaviour which you think requires further observation and assessment.
References/bibliography: list details of all the books used to complete your assessment.

 **Key Task**

Observe a pupil during a learning activity. Include the following information in your assessment:

- The type of learning activity observed (for example curriculum subject/area of learning).
- The intended learning goals/objectives for the pupil.
- The actual development and learning skills demonstrated by the pupil.
- The pupil's communication skills and behaviour during the activity.
- Suggestions for extending the pupil's development and learning in this area.

You could use the developmental charts in this chapter to help you with your assessment. Remember your school's guidelines for pupil observations.

NOS Links:

Level 3:   STL 18.1   STL 27.3   STL 29.1

Planning provision to promote development

As directed by the teacher, you may be involved in planning provision for the pupils you work with based on assessments of their developmental progress. You should recognise that developmental progress depends on each pupil's level of maturation and their prior experiences. You should take these into account and have realistic expectations when planning activities to promote pupils' development. This includes regularly reviewing and updating plans for individual pupils and ensuring that plans balance the needs of individual pupils and the group as appropriate to your school. You should know and understand that pupils develop at widely different rates but in broadly the same sequence. When planning provision to promote pupils' development you need to recognise that children's development is holistic even though it is divided into different areas: **S**ocial; **P**hysical; **I**ntellectual; **C**ommunication and language; **E**motional. Remember to look at the 'whole' child, you need to look at *all* areas of children's development in relation to the particular aspect of development or learning you are focusing on when planning provision to promote pupils' development.

The planning cycle

Following observations and assessments of a pupil's development, learning and/or behaviour, the recommendations can provide the basis for planning appropriate activities to encourage and extend the pupil's skills in specific areas. Effective planning is based on individual needs, abilities and interests, hence the importance of accurate and reliable child observations and assessments. You will also support the teacher in planning provision based on the requirements for the relevant curriculum frameworks.

 **key words**

Holistic: looking at the 'whole' child or young person; *all* aspects of the child or young person's development.

When planning learning activities, your overall aims should be to: support the development and learning of *all* the pupils you work with; ensure every pupil has full access to the appropriate curriculum; meet pupils' individual developmental and learning needs; and build on each pupil's existing knowledge, understanding and skills. (For detailed information on planning learning activities see Chapter 6.)

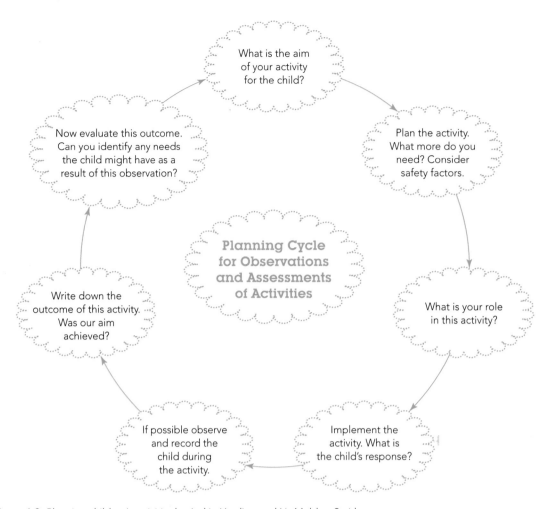

Figure 1.3: *Planning children's activities* by Jackie Harding and Liz Meldon-Smith

 **Activity!**

Describe how *you* help to plan, implement and evaluate activities to promote pupils' development in your school. Include examples of any planning sheets you use.

Implementing and evaluating plans to promote development

Good preparation and organisation are essential when implementing plans to promote pupils' development including: having any instructions and/or questions for the pupil or group of pupils ready, for example prompt cards, worksheet, work card or written on the board; ensuring sufficient materials and equipment including any specialist equipment; setting out the materials and equipment on the table ready or letting the pupils get the resources out for themselves depending on their ages and abilities. Implementing an activity may involve: giving out any instructions to the pupils; showing pupils what to do, for example demonstrating a new technique; keeping an individual pupil and/or group of pupils on task; clarifying meaning and/or ideas; explaining any difficult words to the pupils; assisting pupils with any special equipment, for example a hearing aid or a Dictaphone; providing any other appropriate assistance; encouraging the pupils to tidy up afterwards as appropriate to the ages and abilities and remembering to maintain the pupils' safety at all times.

After you have planned and/or implemented an activity you will need to evaluate it. Some evaluation also occurs during the activity, providing continuous assessment of a pupil's performance. It is important to evaluate the activity so that you can: assess whether the activity has been successful, that the aims and objectives have been met; identify possible ways in which the activity might be modified/adapted to meet the individual needs of the pupil or pupils; and provide accurate information for the teacher, SENCO or other professionals about the successfulness of a particular activity. The teacher or your college tutor/assessor should give you guidelines on how to present your activity plans. If not, you might find this suggested format useful:

Suggested format for planning activities

Title: brief description of the activity
Date and time: the date and time of the activity
Plan duration: how long will the activity last?
Aim and rationale: the main purpose of the activity including how it will encourage development, learning and/or behaviour. The rationale should outline why this particular activity has been selected (e.g. identified particular pupil's need through observation; links to topics/themes within the group, class or setting). How does the activity link with any curriculum requirements?
Staff and setting: the roles and number of staff involved in the activity plus the type of setting and the age range of the setting.
Details of the pupils(s): activity plans involving an individual pupil or small group of pupils should specify first name, age in years and months, plus any relevant special needs; activity plans involving larger groups should specify the age range and ability levels.
Learning objectives for the pupil(s): indicate what the child or children could gain from participating in the activity in each developmental area: **SPICE**.
Preparation: what do you need to prepare in advance? (e.g. selecting or making appropriate materials; checking availability of equipment) Think about the instructions and/or questions for the pupil(s); will these be spoken and/or written down, e.g. on a worksheet/card or on the board? Do you need prompt cards for instructions or questions?
Resources: what materials and equipment will you need? Where will you get them from? Are there any special requirements? Remember equal opportunities including special needs. How will you set out the necessary resources (e.g. setting out on the table ready or the pupils getting materials and equipment out for themselves)?
Organisation: where will you implement the activity? How will you organise the activity? How will you give out any instructions the pupils need? Will you work with pupils one at a time or as a group? Are there any particular safety requirements? How will you organise any tidying up after the activity? Will the pupils be encouraged to help tidy up?
Implementation: describe what happened when you implemented the activity with the pupil(s). Include any alterations to the original plan, e.g. changes in timing or resources.
Equal opportunities: indicate any multicultural aspects to the activity and any additional considerations for pupils with special needs.

Review and evaluation: review and evaluate the following:

- The aims and learning outcomes/objectives.
- The effectiveness of your preparation, organisation and implementation.
- What you learned about development and learning.
- What you learned about planning activities.
- Possible modifications for future similar activities.

References and/or bibliography: the review and evaluation may include references appropriate to development, learning and behaviour. Include a bibliography of any books used as references or for ideas when planning the activity.

 Key Task

Use your suggestions from your previous observation of a pupil during a learning activity to plan an activity to extend the pupil's skills in a specific area. After discussing your plan with the class teacher, implement and then evaluate the activity.

NOS Links:

| Level 3: | STL 18.1 | STL 23.1 | STL 23.2 | STL 23.3 | STL 24.1 | STL 24.2 |
| | STL 27.1 | STL 27.2 | STL 27.3 | STL 29.2 | | |

Understanding child and young person development

When supporting child and young person development, it is essential to always look at the 'whole' child or young person. This means looking at *all* areas of their development in relation to the particular aspect of development or learning you are focusing on. We therefore refer to child and young person development as holistic with each area being interconnected. For example, when observing a pupil's writing skills as well as looking at their intellectual development you will need to consider the pupil's:

- Physical development (fine motor skills when using a pencil or pen).
- Language development and communication skills (vocabulary and structure of language used during their writing).
- Social and emotional development (interaction with others and behaviour during the writing activity).

The basic patterns of child and young person development

It is more accurate to think in terms of sequences of children and young people's development rather than stages of development. This is because stages refer to development that occurs at *fixed ages* while sequences indicates development that follows the same basic pattern *but not necessarily at fixed ages*. You should really use the term 'sequences' when referring to all aspects of development. However, the work of people such as Mary Sheridan provides a useful guide to the milestones of *expected* development, that is, the usual patterns of development or norms. As well as their chronological age, children and young people's development is affected by many other factors, for example maturation, social interaction, play opportunities, early learning experiences and special needs. The developmental charts below *do* indicate specific ages, but only to provide a framework to help you understand the basic patterns of development. *Always remember that all children and young people are unique individuals and develop at their own rate.*

 Activity!

- What are the principles of child and young person development?
- Describe the basic patterns of development.

The sequences of development 0 to 16 years

The sequence of children's development for each age range is divided into five different aspects:

* **S**ocial * **P**hysical * **I**ntellectual * **C**ommunication and language * **E**motional.

The sequence of children's development: 0 to 3 months

Social development

- Cries to communicate needs to others; stops crying to listen to others.
- Responds to smiles from others; responds positively to others, e.g. family members and even friendly strangers unless very upset (when only main caregiver will do!).
- Considers others only in relation to satisfying own needs for food, drink, warmth, sleep, comfort and reassurance.

Physical development

- Sleeps much of the time and grows fast.
- Tries to lift head.
- Starts to kick legs with movements gradually becoming smoother.
- Starts to wave arms about.
- Begins to hold objects when placed in hand, e.g. an appropriate size/shaped rattle.
- Grasp reflex diminishes as hand and eye coordination begins to develop.
- Enjoys finger play, e.g. simple finger rhymes.
- Becomes more alert when awake.
- Learns to roll from side on to back.
- Sees best at distance of 25 cm then gradually starts watching objects further away.
- Needs opportunities to play and exercise, e.g. soft toys, cloth books and play-mat with different textures and sounds.

Intellectual development

- Recognises parents; concentrates on familiar voices rather than unfamiliar ones.
- Aware of different smells.
- Explores by putting objects in mouth.
- Observes objects that move; responds to bright colours and bold images.
- Stores and recalls information through images.
- Sees everything in relation to self (is egocentric).

Physical development

- Is now very mobile e.g. crawls, bottom-shuffles, cruises, walks.
- Starts to go upstairs (with supervision) but has difficulty coming down.
- Needs safe environment in which to explore as becomes increasingly mobile, e.g. remember safety gates on stairs, etc.
- Throws toys deliberately.
- Watches ball rolling towards self and tries to push it back.
- Has mature pincer grasp and can scribble with crayons.
- Points to objects using index finger.
- Places one (or more) bricks on top of each other to make a small tower.
- Holds a cup and tries to feed self.
- Continues to enjoy finger rhymes plus action songs.
- Needs space, materials and opportunities to play alongside other children.

Intellectual development

- Explores immediate environment using senses, especially sight and touch; has no sense of danger.
- Concentrates more, due to curiosity and increased physical skills, but still has short attention span.
- Follows one-step instructions and/or gestured commands.
- Observes other people closely and tries to imitate their actions.
- Uses 'trial and error' methods when playing with bricks, containers.
- Searches for hidden or dropped objects (aware of object permanence).
- Learns that objects can be grouped together.
- Continues to store and recall information through images.
- Is still egocentric.

Communication and Language Development

- Continues to imitate sounds; starts jargoning, e.g. joins up syllables so more like 'sentences' such as 'Maama-baaba-daa'.
- Learns to say first real words, usually the names of animals and everyday things.
- Uses gestures to emphasise word meanings.
- Uses vocabulary of between 3 and 20 words.
- Participates in simple finger rhymes; continues to enjoy books.
- Over-extends words, that is, uses same word to identify similar objects, e.g. *all* round objects are called 'ball'.

Emotional development

- Likes to get own way; gets very angry when adult says 'No!'.
- Has emotional outbursts ('temper tantrums') when does not get own way or is otherwise frustrated, e.g. unable to do activity because of physical limitations.
- Shows fear in new situations, e.g. attending parent/toddler group, visiting somewhere new such as the farm or nature centre.
- Relies on parent/carer for reassurance and support in new situations.
- Is upset by the distress of other children (even if they caused it).
- Seeks reassurance and contact with familiar adults throughout waking hours.

The sequence of children's development: 18 months to 2 years

Social development

- Responds positively to others, e.g. plays alongside other children and enjoys games with known adults.
- Communicates more effectively with others; responds to simple instructions.
- Wants to help adults and enjoys imitating their activities.
- May be interested in older children and their activities; imitates these activities.
- May unintentionally disrupt the play of others, e.g. takes toys away to play with by self.
- Becomes very independent, e.g. wants to do things by self.
- Still demonstrates egocentric behaviour; wants own way and says "No!" a lot.

Physical development

- Starts using potty but has difficulty keeping dry.
- Can feed self.
- Walks well and tries to run but has difficulty stopping.
- Comes downstairs on front with help.
- Learns to push a pedal-less tricycle or sit-and-ride toy with feet.
- Tries to throw ball but has difficulty catching.
- Bends down to pick things up.
- Uses several bricks to make a tower.
- As fine motor skills improve continues to scribble and can do very simple jigsaw puzzles.
- Enjoys action songs and rhymes.
- Needs space, materials and opportunities to play alongside other children.

Intellectual development

- Recognises objects from pictures and books.
- Points to desired objects; selects named objects.
- Matches basic colours; starts to match shapes.
- Does very simple puzzles.
- Follows one-step instructions.
- Concentrates for longer, e.g. searching for hidden object, but attention span still quite short.
- Shows lots of curiosity and continues exploring using senses and 'trial and error' methods.
- Processes information through images and increasingly through language too.
- Shows preferences and starts to make choices.
- Is still egocentric.

Communication and language development

- Uses language to gain information, e.g. starts asking 'What dat?'.
- Repeats words said by adults.
- Acquires 1–3 words per month; by 2 years has vocabulary of about 200 words.
- Participates in action songs and nursery rhymes; continues to enjoy books and stories.
- Uses *telegraphic speech*, e.g. speaks in 2–3 word sentences such as 'Daddy go' or 'Milk all gone'.

Emotional development

- Begins to disengage from secure attachment, e.g. wants to do things by self 'Me do it!'.
- Still emotionally dependent on familiar adult(s) but this leads to conflict as need for independence grows.
- Has mood swings, e.g. clingy one moment, then fiercely independent the next.
- Becomes very frustrated when unable/not allowed to do a particular activity which leads to frequent but short-lived emotional outbursts ('temper tantrums').
- Explores environment; even new situations are less frightening as long as parent/carer is present.

The sequence of children's development: 2 to 3 years

Social development

- Continues to enjoy the company of others.
- Wants to please and seeks approval from adults.
- Is still very egocentric and very protective of own possessions; unable to share with other children although may give toy to another child if *adult* requests it to please the adult.
- May find group experiences difficult due to this egocentric behaviour.
- Uses language more effectively to communicate with others.

Physical development

- Uses potty and stays dry more reliably
- Comes downstairs in upright position one stair at a time.
- Starts to climb well on play apparatus.
- Kicks a ball, learns to jump and may learn to somersault.
- Learns to pedal a tricycle.
- Can undress self; tries to dress self but needs help especially with socks and fastenings.
- Fine motor skills improving: has increased control of crayons and paintbrush; tries to use scissors.
- Enjoys construction activities and can build more complex structures.
- Continues to enjoy action songs and rhymes.
- Needs space, materials and opportunities to play alongside and with other children.

Intellectual development

- Identifies facial features and main body parts.
- Continues to imitate other children and adults.
- Follows two-step instructions.
- Matches more colours and shapes including puzzles and other matching activities.
- Points to named object in pictures and books.
- Develops understanding of big and small.
- Begins to understand concept of time at basic level, e.g. before/after, today/tomorrow.
- Enjoys imaginative play; able to use symbols in play, e.g. pretend a doll is a real baby.
- Concentrates on intricate tasks such as creative activities or construction, but may still have short attention span especially if not really interested in the activity.
- Is very pre-occupied with own activities; still egocentric.
- Shows some awareness of right and wrong.
- Processes information through language rather than images.

Communication and language development

- Has vocabulary of about 300 words.
- Uses more adult forms of speech, e.g. sentences now include words like that, this, here, there, then, but, and.
- Can name main body parts.
- Uses adjectives, e.g. big, small, tall; words referring to relationships, e.g. I, my, you, yours.
- Asks questions to gain more information.
- Sings songs and rhymes; continues to participate in action songs and enjoy books/stories.
- Can deliver simple messages.

Emotional development

- May still rely on parent/carer for reassurance in new situations or when with strangers.
- Still experiences emotional outbursts as independence grows and frustration at own limitations continues, e.g. aggressive towards toys that cannot get to work.
- Begins to understand the feelings of others but own feelings are still the most important.
- Has very limited understanding of other people's pain, e.g. if hits another child.
- Feels curious about their environment but has no sense of danger, e.g. that they or other people can be hurt by their actions.

The sequence of children's development: 3 to 5 years

Social development

- Enjoys the company of others; learns to play *with* other children, not just alongside them.
- Uses language to communicate more and more effectively with others.
- Develops self-help skills (e.g. dressing self, going to the toilet) as becomes more competent and confident in own abilities.
- Still wants to please and seeks approval from adults.
- Observes closely how others behave and imitates them.
- Still fairly egocentric; may get angry with other children if they disrupt play activities or snatch play items required for own play; expects adults to take *their* side in any dispute.
- Gradually is able to share group possessions at playgroup or nursery.

Physical development

- Usually clean and dry but may have occasional 'accidents'.
- Able to run well – and stop!
- Competent at gross motor skills such as jumping, riding a tricycle, climbing play apparatus, using a swing.
- Throws and catches a ball but is still inaccurate.
- Fine motor skills continue to improve, e.g. can use scissors.
- Continues to enjoy action songs plus simple singing and dancing games.
- Needs space, materials and opportunities to play cooperatively with other children.

Intellectual development

- Learns about basic concepts through play.
- Experiments with colour, shape and texture.
- Recalls a simple sequence of events.
- Follows two or three-step instructions including positional ones, e.g. 'Please put your ball in the box under the table'.
- Continues to enjoy imaginative and creative play.
- Interested in more complex construction activities.
- Concentrates on more complex activities as attention span increases.
- Plays cooperatively with other children; able to accept and share ideas in group activities.
- Shows some awareness of right and wrong, the needs of others.
- Holds strong opinions about likes and dislikes.
- Processes information using language.

Communication and language development

- Has vocabulary of between 900 and 1500 words.
- Asks lots of questions.
- Uses language to ask for assistance.
- Talks constantly to people known well.
- Gives very simple accounts of past events.
- Can say names of colours.
- Begins to vocalise ideas.
- Continues to enjoy books, stories, songs and rhymes.
- Listens to and can follow simple instructions; can deliver verbal messages.

Emotional development

- Less reliant on parent/carer for reassurance in new situations.
- May be jealous of adult attention given to younger sibling or other children in a group.
- Argues with other children but is quick to forgive and forget.
- Has limited awareness of the feelings and needs of others.
- May be quite caring towards others who are distressed.
- Begins to use language to express feelings and wishes.
- Still has emotional outbursts especially when tired, stressed or frustrated.

The sequence of children's development: 5 to 7 years

Social development

- Enjoys the company of other children; may have special friend(s).
- Uses language even more effectively to communicate, share ideas, engage in more complex play activities.
- Appears confident and competent in own abilities.
- Cooperates with others, takes turns and begins to follow rules in games.
- Seeks adult approval; will even blame others for own mistakes to escape disapproval.
- Observes how others behave and will imitate them; has a particular role model.
- May copy unwanted behaviour, e.g. swearing, biting or kicking to gain adult attention.

Physical development

- Clean and dry but may still have occasional 'accidents' if absorbed in an activity or upset.
- Can dress/undress self but may still need help with intricate fastenings and shoelaces.
- Has improved gross motor skills and coordination so is more proficient at running, jumping, climbing and balancing but may have some difficulty with hopping and skipping.
- Has improved ball skills, but still learning to use a bat.
- May learn to ride a bicycle (with stabilisers).
- Enjoys swimming activities.
- Fine motor skills continue to improve: has better pencil/crayon control; is more competent at handling materials and making things.
- Continues to enjoy action songs plus singing and dancing games.
- Needs space, materials and opportunities to play cooperatively with other children.

Intellectual development

- Is very curious and asks lots of questions.
- Continues to enjoy imaginative and creative play activities.
- Continues to enjoy construction activities; spatial awareness increases.
- Knows, matches and names colours and shapes.
- Follows three-step instructions.
- Develops interest in reading for themselves.
- Enjoys jigsaw puzzles and games.
- Concentrates for longer, e.g. television programmes, longer stories and can recall details.
- Shows awareness of right and wrong, the needs of others.
- Begins to see other people's points of view.
- Stores and recalls more complex information using language.

Communication and language development

- May use vocabulary of about 1500 to 4000 words.
- Uses more complex sentence structures.
- Asks even more questions using what, when, who, where, how and especially why!
- Develops early reading and writing skills.
- Continues to enjoy books, stories and poetry; by age 7 can recall the story so far if book read a chapter at a time.
- Shows interest in more complex books and stories; continues to enjoy songs and rhymes.
- Gives more detailed accounts of past events.
- Vocalises ideas and feelings.
- Can listen to and follow more detailed instructions; can deliver more complex verbal messages.

Emotional development

- Becomes more aware of the feelings and needs of others.
- Tries to comfort others who are upset, hurt or unwell.
- May occasionally be aggressive as still learning to deal with negative emotions.
- Uses language to express feelings and wishes.
- Uses imaginative play to express worries and fears over past or future experiences, e.g. hospital visits, family disputes, domestic upheaval.
- Has occasional emotional outbursts when tired, stressed or frustrated.
- Argues with other children but may take longer to forgive and forget.
- Confidence in self can be shaken by 'failure'.
- May have an 'imaginary friend'.

The sequence of children's development: 7 to 12 years

Social development

- Enjoys company of other children; wants to belong to group; has at least one special friend.
- Uses language to communicate very effectively, but may use in negative ways, e.g. name-calling or telling tales, as well as positively to share ideas and participate in complex play activities often based on television characters or computer games.
- Is able to play on own; appreciates own space away from others on occasion.
- Becomes less concerned with adult approval and more concerned with *peer* approval.
- Is able to participate in games with rules and other cooperative activities.

Physical development

- Can dress/undress self including fastenings and shoelaces.
- Grows taller and thinner; starts losing baby teeth.
- Improved gross motor skills and coordination leads to proficiency in climbing, running, jumping, balancing, hopping and skipping.
- Can hit a ball with a bat.
- Learns to ride a bicycle (without stabilisers).
- Learns to swim (if taught properly).
- As fine motor skills improve, handwriting becomes easier and more legible.
- Can do more complex construction activities.
- Continues to enjoy singing and dancing games.
- Needs space, materials and opportunities to play cooperatively with other children.

Intellectual development

- Learns to read more complex texts and continues to develop writing skills.
- Enjoys number work, but may still need real objects to help mathematical processes.
- Enjoys experimenting with materials and exploring the environment.
- Develops creative abilities as coordination improves, e.g. more detailed drawings.
- Begins to know the difference between real and imaginary, but still enjoys imaginative play.
- Interested in more complex construction activities.
- Has longer attention span; does not like to be disturbed during play activities.
- Follows increasingly complex instructions.
- Enjoys board games and other games with rules; also computer games.
- Develops a competitive streak.
- Has increased awareness of right and wrong, the needs of others.
- Sees other people's points of view.
- Seeks information from various sources, e.g. encyclopaedia, internet.
- Processes expanding knowledge and information through language.

Communication and language development

- Has extensive vocabulary of between 4000 and 10,000 words.
- Uses more complex sentence structures.
- Develops more complex reading and writing skills including improved comprehension, more accurate spelling, punctuation and joined-up writing.
- Continues to enjoy books, stories and poetry.
- Gives very detailed accounts of past events and can anticipate *future* events.
- Vocalises ideas and feelings in more depth.
- Listens to and follows more complex instructions.
- Appreciates jokes due to more sophisticated language knowledge.
- Uses literacy skills to communicate and to access information, e.g. story and letter writing, use of dictionaries, encyclopaedia, computers, internet, email.

Emotional development

- Becomes less egocentric as understands feelings, needs and rights of others.
- Still wants things that belong solely to them, e.g. very possessive of own toys.
- Becomes more aware of own achievements in relation to others but this can lead to a sense of failure if feels does not measure up; hates to lose.
- May be very competitive; rivalry may lead to aggressive behaviour.
- Argues with other children but may take even longer to forgive and forget.
- Aware of wider environment, e.g. weather, plants, animals, and people in other countries.

The sequence of children's development: 12 to 16 years

Social development

- Continues to enjoy the company of other children/young people; individual friendships are still important; belonging to group or gang becomes increasingly important.
- The desire for peer approval can overtake the need for adult approval and may cause challenges to adult authority at home, school or in the setting particularly in teenage years.
- Participates in team games/sports or other group activities including clubs and hobbies.
- May be strongly influenced by role models in media, e.g. sports celebrities, film/pop stars.
- Communicates effectively and uses language to resolve difficulties in social interactions.
- Can be very supportive towards others experiencing difficulties at home or school, etc.

Physical development

- Can dress/undress self including intricate fastenings and shoelaces.
- Grows taller and thinner; continues losing baby teeth, physical changes of puberty.
- Enjoys team games and sports.
- Rides a bicycle with competence and confidence.
- Improved fine motor skills makes handwriting easier and more legible.
- Can do more complex construction activities.
- Enjoys singing and dancing but performs set dance routines instead of dancing games.
- Needs space, materials and opportunities to play cooperatively with other children.

Intellectual development

- Reads more complex texts with improved comprehension and extends writing skills.
- Understands more abstract mathematical/scientific processes, e.g. algebra, physics.
- Develops more creative abilities, e.g. very detailed drawings and stories.
- Knows the difference between real and imaginary.
- Has increased concentration levels and continues to follow more complex instructions.
- Continues to enjoy board games and computer games which require strategy skills.
- Has well-defined understanding of right and wrong; can consider the needs of others.
- Sees other people's point of view.
- Continues to seek information from various sources, e.g. encyclopaedia, internet.
- Continues to process increasing knowledge and information through language.

Communication and language development

- Has an extensive and varied vocabulary of between 10,000 and 20,000 words.
- Uses appropriate language styles for different occasions, e.g. standard English.
- Has more complex reading skills including detailed comprehension skills.
- Writing skills include accurate spelling and punctuation; neat and legible joined-up writing.
- Can use different writing styles including word-processing on a computer.
- Continues to enjoy more complex texts including fiction, poetry and factual books.
- Gives very detailed accounts of past events using varied expression and vocabulary.
- Can anticipate future events *and* give detailed reasons for possible outcomes.
- Vocalises ideas and feelings in greater depth including justifying own views and opinions.
- Listens to and follows complex sets of instructions; appreciates complex jokes/word play.
- Continues to use literacy skills to communicate and to access information, e.g. taking notes, writing essays/letters; using dictionaries/thesaurus, encyclopaedia; computers, internet, email.

Emotional development

- Sensitive to own feelings and those of others with a growing understanding of the possible causes for why people feel and act as they do.
- Emotional changes due to puberty.
- Understands issues relating to fairness and justice.
- Can anticipate people's reactions and consider the consequences of own actions.
- Is increasingly able to see different viewpoints to resolve difficulties in relationships.
- Has confidence in own skills/ideas; able to be assertive rather than aggressive or passive.
- May have very strong opinions or beliefs, leading to arguments with adults and peers; may hold grudges and find it difficult to forgive or forget.
- Has more understanding of complex issues, e.g. ethics, philosophy, religion, politics.

 **Activity!**

- Describe the different aspects of development (SPICE).
- Outline the sequences of development for the age group you currently work with.

Supporting social development

Children and young people's social development involves developing social skills such as: demonstrating acceptable behaviour patterns including self-control and discipline; developing independence including self-help skills, for example feeding, toileting, dressing, etc; showing awareness of self in relation to others; developing positive relationships with others; understanding the needs and rights of others; developing moral concepts, for example understanding the difference between right and wrong and making decisions based on individual morality.

The socialisation process

Socialisation determines how children relate socially and emotionally to others. Children need to learn how to deal appropriately with a range of people, situations and emotions. (See section on supporting pupils in developing relationships in Chapter 3.) An essential aspect of

 **key words**

Socialisation: how children relate socially and emotionally to other people.

socialisation is encouraging children to behave in socially acceptable ways without damaging their self-esteem. That is, rejecting the children's unacceptable behaviour not the children themselves. Socialisation begins from birth as babies interact with the people around them and respond to their environment. Babies develop an awareness of others in relation to themselves, for example people who fulfil their needs for food and drink, warmth and shelter, rest and sleep, physical comfort and entertainment.

Developing independence

Children need the freedom to develop their independence in ways that are appropriate to their overall development. Some children may need more encouragement than others to become increasingly independent and less reliant on other people. Children gain independence by:

 **Key Task**

- Plan a play activity which encourages or extends a pupil's social development. For example, encouraging the pupil to use a variety of social skills such as: demonstrating positive behaviour; being independent (using self-help skills or making choices); using effective communication skills; sharing resources; or understanding the needs and feelings of others.
- Use the assessment from your previous observation of a pupil's social development as the basis for your planning.
- Consider how you could meet the needs of a pupil with behavioural difficulties with this activity (see Chapter 13).
- If possible, ask the class teacher for permission to implement the activity. Evaluate the activity afterwards.

NOS Links:

Level 3:   STL 18.1   STL 18.2   STL 23.1   STL 23.2   STL 23.3   STL 24.1
            STL 24.2   STL 27.1   STL 27.2   STL 27.3   STL 29.2   STL 37.1   STL 38.2

Supporting physical development

As young children grow they go through striking changes in body shape and features from helpless baby to wobbly toddler to physically competent 4 year old. At birth a baby's head accounts for about 25 per cent of the full body length. During childhood a child's head grows the least compared to the growth of the rest of the body. By adulthood the head is about 12 per cent of body. After the changes of early childhood, the next major changes occur in puberty as girls start becoming mature females and boys start becoming mature males (Lindon, 2007).

As children grow up, their bodies are affected by what they eat and drink as well as how bodies are used. Imbalanced diets and inappropriate exercise all affect children's physical development. Healthy eating and exercise habits should be established in childhood which can then be maintained into adulthood (Lindon, 2007).

As well as growth, physical development also involves children's increasing ability to perform more complex physical activities involving gross motor skills, fine motor skills and coordination.

Developing gross motor skills

Gross motor skills involve whole body movements. Examples of gross motor skills include walking, running, climbing stairs, hopping, jumping, skipping, cycling, swimming, climbing play apparatus, playing badminton, basketball, football, hockey, netball, rugby or tennis. Children need strength, stamina and suppleness to become proficient in activities involving gross motor skills.

Developing fine motor skills

Fine motor skills involve whole hand movements, wrist action or delicate procedures using the fingers, for example the palmar grasp (grabbing and holding a small brick), the pincer grip (using the thumb and index finger to pick up a pea), tripod grasp (holding a crayon, pencil or pen). Examples of fine motor skills include drawing, painting, writing, model-making, playing with wooden/plastic bricks or construction kits, cutting with scissors, doing/undoing buttons, shoelaces and other fastenings. Children need good concentration levels and hand–eye coordination (see below) to become proficient in activities involving fine motor skills.

Developing coordination

Coordination involves hand–eye coordination, whole body coordination and balance. Examples of hand–eye coordination include drawing, painting, using scissors, writing and threading beads. Examples of whole body coordination include crawling, walking, cycling, swimming and playing football or netball. Examples of balance include hopping and gymnastics. Coordination plays an important part in developing children's gross and fine motor skills. Coordination and balance are needed to improve children's gross motor skills.

You should provide appropriate play and learning activities for children to develop their physical skills. Remember that some children may be limited in their physical abilities due to physical disability, sensory impairment or other special needs.

Developing physical skills through activities and routines

Children need opportunities for both indoor and outdoor activities to: practise physical skills and develop competence; develop balance, skills and coordination of large muscles; support fine motor skills; develop hand–eye coordination. Physical activities that can help children develop their gross motor skills, fine motor skills and coordination include: indoor play opportunities such as sand/water play, drawing and painting, play dough, pretend play; outdoor play opportunities including larger play apparatus; jigsaw puzzles and construction materials; ball games; action songs and movement sessions; swimming and outings to local parks and playgrounds. Routines to help children develop their fine motor skills and hand–eye coordination include: dealing with fastenings and shoelaces; using a cup; using a spoon, fork or knife; helping prepare or serve food and helping to set out and/or clear away play and learning equipment.

Children involved in physical activities should wear appropriate clothing for their comfort and safety such as: comfortable, loose clothing; appropriate footwear, for example pumps or trainers for ball games, bare feet for movement sessions; no belts, ties or scarves when using play apparatus, for example climbing equipment; and waterproof aprons for sand, water or painting activities. Adults should ensure that children are given 'warm up' opportunities, for example appropriate stretching exercises such as 'Pretend you are waking up in the morning, yawn and stretch your arms out as high as you can'. Remember 'wind down' opportunities afterwards, for example a big stretch then curling up as small as a mouse or lying down with eyes closed and imagining they are on the beach listening to the sea.

During physical activities and routines children should be encouraged to extend their range and level of skills and be rewarded for their efforts and achievements. Activities should be inclusive and available to all children; adults may need to adapt plans as necessary to meet individual needs (see information on supporting pupils with sensory and/or physical needs in Chapter 13). In addition, adults should adequately assess risk, in line with organisational policy, without limiting opportunities to extend and challenge children's skills and experience. (See section on maintaining health and safety in Chapter 5.) As well as space to move freely (and safely) while playing both indoors and outdoors, children also need space to rest and recover from physical exercise such as quiet corners to look at attractive books or engage in imaginative play.

Figure 1.5: *Playing on a swing*

Key Task

Observe a pupil involved in a physical activity, e.g. indoor movement session or outdoor play. Focus on the physical skills demonstrated by the pupil. In your assessment comment on:

- The pupil's gross motor skills.
- The pupil's fine motor skills.
- The pupil's coordination skills.
- The pupil's ability to cooperate and/or take turns.
- The role of the adult in promoting the pupil's physical development.
- Suggestions for further activities to encourage or extend the pupil's physical development.

NOS Links:

Level 3:   STL 18.1   STL 27.3   STL 29.1

The teaching assistant's role in promoting children's physical development

As a teaching assistant, you should support the teacher in promoting children's physical development and physical well-being by providing routines and activities appropriate to the children's ages and levels of development. You should provide opportunities for fresh air and exercise including outdoor play and outings. You must also protect the children from infection and injury by, for example, recognising symptoms of common childhood illnesses, handling emergency situations and administering first aid (see Chapter 5).

Five ways to promote children's physical development

You can help to promote children's physical development by:

1. **Providing play opportunities for children to explore and experiment** with their gross motor skills both indoors and outdoors, with and without play apparatus or other equipment. Helping children to practise fine motor skills (with, for example, bricks, jigsaws, play dough, sand, construction kits, drawing) and to develop body awareness through action songs such as 'Head, shoulders, knees and toes'.

2. **Maintaining the children's safety** by supervising the children at all times and checking any equipment used meets required safety standards and is positioned on an appropriate surface. Ensure the children know how to use any equipment correctly and safely.

3. **Selecting activities, tools and materials** that are appropriate to the ages and levels of development of the children to help the children practise their physical skills. Encourage children to persevere with tackling new skills that are particularly difficult and praising the children as they become competent in each physical skill.

4. **Using everyday routines** to develop the children's fine motor skills, such as getting dressed, dealing with fastenings and shoelaces, using a cup, using a spoon, fork or knife, helping prepare or serve food, setting the table, washing up. (Remember safety.)

5. **Allowing the children to be as independent as possible** when developing their physical skills, including adapting activities and/or using specialist equipment for children with special needs to enable their participation in physical activities as appropriate.

 Key Task

- Plan an activity which encourages or extends a pupil's physical development. For example, encouraging the pupil to use a variety of physical skills such as: extending the range and level of gross motor skills, fine motor skills and/or coordination skills.
- Use the assessment information from your previous observation of a pupil's physical skills as the basis for your planning.
- Consider how you could meet the needs of a pupil with physical disabilities with this activity (see Chapter 13).
- If possible, ask the class teacher for permission to implement the activity. Evaluate the activity afterwards.

NOS Links:

Level 3:	STL 18.1	STL 18.2	STL 23.1	STL 23.2	STL 23.3	STL 24.1
	STL 24.2	STL 27.1	STL 27.2	STL 27.3	STL 29.2	STL 38.2

Supporting intellectual development

Intellectual development involves the processes of gaining, storing, recalling and using information. To develop as healthy, considerate and intelligent human beings, all children require intellectual stimulation as well as physical care and emotional security. Children are constantly thinking and learning, gathering new information and formulating new ideas about themselves, other people and the world around them. The inter-related components of intellectual development are: sensory perception; thinking; language; problem-solving; concepts; memory; concentration; imagination and creativity.

Developing sensory perception

Sensory perception involves the ability to use our senses to identify the differences between objects or sounds. There are two types of sensory perception: auditory perception – differentiating between sounds; and visual perception – differentiating between objects or the distance between objects.

Research shows that babies are born with a wide range of sensory skills and perceptual abilities which enable them to explore their environment in a variety of ways. Children use their senses (hearing, sight, touch, sound, taste and smell) to: explore objects and the environment; investigate and participate in new experiences; develop new skills and abilities and discover how things work in the world around them.

Babies' responses initially consist of automatic reflexes such as grasping and sucking. Within a few months babies are able to explore objects in more purposeful and controlled ways. Gradually children use different strategies for exploring their environment as they mature, gain more experience and develop their physical skills. The more opportunities children have to explore, the more they will develop their sensory perception. As their senses develop, children begin to *make sense* of the world around them as they perceive and process information in their environment.

Developing thinking skills

Thinking can be defined as the intellectual process of using information to find solutions. We cannot see a person's thoughts because the thinking process is internal. We can see the process and progress of a person's thinking through their actions and communications. Children can develop their thinking skills through a wide range of learning activities including: problem-solving in mathematics; investigating and hypothesising in science and identifying and solving design needs in technology.

The Austrian physician Sigmund Freud believed that very early childhood experiences are responsible for how people think and feel in later life. Depending on these experiences, people are either well or poorly adjusted to their everyday lives. Freud considered that most of our thinking is done on a *sub-conscious* level and is therefore beyond our control. More recently psychologists, such as Carl Rogers, have suggested that most of our thinking is *conscious* and that individuals *are* in control of their own lives.

Jean Piaget was a Swiss biologist who used observations of his own children, plus a wider sample of children, to develop his theories of cognitive development. He believed that children went through different stages of cognitive development based on fixed ages. Piaget believed that children's thinking is an active process rather than one of passive absorption of information.

The Russian psychologist L.S. Vygotsky argued that the social interaction between children and other people enables children to develop the intellectual skills necessary for thinking and logical reasoning. Language is the key to this social interaction. Through language and communication children learn to think about their world and modify their actions accordingly. Vygotsky and also the American psychologist Jerome Bruner viewed adults as supporting children's cognitive development within an appropriate framework. (There is more detailed information about how children think and learn in Chapter 6.)

Developing language skills

Language is an essential component of intellectual development as it enables children to: make sense of the world around them; access new experiences and store new information; make better connections between existing and new information; develop understanding of concepts (see below); communicate more effectively with others, for example ask appropriate questions; verbalise their thoughts and express their opinions and ideas. Language has such a key role to play in children's overall development that it is dealt with separately – see below. (See detailed information about speech, language and communication in Chapter 11 and the section on developing literacy skills in Chapter 12.)

Developing problem-solving skills

Problem-solving involves: using the intellectual processes of logic and reasoning to make personal judgements and making connections between existing information and new information. Children use their existing knowledge and past experiences to solve problems. Children often supplement their lack of knowledge or experience by experimenting, i.e. using a process of trial and error. Making mistakes is part of the learning process. By using logic, children can make reasonable assumptions or predictions about what might happen in a particular situation or to a particular object. Logical thinking and problem-solving skills are essential to making mathematical calculations and scientific discoveries. Children need lots of opportunities to develop these scientific skills: observation; investigation; prediction; hypothesising and recording data.

As a teaching assistant you need to help provide activities at the appropriate level for the children's intellectual development. There should be a balance between encouraging children to develop their own problem-solving skills through play with minimal adult intervention *and* complying with the relevant curriculum requirements. (See section on developing numeracy skills in Chapter 12.)

Developing an understanding of concepts

Concepts are the ways in which people make sense of and organise the information in the world around them. Concepts can be divided into two categories: concrete and abstract (see below). Mathematics and science rely on the ability to understand abstract ideas. For young children this means developing a sound knowledge and understanding of concrete concepts first, such as: number; weighing and measuring; volume and capacity; shape; colour; space; textures; growth and physical forces. Experiences with real objects enable young children to develop problem-solving skills and to acquire an understanding of these concepts.

Some concepts require the understanding of other concepts beforehand, for example understanding number and counting comes before addition; understanding addition comes before multiplication. Young children take longer to understand abstract concepts, but this depends on their individual learning experiences. For example, many children

key words

Cognitive: intellectual abilities involving processing information received through the senses.

Concepts: the ways people make sense of and organise information in the world around them.

Problem-solving: activities which involve finding solutions to a difficulty or question.

do understand some moral concepts such as ideas concerning fairness and the rights of people (and animals) to live in freedom if these concepts are linked with *real* events.

Concrete concepts include:

- **Mathematical concepts** including: sorting and counting; matching objects; understanding and using number; number/numeral recognition and formation; number patterns; number operations (addition, subtraction, multiplication, division); shape and colour recognition; weighing and measuring and volume and capacity.
- **Scientific concepts** including: object permanence (understanding that when an object is out of sight it still exists); texture (exploring the tactile qualities of objects); living and growing (understanding the processes of humans, animals, plants); physical forces (understanding the changing properties of materials, for example water can be steam or ice as well as liquid).
- **Positional relationships** including: inside and outside; over and under; same and different; near and far; and high and low.

Abstract concepts include:

- **Moral concepts** including: understanding the difference between right and wrong; making decisions based on individual morality. (For more information see section on moral concepts in section on social development.)
- **The concept of time** including: understanding the sequence of events and the passage of time; knowledge and awareness of: today, tomorrow, yesterday; times of the day (morning, afternoon, evening, night); days of the week, months and seasons; *before* and *after*; *next* – next week, next month, next year; telling the time.
- **Higher number operations** including: understanding and using numbers *without* real objects, for example mental arithmetic, calculations (addition, subtraction, division and multiplication); knowing the times-tables by heart; understanding and using more complex number operations such as algebra and physics.

Developing memory skills

Memory involves the ability to recall or retrieve information stored in the mind. The other intellectual processes would be of little use to children without effective memory skills. Memory skills involve: recalling information about past experiences, events, actions or feelings; recognising information and making connections with previous experiences; and predicting, using past information to anticipate future events. Many intellectual processes involve all three of these memory skills, such as the problem-solving in mathematics and science or the decoding and comprehension skills needed for reading.

A person's mind is like a computer which stores information using a system of files to link different pieces of information together. Relating new information to existing information through this system makes it easier to access and use information. Information is stored in the short-term (or working) memory for about 10–20 seconds; from there the information is either forgotten or is passed on to the long-term memory, where it is linked to existing stored information and 'filed' for future reference. Information is more likely to be stored and remembered if it is repeated several times and is linked effectively to existing information (e.g. through personal experiences).

Young children have a limited number of experiences so their 'filing' system is quite basic. Gradually children create new files and have more complex filing systems to store the ever-increasing amount of information they receive through their own experiences, interaction with others and by developing knowledge and understanding of their environment. There is no limit to the amount of information that can be stored in the long-term memory. The difficulty lies in accessing this stored information.

Most people are unable to recall events or experiences before the age of three. From birth to about three years old memories are stored using our senses (sight, sound, smell, taste and touch) rather than language. Once we develop language, we use words rather than our senses to recall information and lose the ability to remember our earlier sensory memories. It is as if these earlier memories were stored using a card-index file and once we have installed our 'computerised' filing system we no longer require the old card files or cannot find them. As children get older the process of remembering relies more and more on being able to use language to organise and retrieve information effectively.

Developing concentration

Concentration involves the ability to pay attention to the situation or task in hand. A person's concentration level or attention span is the length of time they are able to focus on a particular activity. Some children can concentrate for quite a long time, while some children (and adults!) find their attention starts to wander after just a few minutes. This may be due to a mismatch of activities to the individual's needs, interests and abilities which can lead to boredom and a lack of concentration. Attention Deficit Disorder (ADD) or Attention Deficit Hyperactive Disorder (ADHD) may also be responsible for poor concentration in certain people (see Chapter 13 for more information). Concentration is a key intellectual skill, which is necessary for the development of other intellectual components such as language and understanding concepts.

Being able to concentrate is an important part of the learning process. Children with short attention spans find it more difficult to take in new information; they may also need extra time to complete activities. Children need to be able to focus on one activity at a time without being distracted by other things. This is an essential skill for learning, particularly within schools. Concentrating enables children to get the most out of learning opportunities.

Activities within the setting may require different kinds of concentration, for example: passive concentration, such as listening to instructions, listening to stories, watching television and assemblies; and active concentration, such as creative activities, construction, puzzles, sand/water play, imaginative play, literacy activities and problem-solving activities including mathematics and science. Some children have no difficulty paying attention to activities requiring passive concentration for quite long periods, for example watching a video or television programme or listening to a story tape. Other children may not be able to pay attention to such activities for long but are totally engrossed in activities requiring active concentration, such as constructing a model or completing a complex jigsaw puzzle.

Developing imagination and creativity

Imagination involves the individual's ability to invent ideas or to form images. Children express their imagination through imitative play to begin with and then gradually through imaginative play, pretend play or role play. As children explore their environment and find out what objects and materials can do, they use their imagination to increase their understanding of the world and their role within it. For example, through imaginative play children can become other people by dressing-up and behaving like them. Imaginative play assists the development of children's imagination through activities such as dressing-up, small scale toys, doll play, shop play and hospital play. (For more information about the role of play in children's learning and development see Chapter 6.)

Creativity is the *use* of the imagination in a wide variety of activities including play, art, design technology, music, dance, drama, stories and poetry. Children can express their creativity through creative activities such as painting, drawing, collage, play dough, clay, cooking, design and model making. Creativity involves a process rather than an end product; it cannot be measured by the end result of an activity, but is based upon *how* the child worked and *why*. Creativity involves: exploring and experimenting with a wide range of materials; learning about the properties of materials, the colour, shape, size and texture; developing fine motor skills to manipulate materials; developing problem-solving techniques; and developing an understanding of the world and our personal contribution to it.

(There is more detailed information about how children think and learn in Chapter 6.)

✏ Activity!

From your experiences of working with pupils, provide examples of activities which you think encourage and extend their intellectual skills in each of the following areas:

INTELLECTUAL SKILLS	EXAMPLE ACTIVITIES
Sensory perception	
Thinking	
Language	
Problem-solving	
Concepts	
Memory	
Concentration	
Imagination and creativity	

Figure 1.6: *Teaching assistant supporting pupils*

Key Task

Observe a pupil during a learning activity. Focus on the pupil's intellectual development. In your assessment comment on:

- The pupil's imaginative and creative skills.
- The pupil's level of concentration.
- Any problem-solving skills used by the pupil.
- The pupil's use of language and communication skills.
- The role of the adult in promoting the pupil's intellectual development.
- Suggestions for further activities to encourage or extend the pupil's intellectual development including appropriate resources.

NOS Links:

Level 3:　　**STL 18.1**　　**STL 27.3**　　**STL 29.1**

The teaching assistant's role in promoting children's intellectual development

As a teaching assistant, you should support the teacher in providing learning opportunities to encourage children's intellectual skills. This includes providing opportunities to explore and learn about their environment, such as outings like shopping trips, library visits and going to the park. You should also provide toys and other play equipment that are age-appropriate to stimulate the children's thinking and learning. You should also provide opportunities for the children to share books, stories, rhymes and songs to stimulate new ideas and consolidate existing learning. (See information on supporting learning activities in Chapter 6.)

Five ways to promote children's intellectual development

You can help too promote children's intellectual development by:

1. **Providing opportunities and materials to increase the children's curiosity** e.g. books, games, posters, pictures, play equipment and toys. Encourage children to observe details in the environment, such a colours, shapes, smells and textures. Talk about weather conditions. Take the children on outings. Do gardening and/or keep pets.

2. **Participating in the children's activities to extend their development and learning** by asking questions, providing answers and demonstrating possible ways to use play equipment and other learning resources. Demonstrate how things work or fit together when the children are not sure what to do. Make sure your help is wanted (and necessary). Use verbal prompts where possible to encourage children to solve the problem for themselves.

3. **Providing gradually more challenging play and learning activities** but do not push the children too hard by providing activities which are obviously too complex; instead of extending the children's abilities this will only put them off due to the frustration of not being able to do the activity. Provide repetition by encouraging the children to play with toys and games more than once; each time they play, they will discover different things about these activities. Encourage acceptable risk taking during play opportunities.

4. **Helping the children to develop their concentration and memory skills by**: ensuring the children are *looking* and *listening* attentively when giving new information; explaining how new information is connected to the children's existing experiences and knowledge (by linking activities with a common theme); dividing complex activities into smaller tasks to make it easier for children to concentrate; using memory games to encourage/ extend concentration levels; singing songs and rhymes, for example following a number sequence in songs like 'Five brown teddies', 'Ten green bottles', 'When I was one I was just begun…'.

5. **Encouraging the children to use their senses to experiment with different materials and to explore their environment**, for example by doing arts and crafts; playing with sand, water, clay, dough, wood; playing with manufactured materials such as plastic construction kits; modelling with safe household junk materials; cooking activities; singing rhymes and songs; clapping games; outings to the local park; matching games, jigsaws and lotto.

 **Key Task**

- Plan a learning activity which encourages or extends a pupil's intellectual development such as: imaginative and creative skills; concentration and memory skills; problem-solving skills or language and communication skills.
- Use the assessment information from your previous observation of a child's intellectual development as the basis for your planning.
- Consider how you could meet the needs of a pupil with learning difficulties with this activity (see Chapter 13).
- If possible, ask the class teacher for permission to implement the activity. Evaluate the activity afterwards.

NOS Links:

Level 3: STL 18.1   STL 18.2   STL 23.1   STL 23.2   STL 23.3   STL 24.1
STL 24.2   STL 27.1   STL 27.2   STL 27.3   STL 29.2   STL 38.2
and depending on the learning activity:
STL 8.2 (ICT)   STL 25.1   STL 25.2   STL 25.3 (literacy)   STL 26.1
STL 26.2 (numeracy)

Supporting communication and language development

Language is *the* key factor in all children's development as it provides them with the skills they need to communicate with others, relate to others, explore the environment, understand concepts, formulate ideas and express feelings. The word 'language' is often used to describe the process of speaking and listening, but it is much more than verbal communication.

 **key words**

Community language: main language spoken in a child's home.

Key factor: an essential aspect affecting learning and development.

Modes of language: non-verbal communication; listening; speaking; thinking; reading; writing.

The human ability to utilise language depends on the use of a recognised system of symbols and a common understanding of what those symbols mean. Obviously there are many different systems of symbols, as indicated by the many different languages and alphabet systems used by people throughout the world. At first, very young children are not able to use a complex system of symbols; it takes time to learn the system of their particular community language. People also use other ways to communicate their needs and feelings to other people, for example: body language, gestures and facial expressions.

Developing communication skills

Children (and adults) use a variety of different ways to communicate. These modes of language are essential to being able to communicate effectively with others and to being fully involved in a wide range of social interactions. The different modes of language can be described as: non-verbal communication; thinking; listening; speaking; reading and writing. Each mode of language involves a variety of communication skills which are inter-related; some of the skills are required in more than one mode, for example reading and writing both involve the processing of oral language in a written form.

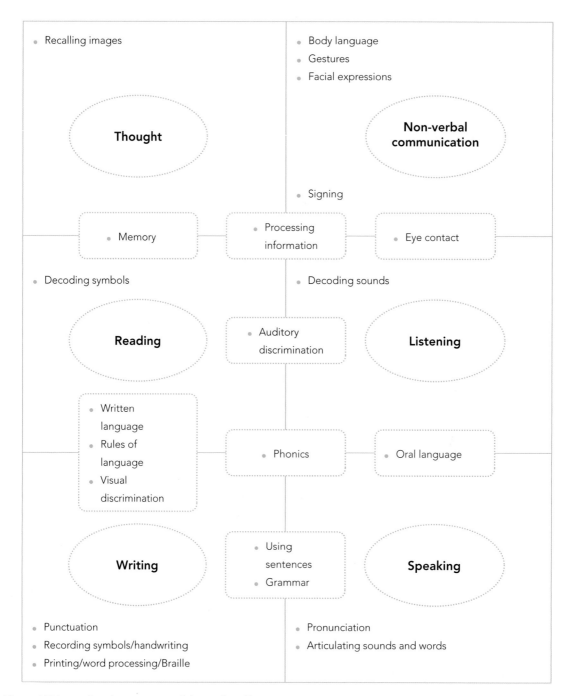

Figure 1.7: Inter-related components of the modes of language

You should provide opportunities for children to develop the necessary communication skills to become competent at using these different modes of language. Opportunities for talk are especially helpful in promoting language development and the use of communication skills. When working with children you must be aware of and provide for appropriate play and learning activities to enable the children to develop effective communication skills. (There is more detailed information about supporting speech, language and communication in Chapter 11.) Remember that some children may be limited in their ability to use some modes of language due to sensory impairment or other special needs (see Chapter 13).

Key Task

Observe a pupil involved in a conversation, discussion or circle time. Focus on the language development and communication skills demonstrated by the pupil. In your assessment comment on:

- The verbal and/or non-verbal communication used by the pupil.
- The complexity of any language used by the pupil.
- The level of social interaction.
- The role of the adult in promoting the pupil's language development.
- Suggestions for further activities to encourage or extend the pupil's language development.

NOS Links:

Level 3:   STL 18.1   STL 27.3   STL 29.1

The teaching assistant's role in promoting children's language development

The teaching assistant plays a vital role in encouraging and extending children's language development and communication skills by providing opportunities for children to talk and to use language as a tool for exploring ideas and experiences. You should be aware of and provide for appropriate language experiences to enable all the children you work with to develop effective communication skills. You should help to provide appropriate opportunities for children to encourage and extend their language and communication skills. This includes communicating effectively at the children's level of understanding and modelling appropriate language for the children (see section on communicating with children and young people in Chapter 3). You should also listen carefully to the children's talk and respond appropriately including considering the mood of the children: sometimes they will not want to talk. You should also provide appropriate opportunities for language including participating in everyday conversations, sharing books and stories, singing rhymes and songs.

Five ways to promote children's language development

You can help to promote children's language development by:

1. **Talking to the children about anything and everything!** Show the children what you are talking about, use real objects/situations, pictures, books, and other visual or audio aids.

2. **Using straightforward sentences** with words appropriate to the children's levels of understanding and development; avoid over-simplifying language; do not use 'baby talk' – children need to hear adult speech to learn language. Use repetition to introduce or reinforce new vocabulary and ideas. Do *not* make the children repeat things back over and over; this is boring and frustrating.

3. **Copying the children's sounds and words** including any extensions or corrections to positively reinforce and extend the children's vocabulary, sentence structures, etc. For example: a child says 'ball', you could reply 'Yes that is Tom's red ball'; or a child may say 'moo!', you could reply 'Yes, the cow goes "moo"!'

4. **Remembering turn taking in language exchanges**. Ask questions to stimulate the children's responses and to encourage or extend their speech. Look at the children when you are talking with them. Remember to be at the children's level, sitting on a low chair or even on the floor; do not tower over them.

5. **Sharing books, stories and rhymes** with children including babies.

 Key Task

- Plan an activity which encourages or extends a pupil's language and communication skills. Include a variety of communication techniques such as: active listening (listening carefully and focusing on what the pupil has to say); leaving time for the pupil to respond/talk; careful phrasing of adult questions and responses.
- Use the assessment information from your previous observation of a pupil's language and communication skills as the basis for your planning.
- Consider how you could meet the needs of bilingual pupils with this activity (see Chapter 11).
- Consider how you could meet the needs of a pupil with communication difficulties with this activity (see Chapter 13).
- If possible, ask the class teacher for permission to implement the activity. Evaluate the activity afterwards.

NOS Links:

Level 3:	STL 18.1	STL 18.2	STL 20.2	STL 23.1	STL 23.2	STL 23.3
	STL 24.1	STL 24.2	STL 25.3	STL 27.1	STL 27.2	STL 27.3
	STL 29.2	STL 35.2	STL 38.2			

Supporting emotional development

Emotional development can be defined as the development of personality and temperament. This includes how each child: develops as a unique individual; sees and feels about themselves; thinks other people see them; expresses their individual needs, desires and feelings; relates to others; and interacts with their environment.

 key words

Personality: distinctive and individual characteristics which affect each person's view of themselves, their needs, feelings and relationships with others.

Temperament: person's disposition or personality, especially their emotional responses.

Nature versus nurture in personality development

Research indicates that genetics plays its part in personality development. For example, babies only a few weeks old already have distinct personalities. Children inherit their particular temperaments which are then influenced by the environment they are raised in. Researchers agree that personality is derived from a combination of inheritance (nature) and environment (nurture).

In the same way as babies inherit their physical characteristics (such as hair and eye colour) they also inherit genetic information which contributes towards their personality development. Studies of young babies show they already have distinct temperaments or personality types: 40 per cent were easy-going, 10 per cent were 'difficult', 15 per cent were 'slow to warm up' and 35 per cent did not fit any category! (Fontana, 1994.) Remember that labelling personalities is not really a good idea as every child is a unique individual.

Environmental factors also affect children's emotional development. Consistent and loving care from a parent/carer who is sensitive to the child's particular needs enables the child to feel secure and to develop self-worth. Physical care is not enough – every child needs love and attention from their parent and/or carer. Having at least one secure and personal relationship with a parent/carer enables a child to form other relationships (see section below on attachments). Different cultures within society may have different cultural expectations relating to behaviour and emotional responses including the expected roles for men and women. For example, parents do treat boys and girls differently (often subconsciously) such as giving girls more cuddles or expecting boys to be tougher. Family size may also affect children's personality, for example children in large families may find it more difficult to get their parents' attention and this may affect their emotional (and social) adjustment in group settings, but may have positive benefits such as increased independence and ability to take turns. Some research studies indicate that the position of children in the family may also affect their personality. For example: first-born or only children are more likely to be conscientious, cooperative, sensitive and academically ambitious; second-born or middle children are more likely to be out-going, aggressive and competitive; the youngest child in the family tends to be the most sociable, spontaneous, passive and lacking in maturity. However, these differences in personality are probably due to the way in which adults treat the children rather than birth order. For example: first time parents are more likely to be anxious and over-protective of their first-born or only child; parents may be more relaxed with the second-born or middle child who in turn may feel they are in the older child's 'shadow'; the youngest child may be 'babied' by the rest of the family.

Children's emotional (and social) development may also be affected by other factors such as: special needs and/or difficulties at birth (such as a premature baby, forceps or caesarean delivery) which are often stated as being the cause for a baby being 'difficult', but this is more likely to be the result of the adult's treatment of the child which then affects the child's behaviour (for example, over-anxiety due to low birth weight of a premature baby or concerns over a child's special needs); family circumstances such as parental separation/divorce, single-parent families, step-families; death, abandonment or other permanent separation from parent; adoption, foster care or other temporary/permanent residential care. These factors do not necessarily have negative effects on children's emotional development; there are usually additional factors (such as financial hardship or inadequate substitute care) which can lead to poor social adjustment and/or emotional difficulties. (See section on supporting pupils with behaviour, emotional and social development needs in Chapter 13.)

Developing attachments

Babies develop strong attachments to the people they see most often and who satisfy their needs. One attachment is usually stronger than the others and this is usually the baby's mother, but the attachment can be to another family member or anyone outside the immediate family who spends a significant amount of time with the young child such as a grandparent or nanny. The security of these early attachments is essential to babies and young children because they provide a firm foundation for promoting emotional well-being, positive relationships with other people and confidence in exploring the environment. These early attachments enable children to feel secure about their relationships and to develop trust in others. Security and trust are important elements in the young children's ability to separate from their parents and carers in order to develop their own independence and ideas. Another essential aspect of promoting children's emotional development is helping children to recognise and deal with their own feelings and those of other people. (See section on encouraging pupils to recognise and deal with feelings in Chapter 3.)

Developing self-esteem

Another essential aspect of emotional development is self-esteem which involves: feelings and thoughts about oneself (positive or negative); respect or regard for self (or lack of it); consideration of self; self-image (perception of self); self-worth (value of self). The development of self-image and identity are strongly linked to self-esteem. Self-image and identity can be defined as: the individual's view of their own personality and abilities and the individual's perception of how other people view them and their abilities. This involves recognising: ourselves as separate individuals; we are unique individuals with characteristics and abilities that make us separate and different from others; the factors that influence how we identify with other people (for example, culture, race, etc.) as part of our own identity. (See information about equality, diversity and inclusion in Chapter 8 and the section on promoting the well-being and resilience of children and young people in Chapter 14.)

Figure 1.8: Child involved in role play

 **Key Task**

Observe a pupil during an imaginative play or creative activity. Focus on the pupil's emotional development. In your assessment comment on:

- The pupil's imaginative and creative skills.
- The pupil's ability to make choices or decisions.
- The pupil's use of language to express needs and/or feelings.
- The role of the adult in promoting the pupil's emotional development.
- Suggestions for further activities to encourage or extend the pupil's emotional development including appropriate resources.

NOS Links:

Level 3:   STL 18.1   STL 27.3   STL 29.1

The teaching assistant's role in promoting children's emotional development

As a teaching assistant, you should support the teacher in providing appropriate routines and activities to promote children's emotional development. This includes creating an environment that fosters the children's trust and self-esteem. You should help to provide continuity and consistency of care by continuing the children's usual routines (as far as is possible and practical) to give the children emotional security and reassurance. You should also help to provide stimulating play opportunities to promote emotional well-being. You must respect each child as a unique individual, including using praise and encouragement for the children's efforts and achievements to develop the children's self-confidence and promote positive self-esteem. You should also support children with transitions within the setting and with other transitions as they occur, such as moving to a different setting, moving house or the arrival of a new baby (see section on supporting children and young people during transitions in their lives in Chapter 14).

Five ways to promote children's emotional development

You can help to promote children's emotional development by:

1. **Using praise and encouragement** to help the pupils focus on what they are good at. Treat every pupil in the school as an individual. Each pupil has unique abilities and needs. Help pupils to maximise their individual potential.

2. **Taking an interest in the pupils' efforts as well as achievements**. Remember the *way* pupils participate in activities is more important than the end results, for example sharing resources, helping others and contributing ideas. Encourage the pupils to measure any achievements by comparing these to their *own* efforts. Foster cooperation between pupils rather than competition.

3. **Giving pupils opportunities to make decisions and choices**. Letting pupils participate in decision-making, even in a small way, helps them to feel positive and important; it also prepares them for making appropriate judgements and sensible decisions later on.

4. **Promote equal opportunities by providing positive images of children and adults** through: sharing books and stories about real-life situations showing children (and adults) the pupils can identify with; providing opportunities for imaginative play that encourage the pupils to explore different roles in positive ways, such as dressing-up clothes, cooking utensils, dolls and puppets.

5. **Being consistent about rules and discipline.** All pupils need consistency and a clearly structured framework for behaviour so that they know what is expected of them. Remember to label the behaviour not the pupils as this is less damaging to their emotional well-being, for example, say 'That was an unkind thing to say' rather than 'You are unkind'.

Key Task

- Plan an activity which encourages or extends a pupil's emotional development. For example, encouraging the pupil to use a variety of emotional abilities such as: imaginative and/or creative skills to express feelings; ability to make choices or decisions; language and communication skills to express needs and/or feelings; or understanding the needs and feelings of others.
- Use the assessment information from your previous observation of a pupil's emotional development as the basis for your planning.
- Consider how you could meet the needs of a pupil with emotional difficulties with this activity (see Chapter 13).
- If possible, ask the class teacher for permission to implement the activity. Evaluate the activity afterwards.

NOS Links:

Level 3:	STL 18.1	STL 18.2	STL 23.1	STL 23.2	STL 23.3	STL 24.1
	STL 24.2	STL 27.1	STL 27.2	STL 27.3	STL 29.2	STL 38.2

Summary of key points in this chapter:

- **Observing children's development** including: the purpose of observation; the basic principles of child observation; confidentiality; observation methods; recording observations and assessments.

- **Planning provision to promote development** including: the planning cycle; implementing and evaluating plans to promote development.

- **Understanding child and young person development** including: the basic patterns of child and young person development; the sequences of development 0 to 16 years covering the five different aspects social, physical, intellectual, communication and emotional.

- **Supporting social development** including: the socialisation process; developing independence; developing socially acceptable behaviour; the teaching assistant's role in promoting children's social development.

- **Supporting physical development** including: developing gross motor skills; developing fine motor skills; developing coordination; developing physical skills through activities and routines; the teaching assistant's role in promoting children's physical development.

- **Supporting intellectual development** including: developing sensory perception; developing thinking skills; developing language skills; developing problem-solving skills; developing an understanding of concepts; developing memory skills; developing concentration; developing imagination and creativity; the teaching assistant's role in promoting children's intellectual development.

- **Understanding communication and language development** including: developing communication skills; the modes of language – non-verbal communication, listening, speaking, thinking, reading and writing; the teaching assistant's role in promoting children's communication and language development.

- **Supporting emotional development** including: nature versus nurture in personality development; developing attachments; developing self-esteem; the teaching assistant's role in promoting children's emotional development.

Further reading

Bentham, S. (2003) *A Teaching Assistant's Guide to Child Development and Psychology in the Classroom.* Routledge.

Bruce, T. (ed) (2009) *Early Childhood: A Guide for Education Students.* Second edition. Sage Publications Ltd.

Harding, J. and Meldon-Smith, L. (2000) *Helping Young Children to Develop.* Hodder & Stoughton.

Harding, J. and Meldon-Smith, L. (2001) *How to make Observations and Assessments.* Second edition. Hodder Arnold.

Hobart, C. and Frankel, J. (2009) *A Practical Guide to Activities for Young Children.* Fourth edition. Nelson Thornes.

Lindon, J. (2007) *Understanding Children and Young People: Development from 5–18 Years.* Hodder Arnold.

2. Safeguarding children and young people

> ## This chapter relates to QCF unit:
>
> CYP Core 3.3 Understand how to safeguard the well-being of children and young people

Safeguarding children and young people from abuse

All schools should establish and maintain a safe environment for pupils and deal with circumstances where there are child welfare concerns. Through their child protection policies and procedures for safeguarding children, schools have an important role in the detection and prevention of child abuse and neglect. This also includes helping children and young people to protect themselves from abuse and dealing with bullying.

What is child abuse?

The Children Act 1989 defines child abuse as a person's actions that cause a child to suffer *significant harm* to their health, development or well-being. Significant harm can be caused by: punishing a child too much; hitting or shaking a child; constantly criticising, threatening or rejecting a child; sexually interfering with or assaulting a child; or neglecting a child, for example by not giving them enough to eat or not ensuring their safety. The Department of Health (DH) defines child abuse as the abuse or neglect of a child by inflicting harm or by failing to prevent harm. Children may be abused by someone known to them, such as a parent, sibling, babysitter, carer or other familiar adult. It is very rare for a child to be abused by a stranger (DfES, 2006).

> ## Types of child abuse:
>
> - **Physical abuse** involves causing deliberate physical harm to a child and may include: burning, drowning, hitting, poisoning, scalding, shaking, suffocating or throwing. Physical abuse also includes deliberately causing, or fabricating the symptoms of, ill health in a child (Munchausen's Syndrome by Proxy).
> - **Emotional abuse** involves the persistent psychological mistreatment of a child and may include: making the child feel inadequate, unloved or worthless; imposing inappropriate

developmental expectations on the child; threatening, taunting or humiliating the child; or exploiting or corrupting the child.

- **Sexual abuse** involves coercing or encouraging a child to engage in sexual activities to which the child does not or cannot consent because of their age or level of understanding. These sexual activities may involve physical contact such as penetrative and/or oral sex or encouraging the child to watch the adult masturbate or to look at pornographic material.
- **Neglect** involves the persistent failure to meet a child's essential basic needs for food, clothing, shelter, loving care or medical attention. Neglect may also include when a child is put at risk by being left alone without proper adult supervision.

(DfES, 2006)

Identifying signs of possible abuse

As a teaching assistant, you need to be aware of the signs and indicators of possible child abuse and neglect and to whom you should report any concerns or suspicions. You may have contact with pupils on a daily basis and so have an essential role to play in recognising indications of possible abuse or neglect such as outward signs of physical abuse, uncharacteristic behaviour patterns or failure to develop in the expected ways.

Indications of possible physical abuse include:

- recurrent unexplained injuries or burns
- refusal to discuss injuries
- improbable explanations for injuries
- watchful, cautious attitude towards adults
- reluctance to play and be spontaneous
- shrinking from physical contact
- avoidance of activities involving removal of clothes, for example swimming
- aggressive or bullying behaviour
- being bullied
- lack of concentration
- difficulty in trusting people and making friends.

Indications of possible emotional abuse include:

- delayed speech development
- very passive and lacking in spontaneity
- social isolation, for example finding it hard to play with other children
- unable to engage in imaginative play
- low self-esteem
- easily distracted
- fear of new situations
- self-damaging behaviour, such as head-banging, pulling out hair
- self-absorbing behaviour, such as obsessive rocking, thumb-sucking
- eating problems, for example overeating or lack of appetite
- withdrawn behaviour and depression.

Indications of possible sexual abuse include:

- sudden behaviour changes when abuse begins
- low self-esteem
- Using sexual words in play activities uncharacteristic for age/level of development
- withdrawn or secretive behaviour
- starting to wet or soil themselves
- demonstrating inappropriate seductive or flirtatious behaviour
- frequent public masturbation
- frightened of physical contact
- depression resulting in self-harm (or an overdose)
- bruises, scratches, burns or bite marks on the body.

Indications of possible neglect include:

- slow physical development
- constant hunger and/or tiredness
- poor personal hygiene and appearance
- frequent lateness or absenteeism
- undiagnosed/untreated medical conditions
- social isolation, for example poor social skills
- compulsive stealing or begging.

(Indications of possible bullying are dealt with below.)

The law regarding protecting and safeguarding children

All practitioners working to safeguard children and young people must understand fully their responsibilities and duties as set out in government legislation, regulations and guidance. *Working Together to Safeguard Children: a Guide to Inter-agency Working to Safeguard and Promote the Welfare of Children* (2010) provides statutory guidance and non-statutory practice guidance on how organisations and practitioners should work together to safeguard and promote the welfare of children and young people in accordance with the Children Act 1989 and the Children Act 2004. This guidance was most recently updated in 2006. This latest revision follows the publication of Lord Laming's report, *The Protection of Children in England: A Progress Report*, in March 2009, the acceptance by the government of all of his recommendations and the government's detailed response and action plan published in May 2009. Many of Lord Laming's recommendations are reflected in or given effect by this revised guidance. It has also been updated to reflect developments in legislation, policy and practice relating to safeguarding children (DCSF, 2010; p.7).

Working Together to Safeguard Children applies to those working in education, health and social services as well as the police and the probation service. It is relevant to those working with children and their families in the statutory, independent and voluntary sectors. The document sets out:

- A summary of the nature and impact of child abuse and neglect.
- How to operate best practice in child protection procedures.
- The roles and responsibilities of different agencies and practitioners.
- The role of Local Safeguarding Children Boards.

- The processes to be followed when there are concerns about a child.
- The action to be taken to safeguard and promote the welfare of children experiencing, or at risk of, significant harm.
- The important principles to be followed when working with children and families.
- Training requirements for effective child protection.

It is not necessary for all practitioners to read every part of *Working Together to Safeguard Children* to understand the principles and to perform their roles effectively. However, those who work regularly with children and young people and who may be asked to contribute to assessments of children in need should read chapters 1, 2 (relevant sections, for example, schools and further education institutions), 5 and 11; it may also be helpful to read 6, 8, 9, 10 and 12. For full text see: **http://publications.dcsf.gov.uk/eOrderingDownload/00305-2010DOM-EN.pdf**.

As a further safeguard to children's welfare, The Protection of Children Act 1999 requires childcare organisations (including any organisation concerned with the supervision of children) not to offer employment, involving regular contact with children, either paid or unpaid, to any person listed as unsuitable to work with children on the Department of Health list and the Department for Education and Employment's List 99. The Criminal Records Bureau acts as a central access point for criminal records checks for all those applying to work with children and young people.

Schools (including independent and non-maintained schools) and further education institutions have a duty to safeguard and promote the welfare of pupils under the Education Act 2002. They should create and maintain a safe learning environment for children and young people, and identify where there are child welfare concerns and take action to address them, in partnership with other organisations where appropriate (DCSF, 2010; p.11).

Policies and procedures for safeguarding children and young people

The school's policy for safeguarding children should include information on the roles and responsibilities of staff members and the procedures for dealing with child protection issues. For example:

1. All staff members should attend child protection training.
2. The school will comply with the Local Safeguarding Children Board (LSCB) procedures.
3. If any member of staff is concerned about a child s/he must inform a senior colleague. The member of staff must record information regarding such concerns on the same day. This record must give a clear, precise and factual account of their observation.
4. Confidentiality is of crucial importance and incidents should only be discussed with the relevant person, for example a senior colleague or external agency.
5. The head teacher will decide whether the concerns should be referred to external agencies, such as the social services and/or the police.
6. The school should work cooperatively with parents unless this is inconsistent with the need to ensure the child's safety.
7. If a referral is made to social services, the head teacher will ensure that a report of the concerns is sent to the social worker dealing with the case within 48 hours.
8. Particular attention will be paid to the attendance and development of any child identified as 'at risk' or who has been placed on the Child Protection Register.

As teaching assistants have close contact with children, they should be aware of the signs of possible abuse or neglect and know what to do if they have concerns about a child's welfare (see below). The school should have clear procedures, in line with the LSCB procedures, on the situations in which teaching assistants should consult senior colleagues and external agencies (such as the social services and the police) when they have concerns about the welfare of a child.

 **Activity!**

Find out about your school's policies and procedures for safeguarding the welfare of children and young people.

The teaching assistant's responsibilities for safeguarding children

All adults who work with children have a duty to safeguard and promote the welfare of children. As a teaching assistant, you need to be aware of: the signs of possible abuse, neglect and bullying; to whom you should report any concerns or suspicions; the school's child protection policy and procedures; the school's anti-bullying policy; the school's procedures for actively preventing all forms of bullying among pupils and the school's procedure to be followed if a staff member is accused of abuse. You may be involved in child protection in the following ways:

- You may have concerns about a pupil and refer those concerns to a senior colleague in the school (who will then refer matters to social services and/or the police as appropriate).
- You may be the senior practitioner who is responsible for referring concerns about a child's welfare to social services or the police.
- You may be approached by social services and asked to provide information about a child or to be involved in an assessment or asked to attend a child protection conference. This may happen regardless of who made the referral to social services.
- You may be asked to carry out a specific type of assessment, or provide help or a specific service to the child as part of an agreed plan and contribute to the reviewing of the child's progress (including attending child protection conferences).

(DfES, 2006)

Teaching assistants working closely with pupils in schools are well placed to identify the early signs of abuse, neglect or bullying. In addition, many pupils may view the school as neutral territory where they may feel more able to talk with an adult they trust about what is happening to them. If you have concerns that a pupil in your school may be experiencing possible abuse or neglect than you *must* report these concerns promptly to the relevant person, the class teacher, head teacher or teacher responsible for child protection issues.

In practice

Lee is working as a teaching assistant with pupils aged 7 to 8 years. Lee has concerns about a particular pupil's welfare after noticing multiple bruises on the child's arms. What would you do if you had concerns about a pupil's welfare? Who would you report your concerns to? How would you report your concerns?

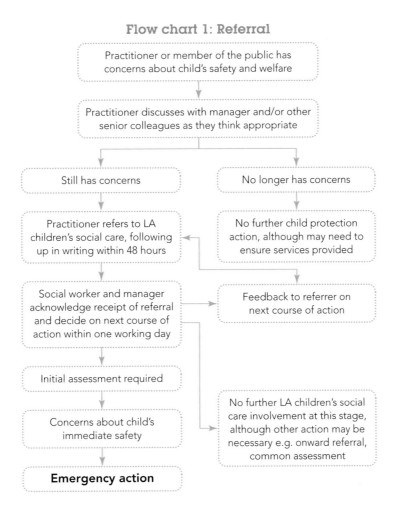

Flow chart 1: Referral

```
Practitioner or member of the public has
concerns about child's safety and welfare
            │
            ▼
Practitioner discusses with manager and/or other
senior colleagues as they think appropriate
            │
    ┌───────┴────────────────┐
    ▼                        ▼
Still has concerns      No longer has concerns
    │                        │
    ▼                        ▼
Practitioner refers to LA    No further child protection
children's social care,      action, although may need to
following up in writing      ensure services provided
within 48 hours
    │                        │
    ▼                        ▼
Social worker and manager    Feedback to referrer on
acknowledge receipt of       next course of action
referral and decide on next
course of action within one
working day
    │
    ▼
Initial assessment required
    │                        No further LA children's social
    ▼                        care involvement at this stage,
Concerns about child's       although other action may be
immediate safety             necessary e.g. onward referral,
    │                        common assessment
    ▼
Emergency action
```

Figure 2.1: Flow chart: Referral process for safeguarding children from *Working Together to Safeguard Children*, 2010; p.186.

Responding to a child's disclosure of abuse

A child may make a personal disclosure to a member of staff relating to an experience in which the child may have been significantly harmed. A child may make a disclosure to you at an inappropriate place or time. If this happens, you should talk again individually to the child before the end of the day. You may be able to discuss the issue with a senior colleague without giving the name of the child. If not, you should follow the setting's confidentiality policy and child protection procedures.

If a child makes a personal disclosure that s/he has been abused in some way, you should:

- Listen to what the child has to say.
- Accept what the child is saying.
- Allow the child to talk openly.
- Listen to the child rather than ask direct questions.
- Not criticise the alleged perpetrator of the abuse.
- Reassure the child that what has happened is not his or her fault.
- Stress to the child that it was the right thing to tell someone.
- Reassure the child but not make promises that you might not be able to keep.

- Not promise the child to keep the disclosed information confidential (as it might be necessary for the matter to be to referred to social services).
- Explain simply to the child what has to be done next and who has to be told.

After a child has made a disclosure to you:

1. Make brief notes as soon as possible after the conversation.
2. Do not destroy the original notes, as the courts may need these.
3. Record the date, time, place and any noticeable non-verbal behaviour as well as the words used by the child.
4. Draw a diagram to indicate the position of any bruising or other injury.
5. Only record statements and observations rather than interpretations or assumptions.

Dealing with a disclosure from a child or being involved in a child protection case can be a very distressing and stressful experience. You may require support for yourself and should discuss with a senior colleague how to access support when dealing with a case of child abuse or neglect.

Allegations of abuse against staff or volunteers

If a pupil, or parent, makes a complaint of abuse against a member of staff or volunteer, the person receiving the complaint must take it seriously and follow the relevant procedures in line with LSCB procedures. Professionals who are independent of the school should investigate all allegations of abuse against staff or volunteers.

If you have reason to suspect that a pupil may have been abused by another member of staff, either in the school or elsewhere, you must immediately inform a senior colleague. You should make a record of the concerns including a note of anyone else who witnessed the incident or allegation. The head teacher will not investigate the incident themselves but will assess whether it is necessary to refer the matter to social services.

If the head teacher decides that the allegation warrants further action through child protection procedures, a referral will be made direct to social services. If the allegation constitutes a serious criminal offence it will be necessary to contact social services and the police before informing the member of staff. If it is decided that it is not necessary to refer the matter to social services then the head teacher will consider whether there needs to be an internal investigation. If the complaint is about the head teacher, then the LSCB should be contacted for information on the necessary procedures to be followed.

 **Activity!**

Find out about your school's procedures for dealing with allegations of abuse against staff members or volunteers.

The confidentiality of information relating to abuse

Child protection raises issues of confidentiality that must be clearly understood by everyone within the school. You must be absolutely clear about the boundaries of your legal and professional role and your responsibilities with regard to the confidentiality of information relating to abuse. A clear and explicit confidentiality policy that staff, pupils and parents can all understand should ensure good practice throughout the school.

Teaching assistants have a legal duty of confidence with regard to the personal information they hold about pupils and their families. Any information you receive about pupils (and their families) in the course of your work should only be shared within appropriate professional contexts. All information, including child protection records, should be kept securely. The law allows the disclosure of confidential personal information in order to safeguard a child or children. Usually personal information should only be disclosed to a third party (such as the social services) after obtaining the consent of the person to whom the information relates. In some child protection matters it may not be possible or desirable to obtain such consent. The Data Protection Act 1998 allows disclosure without consent in some circumstances, for example to detect or prevent a crime, or to apprehend or prosecute an offender.

The safety and well-being of pupils must always be your first consideration. You cannot offer or guarantee absolute confidentiality especially if there are concerns that a pupil is experiencing, or at risk of, significant harm. You have a responsibility to share relevant information about the protection of children with other professionals, particularly the investigative agencies, such as the social services and the police. If a pupil confides in you and requests that the information is kept secret, it is important that you explain to the pupil in a sensitive manner that you have a responsibility to refer cases of alleged abuse to the appropriate agencies for the pupil's sake. Within that context, the pupil should, however, be assured that the matter will be disclosed only to people who need to know about it.

As a teaching assistant you should:

- Be absolutely clear about your school's child protection policy.
- Know and understand your exact role and responsibilities with regard to confidentiality and child protection issues.
- If a pupil asks to speak to you in confidence, s/he should always be told beforehand that unconditional confidentiality may not always be possible if someone is in danger of abuse.
- If confidentiality is to be breached, the pupil needs to know who will be told, why and what the outcome is likely to be and how s/he will be supported.
- Know when and who to contact if further advice, support or counselling is needed.
- Ensure all pupils and their parents/carers are aware of the school's confidentiality policy and how it works in practice.
- Make sure pupils are informed of sources of confidential help such as Childline.

 ## Key Task

- What are your role and responsibilities for reporting information on possible abuse to a senior colleague?
- How and to whom should you pass on information from a pupil's personal disclosure of abuse? For example, your role and your responsibilities for providing information on the disclosure to a senior colleague?
- Find out about your school's policy and procedures with regard to the confidentiality of information in child protection matters.

NOS Links:

Level 3:   STL 3.3

Helping children to protect themselves from abuse

An effective child protection policy will promote a caring and supportive environment in the school and create an atmosphere in which pupils feel that they are secure, valued, listened to and taken seriously. The school's child protection policy should support children's learning and development in ways that foster their security, confidence and independence.

The child protection policy should be regarded as central to the welfare and well-being of all children and incorporate the following aims:

- To encourage children to have positive self-esteem and self-image.
- To help children view themselves as part of the setting and local community.
- To nurture children's abilities to establish and sustain relationships with families, peers, adults and the outside world.
- To provide time, space and opportunities for children to explore, discuss and develop key ideas relating to child protection openly with peers and adults, in a safe and secure environment.
- To equip children with the necessary skills to make reasoned, informed choices, judgements and decisions.
- To work with parents and carers to build an understanding of the setting's responsibility to ensure the welfare and well-being of all children.
- To establish and maintain child protection procedures so that all staff know how to act if they have concerns or need support regarding a particular child.
- To ensure that all staff are aware of local child protection procedures so that information is passed on effectively to the relevant professional or agency.
- To keep members of the setting well informed about child protection issues and to develop effective and supportive liaison with outside agencies.
- To provide a model for open and effective communication between children, parents, childcarers and other adults working with children.

Child protection not only involves the detection of abuse and neglect but also the *prevention* of abuse by helping pupils to protect themselves. As part of this preventive role you should work with the class teacher to help pupils to: understand what is and is not acceptable behaviour towards them; stay safe from harm; speak up if they have worries and concerns; develop awareness and resilience; and prepare for their future responsibilities as adults, citizens and parents.

Being actively involved in prevention helps pupils to keep safe both now and in the future. Pupils need to know how to take responsibility for themselves and to understand the consequences of their actions. Pupils should know and understand:

- That they all deserve care and respect.
- Their rights and how to assert them.
- How to do things safely and how to minimise risk.
- How to deal with abusive or potentially abusive situations.
- When and how to ask for help and support.

Helping pupils to keep themselves safe

Critical thinking and decision-making are also essential for helping pupils to keep themselves safe. You can help them to develop these skills by encouraging them to participate in decision-making within the school and by providing opportunities for cooperation. You should also encourage pupils to trust their own feelings and good judgement in difficult situations. By learning to trust their inner feelings, they can avoid many potential risky situations. Use role play to help them think about what they should do if their friends want them to do something they dislike or feel uncomfortable about, such as going to a party, getting drunk, having sex, shoplifting, taking drugs, etc. Peer pressure can be very strong; encourage them to decide and set limits about what they will and will not do so that they know how to cope before the situation arises. Make sure that pupils understand the dangers of situations that may put their personal safety at risk such as: being left at home alone; playing in deserted or dark places; being out on their own; getting lost, for example when on outings; walking home alone especially in the dark; talking to strangers or accepting lifts from strangers, including hitchhiking.

As pupils get older they need opportunities to explore their environment and to develop their independence. To do this safely they will need to know and understand about acceptable risk taking. Risk taking can be explored through stories (such as *Jack and the Beanstalk*) and television programmes. Pupils can think about and discuss the risks taken by their favourite characters. Encourage them to identify some of the risks they take in their own lives and look at ways they can minimise risk. Puppets and role play can be used to help them deal with potentially risky situations. Ensure the pupils know and understand The Keepsafe Code (see **www.kidscape.org.uk**).

 Activity!

Think about ways of encouraging children to be aware of their own bodies and understand their right not to be abused, for example activities involving discussion about their own bodies, activities to encourage children to help protect themselves, or activities to tackle bullying.

Helping pupils to access appropriate support when necessary

Pupils need to know where to go for help and support in difficult situations. They should be encouraged to identify people in the school and the local community who help them to keep safe, for example worries about bullying or problems at home may be discussed with a member of school staff; if they get lost they can ask a police officer for assistance. Encourage pupils to think of a trusted adult (such as their parents, other relative, best friend, teacher, teaching assistant) they could talk to about a difficult situation, for example abuse, bullying, negative peer pressure, etc. Ensure that they understand that if they go to an adult for help, especially within the school, they will be believed and supported. Provide them with information about other sources of help and support such as Childline, The Samaritans, etc.

 Key Task

Describe the ways your school helps pupils to protect themselves. What sources of help and support are available for children and young people in your setting and the local community?

NOS Link:

Level 3:   STL 46.3

Dealing with bullying

Research suggests that 85 per cent of children aged 5 to 11 years have experienced bullying in some form, e.g. name-calling, being hit or kicked. In 2000, a survey of 11 to 16 year olds, found that '36% of children said they had been bullied in the last 12 months; 26% had been threatened with violence and 13% had been physically attacked' (ATL, 2000). Bullying is such a serious problem that schools must have an anti-bullying policy that clearly sets out the ways in which they try to prevent bullying and deal with bullying behaviour when it happens.

Defining bullying behaviour

Bullying can be defined as behaviour that is deliberately hurtful or aggressive, repeated over a period of time and difficult for victims to defend themselves against. There are three main types of bullying: *physical*: hitting, kicking, taking belongings; *verbal*: name-calling, insulting, making offensive remarks; *indirect*: spreading nasty stories about someone, exclusion from social groups, being made the subject of malicious rumours, sending malicious emails or text messages on mobile phones.

Name-calling is the most common type of bullying. Pupils may be called nasty names because of their individual characteristics, ethnic origin, nationality, skin colour, sexual orientation or disability. Verbal bullying is common amongst both boys and girls. Boys experience more physical violence and threats when being bullied than girls. However, physical attacks on girls by other girls are becoming more common. Girls tend to use more indirect types of bullying, which can be more difficult to detect and deal with. (DfES, 2000.)

Any pupil can experience bullying, but certain factors may make bullying more likely. While there is *never* an acceptable excuse for bullying behaviour, pupils are more likely to experience bullying if they: are shy or have an over-protective family environment; are from a different racial or ethnic group to the majority of pupils; appear different in some obvious respect, for example stammering; have special needs such as a disability or learning difficulty; behave inappropriately, for example are a 'nuisance' or intrude on others' activities; or possess expensive accessories such as mobile phones or computer games.

Recognising when a pupil is being bullied

Pupils who are experiencing bullying may be reluctant to attend school and are often absent. They may be more anxious and insecure than others, have fewer friends and often feel unhappy and lonely. They can suffer from low self-esteem and negative self-image; they may see themselves as failures, as stupid, ashamed and unattractive.

Possible signs that a pupil is being bullied include:

- Suddenly not wanting to go to school when s/he usually enjoys it.
- Unexplained cuts and bruises.
- Possessions that have unexplained damage or are persistently 'lost'.
- Becoming withdrawn or depressed but not saying what the matter is.

While the above signs may indicate that a pupil is being bullied, they may also be symptomatic of other problems such as abuse (see section above about responding to concerns about possible abuse).

Helping pupils who are being bullied

The behaviour of some pupils can lead to them experiencing bullying, though this does not justify the behaviour of the bullies. For example, some pupils may: find it difficult to play with other pupils; be hyperactive; behave in ways that irritate others; bully weaker pupils; be easily roused to anger; fight back when attacked or even slightly provoked; or be actively disliked by the majority of pupils in the school. School staff and the pupil's parents should work together to identify any such behaviour. The pupil needs help to improve personal and social skills including assertiveness techniques and conflict resolution.

You may be able to provide support for a pupil who is being bullied by:

- Encouraging the pupil to talk.
- Listening to the pupil's problems.
- Believing the pupil if they say they are being bullied.
- Providing reassurance that it is not their fault; no one deserves to be bullied.
- Discussing the matter with the pupil's class teacher or form tutor.
- Taking appropriate action, following the school's policy on anti-bullying.

Dealing with persistent and violent bullying

Where a pupil does not respond to the strategies to combat bullying, the school should take tough action to deal with persistent and violent bullying. The school should have a range of sanctions to deal with this type of bullying. Everyone within the school should know what sanctions will be taken. These sanctions should be fair and applied consistently.

You can help deal with bullying behaviour by:

- Knowing the school's policy and strategies for dealing with bullying behaviour.
- Using appropriate sanctions for such behaviour, for example exclusion from certain activities.
- Providing help for the bully so they can recognise that this behaviour is unacceptable, such as discussion, mediation, peer counselling.
- Working with teachers and parents to establish community awareness of bullying.
- Making sure all pupils know that bullying will *not* be tolerated.
- Understanding that the school can permanently exclude pupils who demonstrate persistent bullying behaviour, especially physical violence.

 **key words**

Exclude: to expel or bar from the school as a formal sanction.

 Key Task

- Outline your school's anti-bullying policy and main strategies for dealing with bullying behaviour.
- Give a reflective account of how you have handled concerns about bullying. Remember confidentiality.
- Devise an activity to encourage pupils to speak up about bullying, e.g. a story, discussion, role play, drama or poster making.

NOS Links:

Level 3: STL 3.4   STL 19.1   STL 19.2   STL 20.1   STL 20.2   STL 20.3
          STL 37.1   STL 37.3

Summary of key points in this chapter:

- **Safeguarding children and young people from abuse** including: definitions of child abuse; the different types of abuse.

- **Identifying signs of possible abuse** including the indications of possible physical, emotional, sexual abuse or neglect.

- **The law regarding protecting and safeguarding children** including the Children Act 2004 and statutory guidance in *Working Together to Safeguard Children 2010*.

- **Policies and procedures for safeguarding children** including: the teaching assistant's responsibilities; responding to a child's disclosure of abuse; allegations of abuse against staff or volunteers; the confidentiality of information relating to abuse.

- **Helping children to protect themselves from abuse** including: helping pupils to keep themselves safe; helping pupils to access appropriate support when necessary.

Figure 2.2: Example of a pupil's anti-bullying poster

- **Dealing with bullying** including: defining bullying behaviour; recognising when a pupil is being bullied; helping pupils who are being bullied; dealing with persistent and violent bullying.

Further reading

Beckett, C. (2007) *Child Protection: An Introduction*. Second edition. Sage Publications.

Cheminais, R. (2008) *Every Child Matters: A Practical Guide for Teaching Assistants*. David Fulton Publishers.

Cleaver, H. et al. (2009) *Safeguarding Children: A Shared Responsibility*. Wiley Blackwell.

DfES (2006) *What To Do If You're Worried A Child Is Being Abused*. DfES. (Available from: **http://www.dcsf. gov.uk/everychildmatters/resources-and-practice/IG00182/**.)

Elliott, M. (ed) (2002) *Bullying: A Practical Guide to Coping for Schools*. Pearson Education in association with Kidscape.

Hughes, L. and Owen, H. (2009) *Good Practice in Safeguarding Children: Working Effectively in Child Protection*.

Lee, C. (2004) *Preventing Bullying in Schools: A Guide for Teachers and Other Professionals*. Sage Publications.

Lindon, J. (2008) *Safeguarding Children and Young People: Child Protection 0–18 Years*. Third edition. Hodder Education.

O'Moore, M. and Minton, S.J. (2004) *Dealing with Bullying in Schools: A Training Manual for Teachers, Parents and Other Professionals*. Sage Publications.

Starns, B. and Flynn, H. (2004) *Protecting Children: Working Together to Keep Children Safe*. Heinemann.

to find their own answers as appropriate to their age and level of development. Give them information in an appropriate form, which will increase their vocabulary and add to their knowledge/understanding of their world. Your answers should use words that are appropriate to the pupil. For example, if a younger pupil asks: 'Why does it rain?' you need to give a simple reply such as 'Clouds are full of water which falls back to the ground as drops of rain' while an older pupil can be given a more technical description of cloud formation and rainfall.

⚙ Key Task

Listen to adults talking with children in a variety of situations, both within and outside your school (for example on buses, in shops, in the street, in the playground). Pay particular attention to the questions asked by the adults and the children, and how they are answered. Consider these points:

- Which inter-personal skills were used?
- How effective was the communication?
- Did the adult use active listening skills?
- What did the children learn about language, the activity and/or the environment?

NOS Links:
Level 3:   **STL 20.2   STL 25.3**

The importance of praise and encouragement

Praise and encouragement are essential components when communicating with children. All children (especially young children) need immediate and positive affirmations or rewards to show that their learning and development are progressing in accordance with the adult's (and child's) expectations. Adults should emphasise the positive aspects of children's learning and development. You can support children in managing failure and disappointment by emphasising the importance of taking part, trying their personal best and praising and/or rewarding children for their efforts not just their achievements. Children gain confidence and increased positive self-esteem when they receive praise/rewards for their efforts and achievements, including encouragement to try new activities and experiences.

There are four main methods used to praise and encourage pupils:

1. **Verbal**: for example 'praise' assemblies; positive comments about the child's behaviour or activities such as 'Well done, Tom! This is a lovely story! Tell me what happened next'.
2. **Non-verbal**: for example body language: leaning forward or turning towards a child to show interest in what the child is communicating; facial expressions: smiling; sign language: 'good boy/girl!'.
3. **Symbolic**: for example 'smiley faces' for carefully done work or positive behaviour; stickers for being a good listener or for reading well; stars or merit points for attempting and/or completing tasks.
4. **Written**: for example merit certificates; written comments in head teacher's book; newsletter recording achievements; comments written (or stamped) on child's work such as 'Well done!' or 'Good work!'.

Activity!

What methods do you use to provide positive praise and encouragement for the efforts and achievements of pupils in your school?

Supporting pupils in developing relationships

As a teaching assistant you will support children in developing positive relationships with other children and adults. Observing the behaviour of parents and other significant adults (teachers, teaching assistants, play workers and so on) affects children's behaviour, how children deal with their own and other people's feelings and how children relate to others.

This is why it is so important for adults to provide positive role models for children's behaviour. Positive interactions with adults (and other children) in various settings encourages children to demonstrate positive ways of relating to others and using appropriate social skills. To develop positive relationships every child needs:

- Security
- Praise
- Encouragement
- Communication
- Interaction
- Acceptance
- Love.

You should set limits and firm boundaries as agreed with children, families, colleagues and other professionals. To do this you will need to effectively communicate and exchange information with children according to their ages, needs and abilities. This includes understanding the possible effects of communication difficulties and attention deficit disorders. You will also need to be able to implement agreed behaviour procedures and strategies when dealing with children who continue to demonstrate challenging behaviour.

Supporting pupils in developing agreements about behaviour

Adults should not use aggressive or bullying tactics when trying to encourage appropriate behaviour in children. Firm discipline includes warmth and affection to show children they are cared for and accepted for who they are regardless of any inappropriate behaviour they may demonstrate. The school should provide an appropriate framework for socially acceptable behaviour with rules that have to be followed by all. Language plays an important part in encouraging children to behave in acceptable ways as it enables them to: understand verbal explanations of what is and is not acceptable behaviour; understand verbal explanations of why certain behaviour is not acceptable; express their own needs and feelings more clearly; avoid conflicts when handled by sensitive adults; reach compromises more easily and have a positive outlet for feelings through discussion and imaginative play.

As part of your role as a teaching assistant you will be helping to promote the school's policy, procedures and strategies regarding children's behaviour by consistently and effectively implementing agreements about ways to behave such as ground rules and/or a children's code of conduct (see section on supporting behaviour management strategies in Chapter 7). You will support children in developing agreements about ways of behaving as appropriate to the requirements of the school *and* the children's ages and levels of development.

Agreements about ways of behaving should be introduced following consultation with colleagues, children and parents. A copy of the home–school agreement should be sent home and parents (and if appropriate, children) asked to sign as an indication of agreement and support. The agreement should be displayed throughout the school as appropriate. The agreement should be brief and easy to learn. It should include rules that the school will enforce. The reason for each rule should be obvious, but staff should also explain these as appropriate to the age and level of development of the children they work with. The agreement may be applied to a variety of situations and should be designed to encourage children to develop responsibility for their own behaviour. Developing agreements about ways of behaving should include negotiating appropriate goals and boundaries for behaviour. (See section on setting goals and boundaries in Chapter 7.)

key words

Home–school agreement: a document setting out the responsibilities of the school, parents and pupils which will encourage positive behaviour to support children's development and learning.

Encouraging pupils to recognise and deal with feelings

An essential aspect of supporting children in developing relationships is helping children to recognise and deal with their own feelings and those of other people. Feelings can be defined as: an awareness of pleasure or pain; physical and/or psychological impressions; experience of personal emotions such as anger, joy, fear or sorrow, and inter-personal emotions such as affection, kindness, malice or jealousy.

In British society we are often encouraged to keep our feelings to ourselves. Males may be discouraged from showing the more sensitive emotions; females may be discouraged from demonstrating the more aggressive emotions. Babies and very young children naturally demonstrate clearly how they feel by crying, shouting and rejecting objects. They will openly show affection and other emotions such as jealousy or anger. Young children do not understand that others can be physically or emotionally hurt by what they say or do. Gradually, children become conditioned to accept that the feelings and needs of others *do* matter.

We need to ensure that children do not forget their own feelings and emotional needs by becoming too concerned with the feelings of others or trying to please others. Children need to know that it is natural to feel a wide range of emotions and that it is acceptable to express strong feelings, such as love and anger, openly as long as they do so in positive and appropriate ways.

As a teaching assistant you can help pupils to recognise and express their feelings through:

- **Books, stories and poems** about feelings and common events experienced by other children/young people to help them recognise and deal with these in their own lives.
- **Creative activities** to provide positive outlets for feelings, for example pummelling clay to express anger; painting/drawing pictures or writing stories and poems which reflect their feelings about particular events and experiences.
- **Physical play or sports** involving vigorous physical activity that allow a positive outlet for anger or frustration.
- **Drama or role play** activities to act out feelings, such as jealousy concerning siblings; worries over past experiences; fears about future events such as visit to dentist.

Home-School Agreement example from Oakleigh School, Whetstone, London

Home-School Agreement
Together we will
• Enable the children to make their needs known • Enable the children to know right from wrong • Ensure the children reach their maximum potential • Provide a safe and secure environment where children can grow and develop • Establish open and respectful communication • Share common goals and expectations for the children • Develop consistent approaches for addressing behaviour issues where appropriate • Encourage the children to value and respect people from all cultures and communities
The school will
• Set accurate individual targets together with the family • Recognise and build on each child's individual strengths • Keep the family informed of children's progress and achievements in a variety of ways • Provide support ideas and access to expertise for families • Provide an open, welcoming environment for families and ensure their knowledge, expertise and opinions are valued • Endeavour to make school events/meetings as welcoming and accessible as possible to all families • Notify families of any change in circumstances that may affect their child • Make at least one home visit a year • Make every effort to provide translated documents and interpreters where necessary • Provide daily feedback on the child's experiences that day using the home/school chat book or an alternative
The family will
• Make sure that their child attends regularly and provide a note of explanation if the child is absent • Ensure that the child is well enough to attend school • Support the school's homework policy • Make sure that a named adult is at home to receive children from school transport • Attend school events and meetings when possible • Mark the children's clothes and belongings with their name • Notify the school of any change of circumstances that may affect the child • Acknowledge daily feedback using the home/school chat book or an alternative
Signed: (Family)   Date: Signed: (Headteacher) Date:

Figure 3.2: Example of home–school agreement

Babies and very young children are naturally egocentric; their belief that the world revolves around them and their wishes often makes them appear selfish and possessive. As children develop they begin to think and care about others as well as themselves. We have all experienced jealousy in our relationships with others, perhaps with siblings, friends, neighbours, colleagues or employers. Unchecked jealousy can be a very destructive and hurtful emotion that prevents children (and adults) from developing respect and care for others.

You can help pupils to cope with any feelings of jealousy they may have towards others by:

- **Avoiding comparisons between pupils (especially siblings)**. For example, do not make comments like 'You're not as quiet as your brother' or 'Why can't you behave more like that group of children?'.
- **Encouraging pupils to focus on their own abilities**. Emphasise cooperation and sharing rather than competition. Comparisons should be related to improving their own individual skills.
- **Understanding the reasons for a pupil's jealousy**. Children feel better when adults acknowledge their feelings. Do not make children feel guilty about being jealous.
- **Treating all pupils with respect and fairness**. Take each pupil's individual needs into account. Pupils may require different amounts of adult attention at different times. Equality of opportunity does not mean treating everyone exactly the same, as this would mean ignoring individual needs; it means treating individuals fairly and providing the same *chances*.
- **Reassuring pupils that they are accepted for *who* they are regardless of what they do**. Try to spend a few minutes with each pupil in your group. Give regular individual attention to help reduce jealousy and increase emotional security.

Activity!

Describe an activity which supports pupils in understanding other people's feelings, for example sharing a story or poem about feelings and common events experienced by other children. Give an example from your own experiences of working with pupils.

Dealing with pupils' emotional outbursts

You should work with the teacher to provide a calm and accepting environment which allows pupils to experience and express their feelings safely (see above section on encouraging pupils to recognise and deal with feelings). Sometimes pupils (especially young children) are overwhelmed by their emotions and will act inappropriately or regress to previous patterns of behaviour. When children are unable to use language to express their feelings (for example because they lack the appropriate words, are too worked up, have behavioural/ emotional difficulties or other special needs) they are more prone to demonstrate their emotional responses in physical ways, such as biting, scratching, kicking, shouting, screaming, throwing things, throwing themselves on the floor, etc. An emotional outburst or 'temper tantrum' can be very frightening to the child and others in the group or class. Adults too can find children's emotional outbursts difficult to deal with.

key words

Emotional outburst: uncontrolled expression of intense emotion such as rage or frustration.

When dealing with a pupil's emotional outbursts it is essential that you:

- Remain calm yourself; speak quietly but confidently, shouting only makes things worse.
- Ignore the emotional outburst as much as possible while maintaining pupil safety.
- Avoid direct confrontations.
- Give the pupil time and space to calm down.
- Reassure the pupil afterwards but do not reward them.
- When the pupil has calmed down talk about what upset them in a quiet manner.
- Suggest to the pupil what they could do instead if they feel this way again.

The best way to deal with emotional outbursts is to minimise the likelihood of them happening in the first place: avoid setting up situations where emotional outbursts are likely to happen, such as making unrealistic demands or doing complex activities when a pupil is tired; give advance warning, for example prepare the pupil for new experiences; give a five minute warning that an activity is coming to an end and that you want them to do something else; provide reasonable choices and alternatives to give the pupil a sense of responsibility and control, such as the choice of activity to do next or choice of materials; and encourage the pupil to express their feelings in more positive ways. (See above section on encouraging pupils to recognise and deal with feelings.)

 Key Task

- Outline your school's policy for dealing with a pupil's emotional outburst.
- Describe how *you* have dealt with a pupil's emotional outburst.
- Give examples of opportunities in your school which allow pupils to experience and express their feelings safely.

NOS Links:

Level 3: STL 3.4 STL 19.1 STL 19.2 STL 20.1 STL 20.2 STL 20.3
STL 41.1 STL 41.2 STL 45.1

Helping pupils to deal with conflict situations

All pupils will experience situations where they feel that life is not fair. They will have disagreements and disputes with other pupils. Initially children rely on adults to help resolve these disputes, but gradually they learn how to deal with these for themselves. Pupils need to learn how to use language to reach agreements so that as far as possible their needs and other people's can be met fairly. Pupils need to learn that resolving conflicts does not mean getting your own way all the time (being aggressive) or allowing others to get their own way all the time (being submissive/passive). There is a better way that allows everyone to reach a satisfactory compromise – being assertive.

Ways to resolve conflicts

Fight/Bully = Aggressive ➔ 'I win so you lose'.

Submit/Retreat = Submissive/Passive ➔ 'I lose because you win'.

Discuss/Negotiate = Assertive ➔ 'I win and you win'.

Point out to pupils that shouting or physical violence never resolves conflicts, they usually make matters worse and only demonstrate who is the loudest or strongest or has more power. Conflicts need to be discussed in a calm manner so that a mutually agreed compromise can be reached.

You can use books, stories and videos that depict a potential conflict situation such as:

- sharing or borrowing toys
- deciding on rules for a game or choosing a game
- choosing partners or teams fairly
- knocking over models or spoiling work *accidentally*
- disrupting other children's activities *deliberately*.

Discuss with the pupils afterwards:

- What caused the conflict or disagreement?
- How were they resolved?
- What were the best solutions?
- How would they have resolved it?

Younger pupils can do this with appropriate situations and guidance from sensitive adults. Using puppets and play people can also help. Where pupils are used to doing role-play or drama, adults can get them to act out how to resolve conflicts in peaceful ways.

key words

Assertive: behaving in a way which is neither passive nor aggressive which allows everyone involved to discuss their feelings/opinions and then negotiate to reach a satisfactory compromise.

Conflict situation: verbal or physical disagreement, for example arguments, fighting, disputing rules.

In practice

Curtis is working as a teaching assistant with pupils in a primary school. During one week he helped the pupils to resolve the following conflict situations: two pupils arguing over sharing play equipment; a small group of pupils deciding which game to play; a pupil knocking over models *accidentally*; a pupil disrupting other children's activities *deliberately*. Suggest how these conflict situations could be resolved to achieve a 'win/win' result.

Developing positive working relationships with adults

Developing and promoting positive working relationships with adults is important because this helps to maintain a positive learning environment that benefits pupils, parents and staff. Positive working relationships will also reflect the school's aims such as: providing a caring environment that fosters cooperation and respect; encouraging children's all-round development; delivering play and learning opportunities in stimulating and appropriate ways; working in partnership with parents and the local community.

As a teaching assistant, you should have a strong commitment to pupils, colleagues, parents and the local community. You and your colleagues should behave at all times in a manner that demonstrates personal courtesy and integrity (see code of conduct for staff in Chapter 4). You should actively seek to develop your personal skills and professional expertise (see Chapter 9).

Communicating with adults

You should use language that other adults (including parents/carers, colleagues, parent helpers, volunteers and students) are likely to understand. Try to avoid 'jargon' or technical language unless you are sure that they too understand its meaning. Any requests for information from colleagues or parents that are beyond your knowledge and expertise, or any difficulties in communicating with colleagues or parents, should be referred to the appropriate person, the class/subject teacher, SENCO or head teacher.

key words

Parent: person with parental responsibility for a child (as defined in The Children Act 1989).

Carer: any person with responsibility for the care/education of a child during the parent's temporary or permanent absence.

You may need guidance on how to handle sensitive situations regarding your interactions with some colleagues or parents, especially when a derogatory remark is made about another colleague/parent or when the school policies are disregarded (see section on handling disagreements below).

Sharing information with parents and carers

Parents usually know more about their children and their children's needs so it is important to listen to what parents have to say. You should therefore actively encourage positive working relationships between parents (or designated carers) and the school. As a teaching assistant, you could provide a useful liaison between parents and their children's teacher because some parents may find you easier to talk to than the teacher. Some parents may find you more approachable, especially if you live in the local community and your children go/went to the same school.

Figure 3.3: Sharing information with parents

When communicating with parents use their preferred names and modes of address, for example the correct surname, especially when a woman has changed her name following divorce or remarriage. Only give information to a parent that is consistent with your role and responsibilities within the school – do not give recommendations concerning the pupil's future learning needs directly to the parents if this is the responsibility of the teacher, senior colleague or other professional. Any information shared with parents must be agreed with the teacher and must comply with the confidentiality requirements of the school. When sharing information about a pupil with their parents ensure that it is relevant, accurate and up-to-date.

Some adults may find it difficult to communicate effectively with others, for example those with a hearing impairment or physical disabilities affecting their ability to articulate sounds. Some parents may speak little or no English. Teaching assistants who have additional communication skills, such as being able to use sign language to communicate with an adult who has a hearing impairment, or bilingual teaching assistants who can liaise with parents whose community language is not English, may be very useful in the school. Teaching assistants who share local community languages may help parents and carers to feel more welcome in the school and help to avoid possible misinterpretations concerning cultural differences.

Sharing information is an essential part of working with pupils and their parents or carers. Adults working with pupils need essential information *from* parents including:

- **Routine information** such as medical history/conditions such as allergies; cultural or religious practices which may have implications for the care and education of the pupil such as special diets, exclusion from R.E. and assemblies; who collects the pupil (if applicable) including the transport arrangements (such as taxi or minibus) for a pupil with special needs.
- **Emergency information** such as contact telephone numbers for parents/carers, GP.
- **Other information** such as factors which may adversely affect the pupil's behaviour in the school, including family difficulties and crises such as divorce, serious illness or bereavement.

Remember to pass on information from parents to the relevant member of staff. Always remember confidentiality with regard to information provided by parents or carers (see below).

Adults working with pupils will also need to *give* parents information on:

- the main aims and objectives of the school
- age range of pupils
- class sizes and staff to pupil ratios
- staff names, roles and qualifications
- school hours and term dates/school holidays
- admission and settling in procedures
- record keeping and assessment
- test/examination targets and results
- an outline of approaches to learning (for example, the National Curriculum)
- the facilities for indoor and outdoor play, including arrangements for swimming
- arrangements for pupils with special needs, including the administration of medicines
- school discipline and behaviour management, including rewards and sanctions used

 key words

Confidentiality: professional discretion in keeping and/or disclosing personal information in accordance with the setting's requirements and relevant legislation, for example child protection and data protection.

Ratios: the numbers of adults in relation to children within a group setting, for example three adults with a group of thirty children would be shown as a ratio of 1:10.

- school procedures regarding food, drink, meal/snack times
- rules regarding school uniform, dress code and jewellery.

This information is usually given to parents and carers in the setting's brochure, prospectus or information pack. Information can also be given to parents and carers via letters, notice boards, newsletters and open days.

 Key Task

- Give examples of how your school shares information with parents.
- Get a copy of the school's brochure, prospectus or information pack.
- What are your school's policy and procedures for parents wishing to discuss their child's progress with a teacher?

NOS Links:

Level 3:   STL 20.4   STL 38.3   STL 60.1   STL 60.2

Sharing information with colleagues

You will be working as part of a team with other professionals, including other teaching assistants, teachers and SENCOs. Your colleagues will need regular information about your work, such as feedback about play and learning activities as well as updates about pupil participation and/or developmental progress. Some of this information may be given orally, for example outlining a pupil's participation and developmental progress during a particular learning activity, or commenting on a child's behaviour. Even spoken information needs to be given in a professional manner, to the appropriate person (the teacher), in the right place (not in a corridor where confidential information could be overheard) and at the right time (urgent matters need to be discussed with the teacher immediately while others may wait until a team meeting). Some information will be in written form, such as activity plans, notice boards, newsletters, staff bulletins and records.

Confidentiality matters

Confidentiality is important with regard to sharing information. Only the appropriate people should have access to confidential records. Except where a pupil is potentially at risk, information should not be given to other adults or agencies unless previously agreed. Where the passing of confidential information is acceptable then it should be given in the agreed format. You must always follow the school's policy and procedures regarding confidentiality and the sharing of information. Check with the class teacher or head teacher if you have any concerns about these matters. You should also be aware of any legal requirements with regard to record keeping and accessing information in your school, for example the Data Protection Act.

The basic provisions of the Data Protection Act

Under the Data Protection Act 1998 all settings processing personal information must comply with the eight enforceable principles of good practice. Personal data must be:

- fairly and lawfully processed
- processed for limited purposes
- adequate, relevant and not excessive
- accurate
- not kept longer than necessary
- processed in accordance with the data subject's rights
- secure
- not transferred to countries without adequate protection.

The Data Protection Act also safeguards the storage of data kept on computers, including hard drives and floppy disks. All records relating to personal information must be kept securely within the setting and the person to whom the records refer should have access to them. However, under the Data Protection Act 1998 certain information is exempt from disclosure and should not be shared with other service providers. This includes: material whose disclosure would be likely to cause serious harm to the physical or mental health or emotional condition of the child or someone else; information about whether the child is or has been subjected to or may be at risk of suspected child abuse; information that may form part of a court report; and references about pupils supplied to another school, any other place of education or training, any national body concerned with student admissions.

The school's requirements regarding confidentiality

You may find that the parents or carers of the pupils you work with will talk to you about their problems or give you details about their family. Senior staff at your school may also tell you confidential information to help you understand the needs of particular pupils and so enable you to provide more effective support. Whether a parent or colleague gives you confidential information you must not gossip about it.

However, you may decide to pass on information to colleagues on a 'need to know' basis; for example, to enable other members of staff to support the pupil's care, learning and development more effectively or where the pupil might be in danger. If you think that a pupil is at risk then you *must* pass on confidential information to an appropriate person, for example to the class teacher or the member of staff responsible for child protection issues in your school. If you decide to pass on confidential information then you should tell the person who gave you the information that you are going to do this and explain that you have to put the needs of the child first. Remember that every family has a right to privacy and you should only pass on information in the genuine interests of the child or to safeguard their welfare. (See section the confidentiality of information relating to abuse in Chapter 2.)

 Key Task

- What are the policies and procedures regarding confidentiality in your school?
- Make a list of the key points.

NOS Links:

Level 3: STL 3.2   STL 3.4   STL 20.4   STL 21.1   STL 23.3   STL 24.2   STL 27.3
          STL 29.1   STL 55.1   STL 55.2

Handling disagreements with other adults

As a teaching assistant you need to be able to recognise and respond to any problems that affect your ability to work effectively. This includes dealing appropriately with disagreements and conflict situations that affect your working relationships with other adults. Conflicts and disagreements are a part of everyone's working lives. If communication and working relationships break down, then conflict situations may arise which seriously damage the atmosphere in the school. Conflicts and disagreements can occur between: you and pupils; you and parents or carers; you and colleagues; you and other professionals. Most conflicts in the workplace arise due to: concerns about duties and responsibilities; disagreements about pupil behaviour; disagreements about management issues; clashes concerning different lifestyle choices or clashes between personalities.

Conflicts can also arise due to prejudice or discrimination. Incidents of such attitudes or behaviour must be challenged, as they are not only undesirable but also unlawful. However, it is essential to follow the school's policy and procedures together with any relevant legal requirements when dealing with these issues.

Many disagreements and conflicts can be resolved through open and honest discussion. This will involve arranging a mutually convenient time to talk to the other adult about the problem and may include the class teacher or head teacher. Sometimes another person can act as a mediator to help those involved to reach a satisfactory agreement or compromise. Where serious difficulties or conflict situations cannot be resolved, then the school will have a grievance procedure to deal with it. This usually involves talking to your line manager (for example the class teacher) about the problem in the first instance; they will then refer the matter to the senior management team/head teacher. If the problem concerns your line manager, then you may need to talk to the head teacher directly. You may also need to put your concerns in writing. If the matter cannot be resolved at this stage then, depending on the nature of the conflict, the school governors, the local education authority and relevant trade unions may be involved. Check with your line manager and/or the staff handbook for the exact procedures in your school. (See section on grievances and disciplinary procedures in Chapter 4.)

 **key words**

Mediator: a person who acts as an intermediary between parties in a dispute.

In practice

A parent has approached you directly with a complaint about the class teacher you work with and asked you to do something about it. How would you approach this conflict situation? Remember to be tactful and maintain confidentiality!

You could act this out as a role play with another student or colleague.

Key Task

Describe how you have responded (or would respond) to a disagreement or conflict situation with another adult in your school. (Be tactful and remember confidentiality.)

NOS Links:

Level 3:   **STL 20.4   STL 21.1**

Summary of key points in this chapter:

- **Developing positive working relationships with pupils** including: positive interactions with pupils; ways to develop positive relationships with pupils.

- **Communicating with children and young people** including: effective communication with children; active listening; asking and answering questions; the importance of praise and encouragement.

- **Supporting pupils in developing relationships** including: supporting pupils in developing agreements about behaviour; encouraging pupils to recognise and deal with feelings; dealing with pupils' emotional outbursts; helping pupils to deal with conflict situations.

- **Developing positive working relationships with adults**.

- **Communicating with adults** including: sharing information with parents and carers; sharing information with colleagues.

- **Confidentiality matters** including: the basic provisions of the Data Protection Act; the school's requirements regarding confidentiality.

- **Handling disagreements with other adults**.

Further reading:

DCSF (2008) *Information Sharing: Guidance for Practitioners and Managers*. DCSF & Communities and Local Government. (Available free at: **http://www.teachernet.gov.uk/_doc/13023/isgpm.pdf**)

DfES (2004) *Every Child Matters: Change for Children*. DfES (Available free online at: **http://www.dcsf.gov.uk/everychildmatters/**)

Digman, C. and Soan, S. (2008) *Working with Parents: A Guide for Educational Professionals*. Sage Publications.

Hartley, M. (2005) *The Assertiveness Handbook*. Sheldon Press.

Harvey, N. (2006) *Effective Communication*. Second revised edition. Gill & MacMillan Ltd.

Hobart, C. and Frankel, J. (2003) *A Practical Guide to Working with Parents*. Nelson Thornes.

Kerry, T. (2001) *Working with Support Staff: their roles and effective management in schools*. Pearson Education.

Lindenfield, G. (2000) *Self Esteem: Simple Steps to Developing Self-Reliance and Perseverance*. Harper Collins.

Lowe, C. (2010) *The Support Staff Little Pocket Book*. Third edition. QGP Ltd.

Miller, L. et al. (2005) *Developing Early Years Practice*. David Fulton Publishers.

Morgan, J. (2007) *How to be a Successful Teaching Assistant*. Continuum Publishing.

Ramsey, R. D. (2002) *How to Say the Right Thing Every Time: Communicating Well with Students, Staff, Parents and the Public*. Corwin Press.

Roet, B. (1998) *The Confidence to be Yourself*. Piatkus.

4. Understanding schools as organisations

This chapter relates to QCF unit:

TDA 3.2 Schools as organisations

The education system in the UK

Free full-time education is available and is compulsory for all children aged 5 to 16 years in the UK. In addition, free education is available for all 3 to 4 year olds whose parents want it, but is not compulsory except in Northern Ireland where compulsory education starts at 4 years old. Pupils are encouraged to continue their education to 18 years either in sixth forms, further education institutions or work-based learning (such as apprenticeships), but at the moment this is not compulsory. However, the Education and Skills Act 2008 plans to raise the school leaving age to 18 by 2015.

The state and private sectors in education

In the UK education is provided by both the state and private sectors. Parents may choose to send their children to schools in the state or private sector or they can educate their children by any suitable means approved, such as home schooling. State or maintained schools are funded by the government with no direct financial contribution by parents. State schools are mostly comprehensive in that they accept pupils of all academic abilities; they are also co-educational, meaning they have both boys and girls. In some areas there are still grammar schools which select the more academically able pupils and these tend to be single sex. Many state-funded secondary schools are specialist schools which receive extra funding for providing one or more specialist subject, for example computing, music, science, sport. Nearly all state schools are day schools, although there are a few state-funded boarding schools where the education is paid for by the government but the boarding fees are paid by parents. Some state-funded schools are faith schools such as Christian (mostly Catholic or Church of England) and Jewish, Muslim or Hindu. The private sector consists of independent or public schools where fees are paid by parents. Most of these are boarding schools, although some are day schools. Some boarding schools also include day pupils and weekly boarders (pupils who go home every weekend).

Types of schools

In the UK there are many different types of schools and other education settings for children aged 0 to 18 years. These can be organised into four main phases of education:

1. **Pre-school and nursery education** (0 to 5 year olds) includes: pre-school groups, playgroups, nursery centres, day nurseries, nursery schools, pupils aged 4–5 years in reception classes in primary schools.
2. **Primary education** (5 to 11 year olds) includes: primary schools, infant schools, junior schools, first schools, pupils aged 4–5 years in primary schools in Northern Ireland, pupils aged 8–11 years in middle schools, pupils aged 11–12 years in lower secondary education in Scotland.
3. **Secondary education** (11 to 16 year olds) includes: secondary schools, pupils aged 11–13 years in middle schools, high schools, grammar schools, academies, city technology colleges, pupils aged 12–16 years in lower secondary education in Scotland.
4. **Further education** (16 to 18 year olds) includes: school sixth forms, sixth form centres/colleges, FE colleges, tertiary colleges, specialist colleges, pupils aged 16–18 years in upper secondary education in Scotland.

Some schools may include several education phases in one setting, e.g. special schools for pupils with special needs aged 0 to 18 years.

 **Activity!**

- What type of school or other education setting do you work in?
- What are the ages of pupils you work with?

The school workforce

The school workforce consists of qualified teachers and support staff.

- Qualified teachers in the leadership group, for example head teachers, deputy or assistant head teachers and other qualified teachers.
- Classroom teachers including Qualified Teacher Status (QTS) – newly or recently qualified teachers; Core Teachers – teachers on the main pay scale; Post-Threshold Teachers – teachers on the upper pay scale; Excellent Teachers; Advanced Skills Teachers.
- Support staff including learning support staff, such as Teaching Assistants, Higher Level Teaching Assistants, Nursery Nurses, Sports Technicians/Assistants and Cover Supervisors.
- Pupil support/welfare staff, for example Learning Mentors, Play Workers, Midday Supervisors, Parent Support Advisors.
- Administrative staff, such as School Business Managers, Administrative Assistants, Secretaries, Examination Officers.
- Specialist technicians and assistants, for example Librarians and Library Assistants, Information and Communication Technology Technicians/Assistants, Design and Technology Technicians/Assistants, Food Technicians, Science Technicians.
- Site staff, such as Cleaners, Catering Staff and Cooks, Site/Premises Managers and Caretakers.

(For more information about support staff roles in visit the TDA website: **http://www.tda. gov.uk/support/support_staff_roles.aspx.**)

THE SCHOOL WORKFORCE

QUALIFIED TEACHERS

Leadership Group
Head Teacher
Deputy or Assistant Head Teacher

Classroom Teachers
Newly Qualified Teachers (NQT)
Qualified Teacher Status (QTS)
Core Teachers – teachers on the main pay scale
Post-Threshold Teachers – teachers on the upper pay scale
Excellent Teachers
Advanced Skills Teachers

SUPPORT STAFF

Learning Support Staff
Teaching Assistants
Higher Level Teaching Assistants
Nursery Nurses
Sports Technicians/Assistants
Cover Supervisors

Pupil support/welfare staff
Learning Mentors
Play Workers
Midday Supervisors
Parent Support Advisors

Administrative Staff
School Business Managers
Administrative Assistants
Secretaries
Examination Officers

Specialist and Technical Staff
Librarians and Library Assistants
Information and Communication Technology Technicians/Assistants
Design and Technology Technicians/Assistants
Food Technicians
Science Technicians

Site Staff
Cleaners
Catering Staff and Cooks
Site/Premises Managers
Caretakers

Figure 4.1: The school workforce

School workforce remodelling

Remodelling was a programme designed to help schools implement the reforms required by *Raising Standards and Tackling Workload: A National Agreement* (the National Agreement), which was signed in 2003. The reforms aimed to improve pupil outcomes and reduce the workload of teachers by focusing more of teachers' time on direct teaching and learning as well as providing leadership and support for colleagues with their teaching and learning. They included a series of changes to teachers' contracts; a review of support staff roles and a concerted attack on bureaucracy (DfES, 2003b).

The National Agreement and workforce remodelling was not only about teachers. The number of support staff working in schools has increased dramatically over the last few years and the National Agreement and workforce remodelling have helped to create new support staff roles. The National Agreement recognised that teachers were not always the most appropriate members of school staff to perform certain duties. While teachers have the central role in promoting pupils' learning, new support staff roles have become established in the classroom and in other areas of the school including: higher level teaching assistants (HLTAs); cover supervisors; bursars/school business manager; pastoral managers and invigilation staff. Both new and existing support staff roles are important in supporting teaching and learning in schools. More information on remodelling and the role of support staff can be found on the Training and Development Agency for Schools (TDA) website: **http://www.tda.gov.uk/**.

 **Activity!**

Find out about the different support staff roles in your school.

Roles and responsibilities within the school

The teaching assistant and the teacher need to be aware of their different roles. The teacher's role is to plan lessons, direct and assess pupils' learning. The teaching assistant's role is to assist the teacher by supporting pupils during the teaching of the curriculum. The teaching assistant works with the teacher to support pupils' learning within the whole class or works on their own to support the learning of an individual pupil or small group of pupils. Remember, the teaching assistant always works under the direction of the class or subject teacher.

 **Activity!**

Briefly describe the role of the teaching assistant in relation to the teacher.

Other roles and responsibilities within the school

The school governors have a range of duties and a general responsibility for the conduct of the school to promote high standards of educational achievement including: ensuring the curriculum is balanced and broadly based; setting targets for pupil achievement; managing the school's finances; appointing staff and reviewing staff performance and pay.

The head teacher is responsible for the internal organisation, management and control of the school; and for advising on and implementing the governing body's strategic framework. In particular, head teachers need to formulate aims and objectives, policies and targets for the governing body to consider adopting; and to report to the governing body on progress at least once every school year (DfEE, 2000; p. 2).

While the head teacher is responsible for all the pupils in the school, each class or subject teacher is responsible for all the pupils in their own class. The teacher is responsible for the learning of all pupils including those with special educational needs and Individual Education Plans or Behaviour Support Plans.

The head teacher and the senior management team, that is, the deputy/assistant head teacher(s), the special educational needs coordinator (SENCO) and the key stage coordinators, are responsible for the creation and maintenance of the learning environment throughout the school as a whole. The class or subject teacher is responsible for the preparation and maintenance of an appropriate learning environment within their own classroom and/or subject area. Working as

key words

SENCO: special needs coordinator.
Special educational needs: all children have *individual* needs, but some children may have *additional* needs due to physical disability, sensory impairment, learning difficulty or emotional/behavioural difficulty.

part of a team, the teacher decides how best to use the resources allocated to the class, which includes adult resources such as teaching assistants, nursery nurses and parent helpers as well as the necessary equipment and materials for learning activities. The teacher should ensure that these adults are used to their full potential in order to respond appropriately to the needs of all pupils in the class. As a teaching assistant you must help with the preparation and organisation of the learning environment as directed by the teacher.

 Activity!

Outline the role and responsibilities of: the school governors; the head teacher; deputy/ assistant head teacher(s); SENCO; key stage coordinators; subject coordinators; class/ subject teachers.

The supporting role of the teaching assistant

Adults who work in classrooms alongside teachers have various job titles including: learning support assistant; classroom assistant; special needs assistant and non-teaching assistant. 'Teaching assistant' is now the preferred term for adults (in paid employment) whose main role is to assist the teacher in a primary, secondary or special school.

To function effectively you need to be clear about your role as a teaching assistant. Your role will depend on the school and your experience/qualifications. There may be different requirements between teaching assistants even within the same school. A teaching assistant may have a *general* role working with different classes in a year group/key stage or *specific* responsibilities for a pupil, subject area or age group.

Activity!

Make a list of the things expected from you as part of your role in supporting an individual pupil or group of pupils.

Effectively managed, skilled teaching assistants make a valuable contribution to pupil achievement within the learning environment. Teaching assistants may be needed to attend to a pupil's care needs; or they may have a more educational role working with a pupil or group of pupils under the guidance of the class or subject teacher; or they may be involved in implementing a programme devised by a specialist, such as a speech and language therapist.

The term 'teaching assistant' indicates their central role of supporting the teacher. Teachers are responsible for planning and directing pupils' learning. Teaching assistants give *support* to class or subject teachers by *assisting* with the teaching of pupils in whole-class, small groups or with individuals, but *always* under a teacher's direction.

In order to provide effective support, teaching assistants need to know: teacher and school expectations for pupils' progress; learning objectives for pupils; behaviour expectations and policies for inclusion of pupils with special educational needs. Teaching assistants working with specific pupils need information regarding their special educational needs and provision including details of any statement of special educational needs, Individual Education Plans (IEPs) and/or Behaviour Support Plans.

Teaching assistants *support the individual pupil* by:

- Understanding the pupil's learning support needs.
- Listening to the pupil.
- Enabling the pupil to access the curriculum.
- Respecting and valuing the pupil.
- Gaining the pupil's trust and confidence.
- Responding appropriately to the pupil's physical needs.
- Encouraging independence.
- Promoting acceptance by the rest of the class.
- Using plenty of praise and rewards.

Teaching assistants *support the class or subject teacher* by:

- Working in partnership to prepare and maintain the learning environment.
- Helping to monitor and evaluate pupil progress.
- Providing feedback about pupils' learning and behaviour.
- Helping with classroom resources and pupil records.

Teaching assistants *support the school* by:
- Working with other members of staff as part of a team.
- Attending staff meetings.
- Working in partnership with parents.
- Making contributions to assessments and reviews.
- Knowing and following relevant school policies and procedures.
- Recognising and using personal strengths and abilities.
- Developing skills through in-service training and other courses.

Teaching assistants also provide *support for the curriculum* under the direction and guidance of the class or subject teacher. This involves an awareness and understanding of:

- Theories concerning how pupils think and learn.
- The sequences of expected development.

- Factors affecting pupils' learning progress in learning difficulties.
- National Curriculum documents.
- National Strategies for literacy and numeracy.
- The planning process.

The responsibilities of the teaching assistant

You need to understand clearly what your responsibilities are as a teaching assistant. Your responsibilities should be set out in your job description if you are already employed as a teaching assistant. (If you are a student you should have guidelines from your college.)

When you know what your responsibilities are, you will be clear about what is required from you. You should not be required to perform duties or activities that you are not qualified or not allowed to do, for example give first aid or administer

Figure 4.2: Teaching assistant supporting a pupil

medicines. However, do not refuse to do a task just because it is not in your job description – sometimes it may be necessary for everyone to help out. (There is more information about the role of the teaching assistant in supporting learning activities in Chapter 6.)

Here are some of the *general tasks* you may be expected to do as a teaching assistant:

- Set out or put away equipment.
- Help younger pupils, or older pupils who have physical disabilities get ready for a PE lesson.
- Check pupils' work.
- Encourage pupils to correct their own mistakes.
- Supervise practical work activities.
- Keep an individual pupil and/or group on task.
- Assist the pupil(s) to catch up on any missed work.
- Check equipment for safety.

Teaching assistants also have *specific tasks* that the class or subject teacher asks them to do. For example, supporting pupils' learning during a lesson or activity by:

- Repeating instructions given by the teacher.
- Taking notes for a pupil while the teacher is talking.
- Transcribing a pupil's dictation.
- Clarifying meaning and/or ideas.
- Explaining difficult words to a pupil.
- Promoting the use of dictionaries.
- Reading and clarifying textbook/worksheet activities for a pupil.
- Reading a story to an individual pupil or small group.
- Listening to pupils read.
- Playing a game with an individual pupil or small group.

- Directing computer-assisted learning programmes.
- Assisting pupils with special equipment (such as a hearing aid or a Dictaphone).
- Making worksheets and other resources as directed by the teacher.
- Observing/recording pupil progress during an activity.
- Providing any other appropriate assistance during an activity.
- Reporting problems and successes to the teacher.
- Contributing to planning and review meetings about pupils.

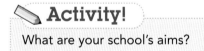 **Activity!**

- Think about your current role and responsibilities. List examples of your own general and specific tasks.
- If you are already employed as a teaching assistant, include your job description in your portfolio of evidence.

The school aims

All schools have a written statement outlining their expectations for both pupils and staff which reflect the purpose and ethos of the school. For example, school aims such as:

- Providing a caring environment that fosters cooperation and respect.
- Encouraging all pupils to fulfil their full potential and prepare for adult life.
- Delivering the National Curriculum in a stimulating and appropriate way.
- Ensuring continuity and progression of learning through carefully planned monitoring and evaluation.
- Working in partnership with parents and the local community.

key words

Ethos: the specific characteristics, beliefs and values of an organisation.

This statement will be available in various documents throughout the school, for example, in the school brochure and the staff handbook.

Activity!

What are your school's aims?

Code of conduct for staff

All members of staff in the school must have a strong commitment to pupils, colleagues, parents, governors and the local community. Staff members should behave at all times in a manner that shows personal courtesy and integrity. Staff members should actively seek to develop their personal skills and professional expertise.

1. With regard to the *pupils* in school you should:
   - Remember that the social, intellectual, physical welfare and emotional well-being of the pupils is the prime purpose and first concern of education.
   - Act with compassion and impartiality.

- Express criticism of pupils in a sensitive manner and avoid hurtful comments of a personal nature.
- Never abuse, exploit or undermine the staff/pupil relationship.
- Respect the confidentiality of information relating to pupils unless the disclosure of such information is either required by law or is in the best interests of that particular pupil.
- Ensure that assessments and reports on all pupils are based on factual, objective and up-to-date information.

2. With regard to *colleagues* in school you should:
- Have a duty of care towards your colleagues.
- Demonstrate an awareness of the work-related needs of others.
- Remember confidentiality in discussions with colleagues concerning problems associated with their work.
- Respect the status of colleagues, particularly when making any assessment or observations on their work.
- Never put down a colleague in the presence of others.
- Use maximum frankness and good faith in all matters relating to appointments to posts.
- If relevant to your role, provide references that are fair and truthful.

3. With regard to the *parents* of pupils in the school you should:
- Seek to establish a friendly and cooperative relationship with the parents of pupils.
- Never distort or misrepresent the facts concerning any aspect of the educational development of pupils.
- Respect the joint responsibility that exists between the school and the parents for the education of their children.
- Respect parental rights to enquiry, consultation and information with regard to the educational development of their children.

4. With regard to the *school governors* you should:
- Establish a friendly and cooperative relationship with the governing body.
- Never distort or misrepresent facts concerning the school.
- Recognise and support the reasonable discharge of the corporate responsibilities and duties of the governing body.

5. With regard to the *local community* you should:
- Promote a good working relationship with parents, governors and elected representatives of the local community.
- Be aware of the involvement of the local community in the life of the school and understand its social, economic, ethnic needs and problems.
- Recognise the need of the local community to use the school facilities subject to the requirements of the school.

6. With regard to your *work commitments* you should:
- Always have proper regard for the health, safety and well-being of pupils, colleagues and yourself. (See the section on the school's health and safety policy.)
- Respect and fulfil your contractual obligations.
- Respect the right of an individual to hold religious or political beliefs and not seek to impose your own personal opinions in such matters.
- Never misrepresent your professional qualifications and work experience.
- Never canvass directly or indirectly in order to secure a post.

- Ensure that other commitments (such as part-time employment or study) do not get in the way of your capacity to fulfil your contractual obligations.
- Make careful and appropriate use of all resources provided.

Grievance and disciplinary procedures

If you have a grievance relating to your employment, you are entitled to invoke the school's grievance procedure (which is part of a Local Education Authority agreement) and is included in the staff handbook. The grievance should be raised initially with your line manager. The grievance should be raised orally in the first instance, although you may be requested to put it in writing. If your grievance relates to your line manager, then your grievance should be referred to their line manager or the head teacher.

The school expects reasonable standards of performance and conduct from all staff members. Details of the disciplinary procedure (which is part of a Local Education Authority agreement) are included in the staff handbook. If you are dissatisfied with a disciplinary decision you should in the first instance contact the head teacher within five working days of the date of the decision.

 Key Task

- Outline the code of conduct in your setting.
- What are the grievance and disciplinary procedures for staff?

NOS Links:

Level 3:   STL 4.4   STL 5.1   STL 20.4   STL 21.1

The organisational structure of the school

You need to be very clear about the organisational structure of the school, as information from different people can be confusing or even contradictory. In particular, you need to know who your line manager is; that is, the person who manages your work in school. Your line manager may not necessarily be the class teacher; depending on the size of the school and the responsibilities of senior staff, your line manager could be the head teacher, deputy head, head of department or key stage coordinator. If your work mostly involves supporting pupils with special educational needs then the SENCO may well be your line manager. Whoever your line manager is, you must always follow the directions of the teacher in whose class you are working with pupils. When the class teacher and your line manager are not the same person, their roles and responsibilities need to be understood both by them and by you.

 **Activity!**

Draw a diagram to show the organisational structure of your school including where you (as a teaching assistant) and your line manager fit into this structure.

Effective planning and organisation within the school

Staff meetings are essential for effective planning and organisation within the school. Such meetings also provide regular opportunities to share day-to-day information and to solve any problems. Staff meetings should be held regularly – about once every 4 to 6 weeks. There should be an agenda for the meeting and minutes of the meeting should be recorded, both of which should be easily accessed by relevant staff. Staff meetings should encourage colleagues to share best practice, knowledge and ideas on developing appropriate learning activities in the school. As well as general staff meetings you may also be involved in regular team meetings for the more detailed planning of activities as well as the allocation of work within your area of responsibility. (For more detailed information on planning activities see Chapters 1 and 6.)

As part of the school's planning and organisation you may be allocated work and responsibilities in a variety of ways. For example, you may have:

- **Responsibility for supporting pupils in a particular age range**: Each teaching assistant (or group of teaching assistants) is responsible for supporting pupils in a particular age range within the school and promoting children's care, learning and development within a particular key stage or year group. The teaching assistant(s) will provide support for the individual needs of the pupils in that key stage or year group including appropriate adult supervision or intervention as and when necessary.
- **Responsibility for supporting pupils in a particular curriculum area**: The teaching assistant may be responsible for a particular curriculum area or activity, for example literacy, numeracy or ICT activities. The teaching assistant stays with the same activity throughout the day/week and is responsible for: selecting and setting out materials or helping pupils to access these for themselves; encouraging pupil interest and participation in the activity; providing appropriate adult supervision or intervention as required and helping pupils to clear away afterwards.
- **Responsibility for supporting a small group of pupils**: Each teaching assistant is responsible for a small group of pupils as their key person or key worker. The teaching assistant helps them to settle into the school. The teaching assistant is responsible for: greeting their group of pupils on arrival; encouraging the children's care, learning and development in the school and establishing and maintaining a special relationship with each child and their family.
- **Responsibility for supporting an individual pupil**: A teaching assistant may have special responsibility for a pupil with a disability. The teaching assistant will be responsible for: ensuring that pupil's particular needs are met in an inclusive way within the school; ensuring the pupil has the necessary materials to participate in routines and activities including any specialist equipment and establishing and maintaining a special relationship with the pupil and their family.

Working in partnership with the teacher

Advanced planning (with clear objectives) and the detailed preparation of work are central to the effective delivery of the curriculum and to providing appropriate support for pupils' learning. Teachers need to involve teaching assistants in the planning and preparation of their work by having regular planning meetings about once a term or every half term. In addition, each day the teacher and the teaching assistant should discuss:

- the teacher's lesson plans
- the learning objectives for the pupils
- the teaching assistant's contribution to the lesson
- the type and level of support for the pupils.

These regular planning meetings and discussions will help to avoid confusion as both the teacher and the teaching assistant will then be clear about the exact tasks to be performed and the level of support to be provided. Short discussions after lessons are also helpful as teaching assistants can provide feedback to the teacher about the progress of pupils during group or individual activities. This feedback can make a valuable contribution to the teacher's assessment of pupils and help with the future planning of learning activities (see Chapter 6).

Teaching assistants also need to be familiar with the ways individual teachers deal with pupils who demonstrate difficult behaviour to avoid giving conflicting messages to pupils. While all staff in a school should work within the framework of the school's behaviour management policy, individual teachers may have different approaches to responding to difficult behaviour based on their own teaching style and the individual needs of their pupils (see Chapter 7).

Working with the special educational needs coordinator

Many teaching assistants are responsible for supporting pupils with special educational needs. As part of this responsibility the teaching assistant should be aware of:

- each pupil's special educational needs
- how these needs affect the pupil
- the special provision and learning support required
- their role in helping the pupil to access the curriculum.

This role will involve working with the teacher responsible for pupils with special educational needs – the special educational needs coordinator (SENCO). Regular meetings, usually once a week, help the teaching assistant and the SENCO to provide effective support for the learning and participation of pupils with special educational needs. Teaching assistants may also be involved in contributing to and reviewing Individual Educational plans or Behaviour Support plans because they spend more time working with individual pupils with special educational needs than the class teacher (see Chapter 13).

 **Key Task**

Give examples of effective planning and organisation of work within your school. With permission, you could include copies of planning sheets, minutes from a staff or team meeting and a work rota.

NOS Links:

Level 3:   **STL 18.1   STL 21.1   STL 23.1   STL 24.1   STL 27.1 (early years)**

Legislation affecting work in schools

There are many laws and codes of practice which affect work in schools including legislation and regulations relating to: health and safety; safeguarding children from abuse; discipline in schools; pupil registration; equality and disability; and curriculum requirements.

Health and safety regulations

The two most important pieces of health and safety legislation affecting schools are the Health and Safety at Work Act 1974 and the Management of Health and Safety at Work Regulations 1999. These set the standards that must be met to ensure the health and safety of all employees and others who may be affected by any work activity. Other regulations also exist to cover work activities that carry specific risks, for example lifting and carrying, computer work and electricity. The main legislation affecting schools includes:

- The Health and Safety at Work Act 1974
- The Management of Health and Safety at Work Regulations 1999
- The Education (School Premises) Regulations 1999
- The Workplace (Health, Safety and Welfare) Regulations 1992
- The Manual Handling Operations Regulations 1992
- The Reporting of Injuries, Diseases and Dangerous Occurrences Regulations 1995
- The Control of Substances Hazardous to Health Regulations 2002
- The Provision and Use of Work Equipment Regulations 1998
- The Health and Safety (First Aid) Regulations 1981.

Health and safety regulations are sometimes supplemented by codes of practice approved and/or issued by the Health and Safety Executive. Approved codes of practice give practical guidance on compliance with the relevant regulations. Failure to comply with an approved code of practice is not an offence in itself, but these codes do have special legal status. So if an employer/employee faces criminal prosecution under health and safety legislation, and it is proved that the approved code of practice was not followed, a court can regard this as evidence of guilt unless the court is satisfied that the employer/employee complied with the law in some other way. Therefore, following approved codes of practice is regarded as best practice. To search for relevant approved codes of practice, go to the HSE Books website: **http://books.hse.gov.uk/hse/public/home.jsf** . Detailed information about health and safety regulations applicable to schools is in Chapter 5. Further information is also available from the Health and Safety Executive's website: **http://www.hse.gov.uk** .

 **Activity!**

Find out about the approved codes of practice relevant to work in schools, for example regarding first aid.

Safeguarding children from abuse

Legislation also affects schools with regard to protecting children from abuse. All school staff members must understand fully their responsibilities and duties for safeguarding children and young people as set out in government legislation, regulations and guidance. *Working*

Together to Safeguard Children: A Guide to Inter-agency Working to Safeguard and Promote the Welfare of Children (2010) provides statutory guidance and non-statutory practice guidance on how organisations and practitioners should work together to safeguard and promote the welfare of children and young people in accordance with the Children Act 1989 and the Children Act 2004. (For more detailed information see Chapter 2.)

Discipline in schools

The Education and Inspections Act 2006 gives all staff in maintained schools in England and Wales new legal rights to discipline pupils. Section 92 of the Act extends the powers of schools to use detentions by making it lawful for schools to place pupils under the age of 18 in detention, without parental consent, outside school hours, such as weekend detentions. Pupils who misbehave can now be required to attend Saturday or Sunday detentions during a school term unless this is a Saturday or Sunday that falls during or at a weekend immediately preceding or immediately following a half-term break. The Act removes the requirement for 24 hours' written notice to be given for lunchtime detentions. However, 24 hours' written notice to parents is still required for all detentions outside normal school hours. The Act now enables schools to make their own applications for parenting orders to ensure parents tackle problem behaviour before a pupil reaches the point of being excluded from school (ATL, 2007; p.1).

The Act also gives all staff in lawful charge of pupils the power to discipline them for inappropriate behaviour or for not following instruction. This means that head teachers can delegate the responsibility of discipline to support staff as well as teaching staff. The Act gives power to school staff to use reasonable force. (See sections on staff responsibilities for managing pupil behaviour and the use of reasonable force to control or restrain pupils in Chapter 7.)

Pupil registration

Pupil registration regulations relate to the admissions and attendance registers that all schools must keep. They also regulate the power of special schools and maintained schools to grant leave of absence. The current regulations, The Education (Pupil Registration) (England) Regulations 2006, came into force on 1 September 2006. By law, schools are required to record in the attendance register once at the beginning of the morning session and once during the afternoon whether the pupil is present, absent, engaged in an approved, supervised educational activity off-site, or unable to attend due to exceptional circumstances as defined in regulation 6(5). If a compulsory school-age pupil is absent, the register must show whether the absence is authorised or unauthorised. It must also record the nature of any approved, supervised educational activities (Teachernet, 2009). Further information is available from the Teachernet website at: **http://www.teachernet.gov.uk/wholeschool/behaviour/attendance/pupilregis/**.

Equality, diversity and inclusion

You must know and understand the basic requirements of legislation relating to equality, diversity and inclusion, for example equal opportunities, disability discrimination and special educational needs. There are three acts which are particularly important for those working in schools: The Special Educational Needs and Disability Act 2001, The Disability Discrimination Act 2005 and The Equality Act 2010. (For detailed information, see the section on legislation relating to equality, diversity and inclusion in Chapter 8.)

Curriculum requirements

Legislation also affects schools with regard to curriculum requirements. You should know the relevant curriculum frameworks for your home country: England, Northern Ireland, Scotland or Wales. For example, in England the curriculum frameworks are the Early Years Foundation Stage (0 to 5 years) and the National Curriculum Key Stages 1 to 4 (5 to 16 years). (For more information see the section on curriculum frameworks in Chapter 6.)

Regulatory bodies

Regulatory bodies relevant to the education sector exist to monitor and enforce the relevant legislations. For example, general bodies such as the Health and Safety Executive are responsible for ensuring the enforcement of health and safety matters in the workplace including schools (see above); while school specific regulatory bodies such as Ofsted are responsible for ensuring standards are maintained in a wide range of education settings. Ofsted is the Office for Standards in Education, Children's Services and Skills. Ofsted regulates and inspects childcare and children's social care. Ofsted also inspects: schools; colleges; initial teacher education; work-based learning and skills training; adult and community learning; education and training in prisons and other secure establishments and the Children and Family Court Advisory Service (Ofsted, 2009).

 **Activity!**

Find out more about the role of regulatory bodies in relation to your setting, such as Ofsted.

School policies and procedures

All schools have policies and procedures that help maintain a structured and consistent learning environment. These policies relate to the legal requirements within schools and provide guidance on the procedures for implementing the policies in the school. Detailed information about key school policies and procedures can be found in the relevant chapter of this book:

- health and safety (Chapter 5)
- child protection/safeguarding children (Chapter 2)
- inclusion/special educational needs (Chapters 8 and 13)
- equal opportunities (Chapter 8)
- behaviour and discipline (Chapter 7)
- anti-bullying (Chapter 2)
- confidentiality (Chapter 3)
- curriculum policies for each subject area (Chapter 6)
- assessment policy (Chapter 10).

Key Task

- Summarise the key policies and procedures schools may have relating to: staff and pupil welfare; teaching and learning; equality, diversity and inclusion; parental engagement.
- How does your setting develop and communicate its policies and procedures?

NOS Links:

Level 3:	STL 3.1	STL 3.2	STL 3.3	STL 3.4	STL 18.1	STL 19.1	STL 19.2
	STL 20.1	STL 20.2	STL 20.3	STL 20.4	STL 21.1	STL 21.2	
	STL 23.1	STL 23.2	STL 23.3	STL 24.1	STL 24.2	STL 30.1	STL 30.2

Summary of the key points in this chapter:

- **The education system in the UK**: the state and private sectors in education; types of schools.
- **The school workforce**: qualified teachers and support staff; school workforce remodelling.
- **Roles and responsibilities within the school**: the roles and responsibilities of others within the school; the supporting role of the teaching assistant; the responsibilities of the teaching assistant; the school aims; code of conduct for staff; grievance and disciplinary procedures.
- **The organisational structure of the school**: effective planning and organisation within the school; working in partnership with the teacher; working with the special educational needs coordinator.
- **Legislation affecting work in schools including**: health and safety regulations; safeguarding children from abuse; discipline in schools; pupil registration; equality and inclusion; curriculum requirements; regulatory bodies; school policies and procedures.

Further reading

ATL (2007) *Statutory Rights: Support Staff in the Maintained Sector*. ATL.

http://www.atl.org.uk/publications-and-resources/factsheets/support-staff-statutory-rights.asp

Balshaw, M. and Farrell, P. (2002) *Teaching Assistants: Practical Strategies for Effective Classroom Support*. David Fulton Publishers.

Brookes, G. (2008) *The Complete Guide for Teaching Assistants in Secondary Education*. Continuum International Publishing Group Ltd.

Dean, J. (2005) *The Teaching Assistant's Guide to Primary Education*. Routledge.

DCSF (2008) *Information Sharing: Guidance for Practitioners and Managers*. DCSF & Communities and Local Government (available free at: **http://www.teachernet.gov.uk/_doc/13023/isgpm.pdf**).

DfES (2004) *Every Child Matters: Change for Children*. DfES (available free online at: **http://www.dcsf.gov.uk/everychildmatters/**).

Harvey, N. (2006) *Effective Communication*. Second revised edition. Gill & MacMillan Ltd.

Hobart, C. and Frankel, J. (2003) *A Practical Guide to Working with Parents*. Nelson Thornes.

Kerry, T. (2001) *Working with Support Staff: Their Roles and Effective Management in Schools*. Pearson Education.

Lowe, C. (2010) *The Support Staff Little Pocket Book*. Third edition. QGP Ltd.

Matheson, D. (2008) *An Introduction to the Study of Education*. Third edition. David Fulton Publishers.

Ramsey, R. D. (2002) *How to Say the Right Thing Every Time: Communicating Well with Students, Staff, Parents and the Public*. Corwin Press.

Sleigh, W.G. (2009) *The Organisation and Curricula of Schools*. Richardson.

Watkinson, A. (2010) *The Essential Guide for New Teaching Assistants*. Routledge.

5. Supporting children and young people's health and safety

This chapter relates to QCF unit:

CYP Core 3.4 Support children and young people's health and safety

Statutory and regulatory health and safety requirements

You will need to know, understand and follow the legal and organisational requirements of the school for establishing and maintaining the health, safety and security of yourself and others (pupils, staff, families and visitors in the school) at all times as well as the procedures for reporting any concerns or problems to the appropriate person. You will also need to use safe working practices in all that you do, which includes ensuring that someone in authority (for example the class teacher and/or your line manager) knows where you are at all times in case of an emergency.

Health and safety legislation places overall responsibility for health and safety with the employer. However, as an employee working within a school, you also have responsibilities with regard to maintaining health and safety. All employees have a responsibility under the Health and Safety at Work Act 1974 to:

- To take reasonable care for the health and safety of themselves and of any person who might be affected by their acts or omissions at work.
- To cooperate with the relevant authorities (for example Ofsted) in meeting statutory requirements.
- To not interfere with or misuse anything provided in the interests of health, safety and welfare.
- To make themselves aware of all safety rules, procedures and safe working practices applicable to their posts. (When in doubt they must seek immediate clarification from the delegated person responsible for health and safety in the setting.)
- To ensure that tools and equipment are in good condition and report any defects to the delegated person.
- To use protective clothing and safety equipment provided and to ensure that these are kept in good condition.

- To ensure that any accidents, whether or not an injury occurs, are reported to the delegated person.
- To report potential hazards or any possible deficiencies in health and safety arrangements to the delegated person.

The Workplace (Health, Safety and Welfare) Regulations 1992 clarify and consolidate existing legislation. They also establish a consistent set of standards for the majority of workplaces. The regulations expand on the responsibilities placed on employers (and others in control of premises) by the Health and Safety at Work Act 1974 including: health and safety in the workplace, welfare facilities for people at work and maintenance of the workplace. The workplace and equipment need to be maintained in an efficient state, in working order, and in good repair. Buildings, including mobile or temporary rooms, should be in a good state of repair and services should be in efficient working order. In general, indoor workplaces should be reasonably comfortable, reasonably clean, properly illuminated and adequately spacious.

The environmental requirements of the regulations apply to the workplace, but existing education standards for children's working space, temperature and ventilation and so on, may be more appropriate for education settings. The Education (School Premises) Regulations 1999 provide the statutory requirements for the minimum standards of both new and existing schools. The regulations include a general requirement that all parts of the school's premises must be reasonably maintained to ensure the health, safety and welfare of all users. These regulations also include the specific requirements for: acoustics, ancillary facilities, drainage, heating, lighting, medical accommodation, playing fields, washrooms, staff accommodation, structural matters, ventilation, water supply and weather protection.

The Management of Health and Safety at Work Regulations 1999 requires a risk assessment of facilities, a safety policy regarding these risks and appropriate health and safety training. You should be able to recognise any risks within the learning environment and take the appropriate action to minimise them, for example reporting potential health and safety hazards to the relevant person. (See section on risk assessment below.)

The Manual Handling Operations Regulations 1992, as amended in 2002, apply to manual handling activities such as lifting, lowering, pushing, pulling and carrying. The load being handled may be a box, trolley, person or animal. The Regulations require employers to:

- *Avoid* the need for hazardous manual handling, so far as is reasonably practicable.
- *Assess* the risk of injury from any hazardous manual handling that cannot be avoided.
- *Reduce* the risk of injury from hazardous manual handling, so far as is reasonably practicable.

The regulations require employees to:

- Follow appropriate systems of work laid down for their safety.
- Make proper use of equipment provided for their safety.
- Cooperate with their employer on health and safety matters.
- Inform the employer if they identify hazardous handling activities.
- Take care to ensure their activities do not put others at risk.

(HSE, 2004)

You should be aware of the risks associated with lifting and carrying children such as possible back injuries. Ensure that you follow your school's procedures for lifting and carrying pupils. The Health and Safety Executive (HSE) provides guidance on manual handling (see Further Reading). (See also section below on risk assessment applicable to the learning environment.)

 **Activity!**

Find out about the statutory and regulatory requirements that apply to your school.

Safety checks in the learning environment

You need to know the location of safety equipment in the different areas of the learning environment. You must be clear about the safety arrangements for the areas and pupils you work with including: the position of fire exits, extinguishers, blanket, first aid boxes; your role during fire drill; what to do in case of fire or other emergency especially the procedures for pupils with physical disabilities or sensory impairments, escape routes and alternatives if blocked by fire, etc.

 **Activity!**

- Where is the safety equipment located in your setting?
- Where are the first aid boxes located?

Checking equipment is safe for use

All equipment in the school should be safe and approved for safety, displaying the BSI Kitemark, European standards markings or BEAB mark of safety. You should know the operating procedures and safety requirements of the school before using any equipment. Operating instructions should be available, and in many cases an experienced/knowledgeable member of staff may show you how to use the equipment beforehand. If not, it is essential to ask, especially when dealing with electrical equipment for safety reasons and the possibility of damaging expensive equipment – you do not want to causes hundreds or even thousands of pounds worth of damage to a computer or photocopier! You should follow any instructions carefully. Allow yourself plenty of time to do this thoroughly. Five minutes before you need to show the group/class a DVD is not the time to start learning how to use the school's DVD player for the first time! As with all learning activities you must plan ahead.

You should check equipment that you use regularly to ensure that it is safe and in proper working order, for example, check the television, video or computer is in working order before you or the pupils need it so that you can sort out any problems in advance. If there is a fault and the equipment is not functioning properly or not at all you need to know the appropriate school procedures for dealing with faults, for example, which can be dealt with by you and which require reporting to the appropriate person. It is also important to check classroom equipment and materials regularly for damage and to report any damage to the appropriate person, such as the class or subject teacher. Serious damage will have to be repaired by a professional (such as a technician or the school caretaker) or the item will have to be replaced.

Storing materials and equipment safely

Storage areas should be kept tidy with sufficient space for the materials and equipment being stored there. Storage facilities should be easily accessible and, where appropriate, lockable. Potentially hazardous materials must be stored away from pupils and locked away. Storage space should be organised so that heavy equipment is stored at a low level. Lightweight equipment may be stored above head level if space is limited. One of your responsibilities as a teaching assistant may be to ensure that all equipment and surfaces are safe, hygienic and usable. If working with pupils who have been using messy materials, such as glue or paint, you will need to wipe tables or easels clean after use and clean any brushes ready for the next time. Any major cleaning tasks that are not part of your responsibilities should be referred to the class or subject teacher for attention. It is also important to ensure proper hygiene and correct use of equipment. For example, using fresh ingredients when doing cooking activities and ensuring pupils wash their hands before and after, or following the correct procedures during science experiments.

Ten important safety points to remember

Remember the following important safety points when establishing a healthy, safe and secure learning environment:

1. **All equipment and materials must be appropriate to the ages/levels of development of the pupils**, for example, small items are potential choke hazards for young children.

2. **Pupils must listen carefully and follow instructions** on the use of equipment and materials during activities, for example handling fragile or breakable objects with care.

3. **Pupils must be told never to put anything in their mouths** during learning activities unless instructed to do so by the adult in charge (they may be allowed to sample food during a cooking or tasting activity).

4. **Safety goggles to British Standard BS2092** (that can also be worn with spectacles) should be worn by pupils engaged in potentially hazardous activities such as sawing, hammering and science experiments involving chemicals.

5. **Pupils should not touch electrical equipment**, especially with wet hands.

6. **When pupils are doing cooking activities** ensure that: ingredients are fresh and in good condition; dried ingredients are stored in airtight containers; cooking utensils and table surfaces are scrupulously clean; and all hands are washed beforehand.

7. **Check if any pupil is prevented from taking part in an activity** due to cultural or religious dietary prohibitions; ensure that individual children are not allergic to any of the ingredients or materials.

8. **Long hair should be tied back** during construction, cooking, PE and science activities.

9. **Pupils should be taught how to use, arrange and store PE apparatus** correctly and safely as appropriate to their age and level of development.

10. **Pupils should report all accidents** to the teacher or teaching assistant.

Figure 5.1: Pupils wearing safety goggles

Maintaining toilet and wash areas

It is important that toilet and wash facilities are maintained in a clean and orderly condition with adequate lighting and ventilation. For children over 2 years old there should be one toilet and hand basin for every ten children. There should be separate toilet facilities for pupils and staff. There should be an adequate supply of drinking water that is easily accessible to pupils. The school should ensure that toilet facilities are maintained to high standards of hygiene. There should be adequate supplies of toilet paper, soap, warm water and disposable paper towels and/or access to hot air driers. The cleaning routines for toilets and washbasins should be regular and thorough to maintain high standards of hygiene. To minimise the spread of infection, the school should advise parents whose children have diarrhoea that the children should stay away from the setting until they no longer have symptoms. Your role might involve checking pupil toilet areas to see that they are used correctly and that pupils wash their hands after using the toilet or before handling food. You may be required to assist very young pupils (or pupils with physical disabilities) with their toileting needs. You should know the school's procedures for dealing with pupils who wet or soil themselves, including the location of appropriate spare clothing.

You may need to provide reassurance and support for a girl who starts menstruation but does not have any sanitary protection. (Girls as young as 8 or 9 can start their first period while at the setting.) You should know the school's procedures for dealing with this situation, including accessing emergency supplies of sanitary protection and its disposal. If you are a male teaching assistant then you must know who to go to for help if this situation occurs.

If you experience any concerns or problems with pupils when carrying out hygiene routines, you should report these to the class teacher. This includes reporting any hazard or unsafe situation you discover when using the school's toilet or wash facilities.

Activity!

- What are your school's procedures for checking toilet and wash areas? What are your responsibilities for checking these areas?
- List 10 important safety points to remember when organising classroom resources.

Maintaining health and safety

You are responsible for the health and safety of the children (and others) under your direct supervision. This includes exercising effective supervision over those for whom you are responsible including children, students, parent helpers and volunteers. You must be aware of and implement safe working practices and set a good example. You should ensure that you and others (under your direct supervision) follow written instructions, warning notices and signs as appropriate. You must ensure appropriate protective clothing and safety equipment are used as required, for example wearing aprons for painting activities. You should provide adequate instruction, information and training in safe working methods as appropriate to your role and responsibilities.

You also need to encourage children to be aware of their own safety, other people's safety and their own personal responsibilities for maintaining health and safety in the setting. The setting should ensure that children (and where appropriate their parents) are aware of their responsibilities through direct instruction, notices and the setting's handbook.

As appropriate to their ages and abilities, all children should be expected to:

- Exercise personal responsibility for the safety of themselves and other children.
- Observe standards of dress consistent with safety and/or hygiene (this precludes unsuitable footwear, knives and other items considered dangerous).
- Observe all the safety rules of the setting, in particular the instructions of adults in the event of a fire or other emergency.
- Use and not wilfully misuse, neglect or interfere with items provided for safety purposes such as fire alarms and fire extinguishers.

You must know and follow the setting's policies and procedures for maintaining child safety at all times, especially during play and learning activities including outings. It is important to provide challenging and exciting play and learning activities that encourage children to develop and explore whilst still maintaining their physical safety and emotional welfare.

Activity!

Find out about your school's policy and procedures for health and safety.

Risk assessment applicable to the learning environment

You must know and understand the importance of pupils being given opportunities to play and learn within an environment that will not harm their health and safety. Adult supervision should be provided as appropriate to the ages/levels of development of the children (for example, very young children need close supervision with a high adult: child ratio). As children grow and develop their physical abilities they need to be provided with activities and experiences that have levels of challenge and risk that will help them to develop confidence and independence.

You need to be able to identify potential hazards (activities likely to cause harm) and assess possible risks (the seriousness of the hazards and their potential to cause actual harm).

1. The purpose of risk assessment is to: undertake a systematic review of the potential for harm; evaluate the likelihood of harm occurring; decide whether the existing control measures are adequate; and decide whether more needs to be done.

2. The sequence for risk assessment is: classify the activity; identify potential hazard(s); evaluate possible risks; evaluate control measures; and specify any further action.

3. Once the risk assessment has been carried out the hierarchy for control measures is: eliminate hazard; reduce hazard; isolate hazard; control hazard.

4. Once the risk assessment and control measures have been completed, no further action needs to be taken unless there is a significant change in that area.

(RoSPA, 2004b)

key words

Hazard: an activity likely to cause harm.

Risk: the seriousness of the hazard and its potential to cause actual harm.

Risk assessment: a systematic review of the potential for harm including identifying hazards, evaluating possible risks, evaluating existing control measures and specifying any further action.

 **Activity!**

Outline the procedures for risk assessment and dealing with hazards in your school.

You must know and understand the basic stages of child development and the implications these have for health, safety and security arrangements. For detailed information go to the Child Accident Prevention Trust (CAPT) website: **www.capt.org.uk** and then clink 'Samples of our leaflets' to access free samples of these age-related safety leaflets:

- *Handle safely*: babies from birth to crawling
- *Active steps to safety*: toddlers up to the age of 5
- *Step safely with a helping hand*: children aged 5 to 7
- *Step safely from the edge*: children aged 7 to 11
- *It's a safety thing*: young people aged 11 to 14.

Remember that, despite the school's procedures to maintain children's safety, there may still be times when accidents or injuries occur. Ensure that you know how to deal with accidents and injuries as well as the arrangements for first aid. (See section below on dealing with accidents and injuries.)

Nikki works at Parkside After-School Club and has started to complete a risk assessment for the outdoor play area. She has used the key below to estimate the Risk (R) by multiplying (X) the Severity (S) by the Likelihood (L) S × L = R

Complete the risk assessment with more examples from your own workplace.

Hazard	Who is at risk?	Severity	Likelihood	Risk estimate = S × L	Controls needed
Entry/exit gates left open	Children	3	2	6	Outside gates locked Constant supervision
Hedging/plants	Children, adults	1	2	2	Cut back hedging regularly
Skipping ropes – tripping	Children	1	2	2	Regular supervision
Footballs – being hit, breakages	Children, adults	1	2	2	Provide sufficient space for games
Sunburn	Children, adults	2	2	4	Provide sun hats Parents/carers to put cream on children

Hazard severity
3 Major
2 Serious
1 Slight

Hazard likelihood
3 High = certain harm will occur
2 Medium = could occur frequently
1 Low = seldom occurs

Figure 5.2: Risk assessment form

Play areas and playgrounds

Accidents are common in children because they are developing and learning rapidly and it can be difficult for adults to keep up with their changing developmental abilities. Accidents also occur because children are naturally curious and want to explore their environment and in doing so may expose themselves to danger. The setting should provide play and learning activities that encourage child curiosity and exploration whilst protecting them from unnecessary harm. Children also need to learn how to deal with risk so that they can keep themselves safe as they grow up. Bumps, bruises, minor cuts and scrapes are all part of play and learning but there is no need for children to suffer serious injuries. To avoid accidents the setting should provide adult care and supervision as well as ensuring safe play equipment design and appropriate modifications to the learning environment (CAPT, 2004a).

The design, location and maintenance of play areas are important to maintaining child safety during play and learning activities. It is essential to remember the following:

- The layout must ensure that activities in one area do not interfere with those in other areas.
- Play areas for younger children should be separated from those for older children.
- Paths must be safely situated away from equipment areas, especially swings.
- Clear sight lines in the play area make it easier to supervise children.
- Secure fencing is required if there are roads, rivers or ponds close to the play area.
- Safe access for children with disabilities should be considered.
- Lighting must be adequate for safety and supervision.
- Repair and replace old or worn play equipment.
- Ensure all play equipment is suitable for the age of the children using it.
- Use impact-absorbing surfaces such as rubber, bark chips and other materials.

(CAPT, 2004b)

Making sure that children are aware of safe behaviour when using play equipment can also help to maintain their safety and protect them from unnecessary accidents. Examples of safe behaviour include:

- No walking in front of swings or other moving equipment.
- No pushing or shoving; being aware of younger children and those with disabilities.
- Removing scarves or other things that could get caught in equipment.
- Taking extra care when using high play equipment such as climbing frames.

(CAPT, 2004b)

There is a duty under Sections 3 and 4 of the Health and Safety at work Act 1974 to ensure the health and safety of users of playground equipment as far as is reasonably practicable (RoSPA, 2004a). Evidence of good practice in ensuring the health and safety of users includes compliance with the relevant safety standards, for example EN 1176 for children's playground equipment and EN 1177 for playground surfaces.

Safety checks for indoor play areas and outdoor play areas/playgrounds include:

1. Inspecting the play area/playground equipment on a regular basis.
2. Reporting any faults to the appropriate person promptly.
3. Ensuring that children do not use the faulty equipment until mended or replaced.
4. Getting the necessary repairs done as quickly as possible.
5. Having an annual inspection by an independent specialist.

Toy safety

Toy safety is also an essential aspect of maintaining child safety. Every year in the UK over 35,000 children under the age of 15 years are treated in hospital following an accident involving a toy (CAPT, 2002). It is essential to provide children with toys and play equipment that are appropriate for their ages and levels of development. Most toys will have a suggested age range. It is a legal requirement for all toys sold in the European Union to carry a CE mark, but this does not necessarily guarantee safety or quality. When

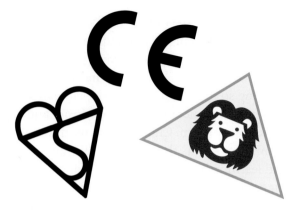

Figure 5.3: Toy safety

selecting toys for children always look for one of these safety marks – European Standard BS EN 71 (indicates the toy has been tested to the agreed safety standards) or the Lion Mark (indicates the toy has been made to the highest standards of safety and quality).

The movement and activity of pupils

You also need to consider the safety of children and adults when *entering* and *exiting* the setting as well as their movement and activity while in the setting. Schools cater for the arrival and departure of children, families, workers and visitors either as pedestrians or in vehicles, including delivery vans and taxis for pupils with special needs. Traffic routes should be properly organised so that both pedestrians and vehicles can move safely in and around the school. Particular care should be taken of everyone using or having access to the premises, especially young children and people with disabilities. The school may have to cope with the large-scale movement of pupils and staff during busy periods, for example, the start and finish of lessons. Care should be taken to avoid accidents such as slips, trips or falls particularly in main corridors and staircases. Floor surfaces should be appropriate for their use and free from hazards or obstructions that might cause people to trip or fall. Particular attention should be given to: holes, bumps and uneven surfaces; wear and tear on carpeted areas; procedures for dealing with spillages; snow and ice on external pathways and precautionary measures prior to repairs, such as barriers, alternative routes.

Security arrangements for pupil arrival and departure

You must know and follow the school's policy and procedures for gaining access to the premises, such as entry systems, visitors' book and identity tags for visitors in the school. Security arrangements should include a registration system, such as a record of the time of arrival and departure of pupils and staff; a visitors' book to record name of visitor, who they are/who they work for, time of arrival, who they are visiting, car registration if applicable, and time of departure. Anyone visiting the school for the first time should provide proof of identity. Pupils should never be left unattended with an adult who is not a member of staff.

A pupil must not be allowed to leave the school with an adult who does not usually collect the pupil without prior permission. You should also know and follow your school's policy and procedures for uncollected pupils or late arrival of a parent or carer to collect younger pupils.

Following procedures for missing pupils

A register of pupils attending each class in the school should be taken at the start of each session. A register should also be taken for pupils participating in outings/visits away from the school, with a duplicate left with the head teacher. Pupils should be made aware (or reminded) of the boundaries of the school at each session. Pupils should be appropriately supervised at all times. However, despite these safeguards, pupils may still go missing from the school.

You need to be aware of the school's procedures for dealing with missing pupils. These procedures may include: contacting the class teacher or head teacher immediately; calling the register to check which pupil is missing; searching classrooms, play areas and school grounds to ensure the pupil has not hidden or been locked in anywhere within the school and the head teacher contacting the police and the parent/carers.

If a pupil is found to be missing while on an outing the teaching assistant should: contact the class teacher immediately; check the register again; keep the rest of the group together while searching the area and contact the class teacher again (who will contact the head teacher, the police and the pupil's parents/carers).

 Activity!

Briefly outline your school's procedures for dealing with missing pupils.

 Key Task

- Outline your school's policies and procedures for maintaining health and safety.
- What are your responsibilities for dealing with the following types of possible hazards that can occur in the school: unsafe buildings, fixtures and fittings; unsafe equipment including play and learning resources; hazardous substances, such as cleaning materials; hygiene hazards in toilet or kitchen areas; security hazards, for example inadequate boundaries, unauthorised visitors?

NOS Links:

Level 3:   STL 3.1   STL 31.1   STL 31.2   STL 31.3   STL 45.3   STL 46.1

Following emergency evacuation procedures in the school

You need to know about the fire and emergency evacuation procedures for the school. The purpose of fire and emergency evacuation procedures is to prevent panic and to ensure the safe, orderly and efficient evacuation of all occupants of the school using all the exit facilities available and to help individuals to react rationally when confronted with a fire or other emergency either at the school or elsewhere. **In the event of a fire or other emergency (such as a bomb scare) all staff should know and understand that their first consideration must be the evacuation of all the pupils to a place of safety**.

The sequence for fire and emergency evacuation procedures should be as follows:

1. Sound the fire alarm.
2. Evacuate the building.
3. Call the fire brigade.
4. Assemble at the designated assembly point.
5. Take a roll call using registers if possible.

The fire alarm signals the need to evacuate the building. You should give calm, clear and correct instructions to the people involved in the emergency as appropriate to your role in implementing emergency procedures within the school. You will need to make sure that any pupils for whom you are responsible leave the building in the appropriate manner, that is walking, no running or talking. This will help to maintain calm and minimise panic as the pupils focus on following the appropriate evacuation procedures. All rooms must have evacuation instructions, including exit routes, prominently displayed.

You also need to know what to do if there is a bomb scare or an intruder in the school. Evacuation procedures would usually be the same as for a fire. You should report any problems with emergency procedures to the relevant colleague, such as the class teacher. Visitors to the school should normally be asked to sign in (and out) so that the people responsible for health and safety know who is in the building (and where) in case of emergencies.

If you work with pupils with special needs, you must know how to assist them in the event of an emergency, for example, a pupil with physical disabilities may need to leave the building via a special route or require access to a lift. You should check with the class teacher or SENCO about the exact procedures to follow. You should know where the fire alarm points and fire exits are, the location of fire extinguishers and fire blankets and their use. There may be different types of extinguishers for use with different hazardous substances, for example in the kitchens – water must not be used to put out oil or electrical fires as this can make the situation worse. Carbon dioxide extinguishers will be located in the necessary places.

Figure 5.4: Fire evacuation instructions

 **Activity!**

- Find out about your school's emergency evacuation procedures.
- Briefly outline the school's procedures in the event of a fire or other emergency evacuation, including your specific role.

Dealing with accidents and injuries

When responding to accidents or injuries that occur within the school, you should remain calm and follow the relevant procedures. You must immediately call for qualified assistance (the designated first aider or the emergency services) and take appropriate action in line with your role and responsibilities within the school. If you are a designated first aider than you can administer first aid; if not, you can comfort the injured person by your physical presence and talking to them until the arrival of a designated first aider, doctor, paramedic or the ambulance staff. You will then help to establish and maintain the privacy and safety of the area where the accident or injury occurred and provide support for any other people involved. When qualified assistance arrives you should give them clear and accurate information about what happened. Afterwards, you will need to follow the school's procedures for recording accidents and injuries. This will normally involve recording the incident in a special book. Serious accidents are usually recorded on an official form. Accuracy in recording accidents and injuries is essential because the information may be needed for further action by senior staff or other professionals. Certain types of accidents and injuries must be reported to an official authority under the Reporting of Injuries, Diseases and Dangerous Occurrences Regulations 1995, for example: local authority and school playgrounds must report to the Health and Safety Executive.

 key words

Designated first aider: a person with appropriate first aid training and a qualification approved by the Health and Safety Executive (such as first aid at work) who has a specific duty to provide first aid within the setting.

You must follow basic good hygiene procedures and take the usual precautions for avoiding cross infection. You should use protective disposable gloves and be careful when dealing with spillages of blood or other body fluids including the disposal of dressings etc. You should be aware of issues concerning the spread of hepatitis, HIV and AIDS (see page 114).

Following first aid arrangements

You must know and understand the first aid arrangements that apply in the school, including the location of first aid equipment/facilities and the designated first aider(s). A designated first aider must complete a training course approved by the Health and Safety Executive. Remember, that even if you have done first aid as part of your teaching assistant training, your first aid certificate should be updated every three years.

First aid notices should be clearly displayed in all rooms; make sure you read this information. First aid information is usually included in induction programmes to ensure that new staff and pupils know about the school's first aid arrangements. Detailed information on the school's first aid policy and procedures will also be in the staff handbook.

Accident/Incident Report Form

Date: Time:

Location of accident/incident:

Address:

Person reporting the accident/incident:

Address:

Details of the accident/incident: (Continue on reverse and additional sheets if necessary)

Action taken: (Continue on reverse and additional sheets if necessary)

Witnesses or others informed of accident/incident: (Continue on reverse and additional sheets if necessary)

1. Name:

Address:

2. Name:

Address:

Any further action required: (Continue on reverse and additional sheets if necessary)

Signed: Date of report:

Number of additional sheets:

Figure 5.5: Accident/incident report form

Activity!

- Find out about your school's policy and procedures for dealing with accidents and injuries, including the provision of first aid.
- Undertake basic first aid procedures, for example gain/update a first aid qualification.

The aims of first aid

1. To preserve life by:
- providing emergency resuscitation
- controlling bleeding
- treating burns
- treating shock.

2. To prevent the worsening of any injuries by:
- covering wounds
- immobilising fractures
- placing the casualty in the correct and comfortable position.

3. To promote recovery by:
- providing reassurance
- giving any other treatment needed
- relieving pain
- handling gently
- moving as little as possible
- protecting from the cold.

The priorities of first aid

A is for **Airway**:
- Establish an open airway by tilting the forehead back so the child can breathe easily.

B is for **Breathing**:
- Check that the child is breathing by listening, looking and feeling for breath.

C is for **Circulation**:
- Apply simple visual checks that the child's blood is circulating adequately by watching for improved colour, coughing or eye movement.

First aid equipment

First aid equipment must be clearly labelled and easily accessible. All first aid containers must be marked with a white cross on a green background. There should be at least one fully stocked first aid container for each building within the setting, with extra first aid containers available on split-sites/levels, distant playing fields/playgrounds and any other high risk areas (such as kitchens), and for outings or educational visits.

Here are some suggestions for the contents of a first aid box:

- A first aid manual or first aid leaflet.
- Assorted bandages, including a wrapped triangular bandage, a one-inch and a two-inch strip for holding dressings and compresses in place.
- Medium and large individually wrapped sterile unmedicated wound dressings.
- Two sterile eye pads.
- Safety pins.
- Adhesive tape.
- Sterile gauze
- A pair of sharp scissors; tweezers.
- Child thermometer.
- Disposable gloves.

Recognising and dealing with common childhood illnesses

Babies and young children should be vaccinated against diseases including: diphtheria, measles, meningitis, mumps, polio, rubella, tetanus and whooping cough. The first immunisations start when a baby is two months old. The child's parents will usually receive appointments by post to attend their local clinic or GP surgery. You need to be aware of the range of common illnesses that may affect children. These include: allergies, asthma, bronchitis, chicken pox, colds, diabetes, diarrhoea, earache, flu, glandular fever, headache, measles, meningitis, mumps, sore throat and worms.

Recognising signs and symptoms

By knowing the usual behaviour and appearance of the pupils you work with, you will be able to recognise any significant changes that might indicate possible illness. You need to be able to recognise the differences between pupils who are: pretending to be ill; feeling 'under the weather'; or experiencing a health problem. The signs of possible illness in children include:

- Changes in facial colour, becoming pale or very red.
- Changes in temperature, becoming very hot or cold, becoming clammy or shivering. (A fever usually indicates that the child has an infection.)
- Changes in behaviour, not wanting to play when would usually be very keen.
- Being upset or generally distressed.
- Having reduced concentration levels or even falling asleep.
- Scratching excessively. (Check the setting's policy regarding head lice.)
- Complaining of persistent pain, such as headache or stomach-ache.
- Coughing or sneezing excessively.

ILLNESS	INCUBATION PERIOD	INFECTIOUS PERIOD	HOW TO RECOGNISE IT	WHAT TO DO
	(The time between catching an illness and becoming unwell)	(When your child can give the illness to someone else)		
CHICKENPOX	11–21 days	From the day before the rash appears until all the spots are dry.	Begins with feeling unwell, a rash and maybe a slight temperature. Spots are red and become fluid-filled blisters within a day or so. Appear first on the chest and back, then spread, and eventually dry into scabs, which drop off. Unless spots are badly infected, they don't usually leave a scar.	No need to see your GP unless you're unsure whether it's chickenpox, or your child is very unwell and/or distressed. Give plenty to drink. Paracetamol will help bring down a temperature. Baths, loose, comfortable clothes and calamine lotion can all ease the itchiness. You should also inform the school/nursery in case other children are at risk. Keep your child away from anyone who is, or who is trying to become, pregnant. If your child was with anyone pregnant just before he or she became unwell, let that woman know about the chickenpox (and tell her to see her GP). Sometimes chickenpox in pregnancy can cause miscarriage or the baby may be born with chickenpox.
MEASLES	7–12 days	From a few days before until 4 days after the appearance of the rash.	Begins like a bad cold and cough with sore, watery eyes. Child becomes gradually more unwell, with a temperature. Rash appears after third or fourth day. Spots are red and slightly raised; may be blotchy, but are not itchy. Begins behind the ears, and spreads to the face and neck and then the rest of the body. Children can become very unwell, with cough and high temperature. The illness usually lasts about a week.	See your GP. If your child is unwell give him or her rest and plenty to drink. Warm drinks will ease the cough. Paracetamol will ease discomfort and lower the temperature. Vaseline® around the lips protects the skin. Wash crustiness from eyelids with warm water.
MUMPS	14–21 days	From a few days before becoming unwell until swelling goes down. Maybe 10 days in all.	At first, your child may be mildly unwell with a bit of fever, and may complain of pain around the ear or feel uncomfortable when chewing. Swelling then starts under the jaw up to the ear. Swelling often starts on one side, followed (though not always) by the other. Your child's face is back to normal size in about a week, it's rare for mumps to affect boys' testes (balls). This happens rather more often in adult men with mumps. For both boys and men, the risk of any permanent damage to the testes is very low.	Your child may not feel especially ill and may not want to be in bed. Baby or junior paracetamol will ease pain is the swollen glands. Check correct dosage on pack. Give plenty to drink, but not fruit juice. This makes the saliva flow, which can hurt. No need to see your GP unless your child has stomach ache and is being sick, or develops a rash of small red/purple spots or bruises.
PARVOVIRUS B19 (ALSO CALLED FIFTH DISEASE OR SLAPPED CHEEK DISEASE)	Variable 1–20 days	It is most infectious in the days before the rash appears.	Begins with a fever and nasal discharge. A bright red rash similar to a slap appears on the cheeks. Over the next 2–4 days, a lacy type of rash spreads to the trunk and limbs.	Although this is most common in children, it can occur in adults. in the majority of cases it has no serious consequences, but it may cause complications for people with chronic anaemic conditions (e.g. sickle cell disease). Rarely, in pregnant women who are not immune to the disease, the intention may result in stillbirth or affect the baby in the womb. Pregnant women who come into contact with the infection or develop a rash should see their GP as soon as possible.
RUBELLA (GERMAN MEASLES)	14–21 days	One week before and at least 4 days after the rash first appears.	Can be difficult to diagnose with certainty. Starts like a mild cold. The rash appears in a day or two, first on the face, then spreading. Spots are flat. On a light skin, they are pale pink. Glands in the back of the neck may be swollen. Your child won't usually feel unwell.	Give them plenty to drink. Keep your child away from anybody you know who's up to 4 months pregnant (or trying to get pregnant). If your child was with anyone pregnant before you knew about the illness, let her know. If an unimmunised pregnant woman catches German measles in the first 4 months of pregnancy, there is a risk of damage to her baby. Any pregnant woman who has had contact with German measles should see her GP. The GP can check whether or not she is immune and, if not, whether there is any sign of her developing the illness.
WHOOPING COUGH	7–14 days	From the first signs of the illness until about 6 weeks after coughing starts. If an antibiotic is given, the infectious period is up to 5 days after beginning the course of treatment.	Begins like a cold and cough. The cough gradually gets worse. After about 2 weeks, coughing bouts start. These are exhausting and make it difficult to breathe. Your child may choke and vomit. Sometimes, but not always, there's a whooping noise as the child draws in breath after coughing. It takes some weeks before the coughing fits start to die down.	If your child has a cough that gets worse rather than better and starts to have longer fits of coughing more and more often, see your doctor. It's important for the sake of other children to know whether or not it's whooping cough. Talk to your GP about how best to look after your child and avoid contact with babies, who are most at risk from serious complications.

Figure 5.6: Childhood illnesses

- Diarrhoea and/or vomiting.
- Displaying a rash. (This could indicate an infection or allergic reaction. Make sure you are aware of any children who may have severe allergic reactions – see section on supporting pupils with long-term medical needs.)

(Watkinson, 2003)

Responding to signs and symptoms

You should know what to do if pupils come to the setting when they are unwell. The most common illness in children is the common cold. A young child may have as many as 5 to 6 colds a year. Pupils do not need to be kept away from school because of a cold unless their symptoms are very bad. Make sure that a box of tissues is available for pupils to use and that used tissues are disposed of properly to avoid the spread of germs. Colds and flu are caused by viruses and so cannot be helped by antibiotics. However, cold and flu viruses can weaken the body and lead to a secondary bacterial infection such as tonsillitis, otitis media (middle ear infection), sinusitis, bronchitis and pneumonia. These bacterial infections require antibiotic treatment. You also need to know what to do if a pupil becomes ill while at the setting. You should seek medical advice if you have concerns about any of the following:

- The child's high temperature lasts for more than 24 hours.
- The child has a persistent cough with green or yellow catarrh (possible bronchitis or pneumonia).
- The child has pain above the eyes or in the face (possible sinusitis).
- The child has a severe sore throat (possible tonsillitis).
- The child has a bad earache (possible ear infection).

Seek medical advice *immediately* if:

- You think the child may have meningitis.
- The child has breathing difficulties.
- The child's asthma deteriorates.
- The child has a convulsion.
- The child has very poor fluid intake or cannot swallow liquids.
- A baby persistently refuses to take feeds.
- The child has been to a country where there is a risk of malaria, in the last 12 months.

Recording and reporting signs of illness

Ensure that you know what to do when pupils are sick, for example where or to whom to send sick pupils. You may need to stay with a sick pupil while someone else summons assistance. If you have any concerns regarding the health of the pupils you work with, you should always inform the class teacher. You need to be able to recognise any changes to a pupil's behaviour or appearance that may indicate a possible health problem and report these appropriately. Whatever the illness, you should know where and when to seek assistance. You should also know what types of written records are required and to whom you should report any concerns regarding any pupil's health. Check whether you are allowed to contact parents/carers directly regarding a sick pupil or whether this is the responsibility of someone else, e.g. the class teacher or head teacher.

Following the procedures for storing and administering medicines

Parents are responsible for their own children's medication. Children under the age of 16 should not be given medication without their parent's written consent. The head teacher usually decides whether the school can assist a pupil who needs medication during the school day. The school will have a form for the parent to sign if their child requires medication while at school. Many pupils with long-term medical needs will not require medication while at the school. If they do, pupils can usually administer it themselves depending on their age, level of development, medical needs and type of medication. The school's policy should encourage self-administration where appropriate and provide suitable facilities for pupils to do so in safety and privacy. (See section below on supporting pupils with long-term medical needs.)

Teaching assistants have no legal duty to administer medication or to supervise a pupil taking it. This is a voluntary role similar to that of being a designated first aider (see above). The head teacher, parents and relevant health professionals should support teaching assistants who volunteer to administer medication by providing information, training and reassurance about their legal liability. Arrangements should be made for when the teaching assistant responsible for providing assistance is absent or not available.

The health and safety of pupils and staff must be considered at all times. Safety procedures must be in place regarding the safe storage, handling, and disposal of medicines. Some medication (such as a reliever inhaler for asthma or adrenalin device for severe anaphylaxis) must be quickly available in an emergency and should not be locked away. The relevant staff members and the pupils concerned must know where this medication is stored.

 Key Task

- Find out about your school's procedures for: dealing with accidents and injuries; providing first aid; dealing with common childhood illnesses; storing and administering medicines.
- Describe your role and responsibilities in the event of an accident, injury, illness and other emergencies.

NOS Links:
Level 3:   STL 3.2   STL 43 (single element unit)

Supporting pupils with long-term medical needs

All schools will have pupils with medical needs at some time. Some medical needs are short-term, such as a pupil finishing a course of antibiotics or recovering from an accident/surgery. Some pupils may have long-term medical needs due to a particular medical condition or chronic illness. The majority of pupils with long-term medical needs will be able to attend a mainstream setting regularly and can participate in the usual setting activities with the appropriate support from the staff. The medical conditions in children that cause most concern in schools are asthma, diabetes, epilepsy and severe allergic reaction (anaphylaxis).

Asthma

About 1 in 10 children in the UK have asthma. People with asthma have airways that narrow as a reaction to a variety of triggers such as animal fur, grass pollen, house dust mites and viral infections. Stress or exercise can also bring on an asthma attack in a susceptible person. A person with asthma can usually relieve the symptoms of an asthma attack with an inhaler.

It is essential that children with asthma have immediate access to their reliever inhalers in the event of an asthma attack in the setting. Children with asthma should be encouraged from an early age to take charge of their own inhaler and know how to use it. Children who can use their inhalers themselves should be permitted to carry these with them at all times. When a child is too young or immature to be personally responsible for their inhaler, then staff must ensure that the inhaler is kept in a safe but accessible place with the child's name clearly written on it. The symptoms of an asthma attack are: excessive coughing; wheezing; difficulty breathing, especially breathing out; possible anxiety and distress and lips and skin turning blue (in severe attacks). A child having an asthma attack should be prompted to use their inhaler if they not using it already. It is good practice to provide comfort and reassurance (to alleviate possible anxiety and distress) while encouraging the child to breathe slowly and deeply. The child should sit rather than lie down. Medical advice must be sought and /or an ambulance called if: the medication has no effect after 5–10 minutes; the child seems very distressed; the child is unable to talk or the child is becoming exhausted (DfES/DH, 2005). For more detailed information see the Asthma UK website: **www.asthma.org.uk**.

Diabetes

Approximately 1 in 550 children have diabetes. Diabetes is a medical condition where the person's normal hormonal mechanisms do not control their blood sugar level properly. Children with diabetes usually need: to have daily insulin injections; to monitor their blood sugar glucose and to eat regularly. Diabetes in most children is controlled by twice daily injections of insulin and it is not likely that these will need to be administered during school hours. If children do need insulin while at the setting then an appropriate, private area should be provided for this. Most children with diabetes can administer their own insulin injections but younger children will require adult supervision. Children with diabetes need to check that their blood sugar levels remain stable by using a testing machine at regular intervals. They may need to check their levels during lunch time or more frequently if their insulin requires adjustment. The majority of children are able to do this themselves and just need an appropriate place to carry out the checks. Children with diabetes must be allowed to eat regularly throughout the day. This might include eating snacks during lesson time or before physical play activities or PE lessons. Blood sugar levels may fall to too low a level if a child misses a snack or meal or after strenuous physical activity resulting in a hypoglycaemia episode (hypo). A hypo left untreated can lead to a diabetic coma. The symptoms of a hypo include: drowsiness; glazed eyes; hunger; irritability; lack of concentration; pallor; shaking and sweating. If a child experiences a hypo it is important that a fast acting sugar is given immediately, such as glucose tablets, glucose rich gel, a sugary drink or chocolate bar. A slower acting starchy food should be given once the child has recovered, such as a sandwich or two biscuits and a glass of milk. If the child's recovery takes longer than 10–15 minutes, or if there are any concerns about the child's condition, then an ambulance should be called (DfES/DH, 2005). For more detailed information see the Diabetes UK website: **www.diabetes.org.uk**.

Epilepsy

Approximately 1 in 200 children have epilepsy and about 80 per cent of these attend mainstream settings. People with epilepsy have recurrent seizures (commonly called fits). The nature, frequency and severity of seizures will vary between individuals. The majority of seizures can be controlled by medication. Seizures may be *partial* when the person's consciousness is affected but not necessarily lost, or *generalised* where the person does lose consciousness.

Most children with epilepsy have symptoms that are well controlled by medication and seizures are therefore unlikely to occur in the setting. The vast majority of children with epilepsy experience seizures for no apparent reason. However, susceptible children may have seizures triggered by: tiredness and/or stress; flashing or flickering lights; computer games and graphics or some geometric shapes or patterns. The symptoms of epileptic seizures include: having convulsions; losing consciousness; experiencing strange sensations and exhibiting unusual behaviour (such as plucking at clothes or repetitive movements).

Once a seizure has started nothing should be done to stop or change its course except when medication is given by appropriately trained staff. The child should not be moved unless s/he is in a dangerous place, but something soft may be placed under the head. No attempt should be made to restrain the child or to put anything into the mouth. The child's airway must be maintained at all times. When the convulsion has finished the child should be put in the recovery position. Someone should stay with the child until s/he has recovered and become re-orientated. If the seizure lasts longer than usual, or one seizure follows another without the child regaining consciousness, or where there are any concerns about the pupil's condition, then an ambulance should be called (DfES/DH, 2005). For more detailed information see the National Society for Epilepsy website: **www.epilepsynse.org.uk**.

Severe allergic reaction (anaphylaxis)

Children with severe allergies learn from an early age what they can and cannot eat or drink. The most common cause for severe allergies is food, especially nuts, fish or dairy products. Wasp and bee stings can also cause severe allergic reaction. Anaphylaxis is a very severe allergic reaction that requires urgent medical treatment. In its most severe form (anaphylactic shock) the condition is potentially life-threatening, but can be treated with medication. This may include antihistamine, adrenaline inhaler or adrenaline injection depending on the severity of the allergic reaction. Anaphylactic shock is rare in children under 13 years old. People with severe allergic reactions usually have a device for injecting adrenaline that looks like a fountain pen and is pre-loaded with the exact dose of adrenaline required. The needle is not exposed and the injection is easy to administer usually into the fleshy part of the thigh. A child may be responsible for keeping the necessary medication with them at all times. The safety of all children should be taken into account and it might be more appropriate to store the medication in a safe but instantly accessible place, especially if working with younger children. All staff should be aware of any children with this condition and know who is responsible for administering the emergency treatment. Responsibility for giving the injection should be on a voluntary basis and should never be done by a person without appropriate training from a health professional. An allergic reaction will usually occur within a few seconds or minutes of exposure to an allergen. The symptoms of a severe allergic reaction include: metallic taste or itching in the mouth; flushed complexion; abdominal cramps and nausea; swelling of the face, throat, tongue and lips; difficulty swallowing; wheezing or difficulty breathing; rise in heart rate and collapse or unconsciousness. An ambulance should be called immediately, especially if there are concerns about the severity of the allergic reaction or if the pupil does not respond to the medication (DfES/DH, 2005). For more detailed information see the The Anaphylaxis Campaign website: **www.anaphylaxis.org.uk**.

 **Activity!**

List the main symptoms for the following: asthma attack; diabetic hypo; epileptic seizure; severe allergic reaction.

HIV and AIDS

HIV (human immunodeficiency virus) is a virus that damages the body's immune system. The immune system fights the virus and if the body's defences are severely weakened this can lead to AIDS (acquired immune deficiency syndrome). AIDS is the collective name of different diseases that can cause serious illness or death in both adults and children. HIV is very fragile and cannot be easily transmitted. For example, it cannot survive in very hot water, in bleach or in detergent. HIV is transmitted in three ways: through unprotected vaginal or anal intercourse; by infected blood entering the blood stream (such as from a blood transfusion or from needle stick injuries); from a woman with HIV to her baby either during pregnancy, during delivery or from breast feeding. There is no evidence that HIV can be caught from social contact. HIV cannot be spread by: hugs and kisses; coughs and sneezes; shared toilet seats; shared drinking fountains; showers and swimming pools; sweat, tears and saliva; or animals and pets. Details of the HIV status of any pupil must not be passed on without the parent's or child's permission. This means that, in most schools, staff will not know if a pupil is HIV positive. It is therefore essential that health and safety procedures for cleaning up blood and blood-stained body fluids are rigorously adhered to, and that disposable gloves are worn when treating bleeding children. (ATL, 2007) For more detailed information see The Terrence Higgins Trust website: **www.tht.org.uk**.

Strategies for supporting pupils with long-term medical needs

The school will need additional procedures to maintain the health and safety of pupils with long-term medical needs; this may include an individual healthcare plan (see below). The school has a responsibility to ensure that all relevant staff are aware of pupils with long-term medical needs and are trained to provide additional support if necessary. Staff providing support for pupils with long-term medical needs must know and understand: the nature of the pupil's medical condition; when and where the pupil may need additional support; the likelihood of an emergency arising (especially if it is potentially life threatening) and what action to take if an emergency occurs.

The head teacher and other staff must treat medical information in a sensitive and confidential manner. The head teacher should agree with the pupil (if appropriate) and their parents, which staff members should have access to records and other information about the pupil's medical needs in order to provide a good support system. However, where medical information is not given to staff, they should not usually be held responsible if they provide incorrect medical assistance in an emergency but otherwise acted in good faith.

Healthcare plans in schools

Some pupils with long-term medical needs may require a healthcare plan to provide staff with the necessary information to support the pupil and to ensure the pupil's safety. A healthcare plan for a pupil with special medical needs is used to identify the level of support the pupil requires in the school. The healthcare plan is a written agreement between the school and parents that specifies the assistance that the school can provide for the pupil. The plan should be reviewed at least once a year or more if the pupil's medical needs change. A written healthcare plan should be drawn up in consultation with the pupil (if appropriate), their parents and the relevant health professionals. The amount of detail contained in a healthcare plan will depend on the particular needs of the individual pupil. The plan should include: details of the pupil's medical condition; any special requirements such as dietary needs; medication and its possible side effects; how staff can support the pupil in school and what to do and who to contact in an emergency (DfES/DH, 2005).

 **Key Task**

Find out about your school's procedures for supporting pupils with long-term medical needs.

NOS Links:
Level 3:   STL 3.2   STL 43 (single element unit)

Summary of key points in this unit:

- **Statutory and regulatory health and safety requirements** including: an employee's responsibility under the Health and Safety at Work Act 1974; The Management of Health and Safety at Work Regulations 1999; The Manual Handling Operations Regulations 1992, as amended in 2002.
- **Safety checks in the learning environment** including: the location of safety equipment and first aid boxes; checking equipment is safe for use; storing materials and equipment safely; maintaining toilet and wash areas.
- **Maintaining health and safety during play and learning activities** including: risk assessment applicable to the learning environment; play areas and playgrounds; toy safety; the movement and activity of pupils; security arrangements for pupil arrival and departure; following procedures for missing pupils.
- **Following emergency evacuation procedures in the school** including fire and emergency evacuation procedures as well as what to do in the event of a bomb scare or an intruder in the school.

- **Dealing with accidents and injuries** including: following first aid arrangements; first aid equipment.
- **Recognising and dealing with common childhood illnesses** including: recognising signs and symptoms; responding to signs and symptoms; recording and reporting signs of illness; following the procedures for storing and administering medicines.
- **Supporting pupils with long-term medical needs** including: asthma, diabetes, epilepsy, severe allergic reaction (anaphylaxis); strategies for supporting pupils with long-term medical needs; healthcare plans in schools.

Further reading

Dare, A. and O'Donovan, M. (2000) *Good Practice in Child Safety*. Nelson Thornes.

DfEE (1998) *Guidance on First Aid for Settings: A Good Practice Guide*. Department for Education and Employment.

DfEE (1998) *Health and Safety of Children on Educational Visits: A Good Practice Guide*. DfEE.

DfES (2004) *Every Child Matters: Change for Children*. DfES. Available free online at: **http://www.dcsf.gov. uk/everychildmatters/about/**.

DfES/DH (2005) *Managing Medicines in Schools and Early Years Settings*. DfES/Department of Health. Available free from: **www.teachernet.gov.uk**.

HSE (2004) *Getting to Grips with Manual Handling: A Short Guide*. Leaflet INDG143 (rev2) HSE Books.

HSE (2005) *COSHH: A Brief Guide to the Regulations: What You Need to Know About The Control of Substances Hazardous to Health Regulations 2002*. Leaflet INDG136 (rev3). HSE Books.

HSE (2006) *Five Steps to Risk Assessment*. INDG163 (rev2). HSE Books.

HSE (2006) *Health and Safety Law: What You Should Know*. Leaflet. HSE Books.

St. John Ambulance, St. Andrew's Ambulance Association and British Red Cross (2009) *First Aid Manual: The Step by Step Guide for Everyone*. Ninth edition. Penguin.

[Note: Single copies of the above HSE leaflets are available free from: **www.hse.gov.uk**]

6. Supporting learning activities

Understanding pupil development and learning

An understanding of intellectual development is essential for teaching assistants because it helps them to assist the teacher in supporting learning activities through: a well-organised and structured learning environment; careful planning and preparation of learning activities; the provision of appropriate learning resources; effective communication with pupils during learning activities; high adult expectations for learner development and accurate evaluation of learning activities and assessment of pupil abilities.

How children think and learn

Research into how children think and learn has made adults more aware of the need to: observe and assess children's development very carefully; listen to children and the way they express ideas and take account of children's interests and experiences when planning learning opportunities. There are three main approaches to understanding children's development: psycho-dynamic, behaviourist and cognitive.

The psycho-dynamic approach includes the Austrian physician Sigmund Freud who believed that very early childhood experiences are responsible for how people think and feel in later life. Depending on these early experiences, people are either well or poorly adjusted to their everyday lives. Freud considered that most of our thinking is done on a *sub-conscious* level and is therefore beyond our control. More recently, psychologists such as Carl Rogers, have suggested that most of our thinking is *conscious* and that individuals are in control of their own lives.

The behaviourist approach focuses on *behaviour* which can be observed rather than thoughts and feelings which cannot be directly observed. Behaviourists are concerned with how external forces can be used to control behaviour, for example B.F. Skinner considered that all thinking and learning is based on responses to rewards and punishments received within our environment.

The cognitive approach includes psychologists who believe that human behaviour can be understood by studying how people think and learn. This includes the work of Froebel, Montessori, Piaget, Vygotsky and Bruner (see below). In this chapter we concentrate on the cognitive approach to development as this has the most relevance to understanding the development of cognitive or intellectual skills. The other approaches *do* contribute to our knowledge of children's development, but are of more significance to understanding children's behaviour (see Chapter 7) and children's emotional well-being (see Chapter 15).

Cognitive approaches to how children think and learn

Friedrich Wilhelm Froebel was a German educator, and the founder of the *kindergarten* (meaning 'children's garden') system, who devised activities for young children which encouraged learning through play. He thought young women had a special rapport with young children; prior to this, teachers were usually men or older women. Froebel trained many young women to become kindergarten teachers; some of these went to America where they established private kindergartens. The first year of compulsory schooling in the USA and Canada is still called kindergarten today.

Froebel had been a student of Heinrich Pestalozzi, a Swiss teacher and writer. Pestalozzi established many schools for young children and also wrote books demonstrating how basic concepts could be introduced to young children. Froebel was the first educator to really see the importance of play in developing children's thinking and learning (see the section on the role of play in children's learning and development on page 128). He believed that play was central to children's learning and their understanding of concepts. He devised a set of specially designed play materials to encourage children's thinking and learning. Froebel pioneered the idea of hands-on experience which forms the basis of learning through play and active learning. He also believed that childhood was a state in its own right and not just a preparation for adulthood. It was his work that moved early education away from young children sitting in rows and learning by rote.

Maria Montessori was an Italian educator and physician who became one of the best known and most influential early childhood educators. She began by working with children with special needs. She designed carefully graded self-teaching materials which stimulated children's learning through use of their senses. Montessori believed that children learn best by doing things independently without adult interference, and that children concentrate better when engaged in a self-chosen activity. Adults working with young children need to be specially trained to give the appropriate support to children's independent learning. The learning environment was considered to be especially important. Montessori believed the equipment should be specifically designed for children (for example small, child-sized furniture, kitchen utensils, tools) and that children should have freedom to move and explore their environment.

Jean Piaget, a Swiss biologist, used observations of his own children, plus a wider sample of children, to develop his theories of cognitive development. Piaget's theories of cognitive development have had a major influence on early education for over 40 years. Piaget believed that children

 key words

Psycho-dynamic: the study of the interaction of conscious and unconscious mental processes which influence personality, behaviour and attitudes.

Behaviourist: the study of observable and quantifiable aspects of behaviour which excludes subjective things such as emotions or motives.

Cognitive: a psychological approach to development and learning that emphasises internal mental processes such as thinking and perception.

Schemas: a term used mainly by Piaget and Froebel to describe internal thought processes.

went through different stages of cognitive development based on fixed ages. Within these stages the children's patterns of learning, or schemas as he called them, were very different from adult ways of problem-solving.

Piaget also believed in the importance of young children learning through action and exploration of their environment using their sensory motor skills. According to Piaget, children are *actively* involved in structuring their own cognitive development through exploration of their environment. Children need real objects and 'concrete experiences' to discover things for themselves. The adult's role is to provide children with appropriate experiences in a suitable environment to facilitate the children's instinctive ability to think and learn. Cognitive development occurs in four set stages which are universal – they apply to all forms of learning and across all cultures.

Piaget's four stages of cognitive development
Stage 1: Sensori-motor – 0 to 2 years • Babies and young children learn through their senses, physical activity and interaction with their immediate environment. • Babies and very young children understand their world in terms of actions.
Stage 2: Pre-operations – 2 to 7 years • Young children learn through experience with real objects in their immediate environment. • Young children use symbols (e.g. words and images) to make sense of their world.
Stage 3: Concrete operations – 7 to 11 years • Children continue to learn through their experiences with real objects. • Children access information (using language) to make sense of their environment.
Stage 4: Formal operations – 11 years to adult • Older children and adults learn to make use of abstract thinking (e.g. algebra, physics).

Piaget viewed children as thinking and learning in a different way to adults. Not only do children have less experience of the world, but their understanding of it is shaped by this entirely different way of looking at their environment. Children will only learn when they are 'ready' for different experiences as determined by their current stage of cognitive development.

Piaget did not see language and communication as central to children's cognitive development because this development begins at birth *before* children can comprehend or use words. Young children's use of language demonstrates their cognitive achievements, but does not control them. (He did see the importance of language at later stages.) Young children are egocentric, they are unable to see or understand another person's viewpoint, and this also means they are unable to convey information accurately or effectively to others.

Piaget believed that children interact with their environment to actively construct their knowledge and understanding of the world. They do this by relating new information to existing information. Piaget called this interaction: *assimilation* (the need for further information); *accommodation* (the need for organised information); *adaptation* (the need for revised/updated information). All new information has to be built on existing information;

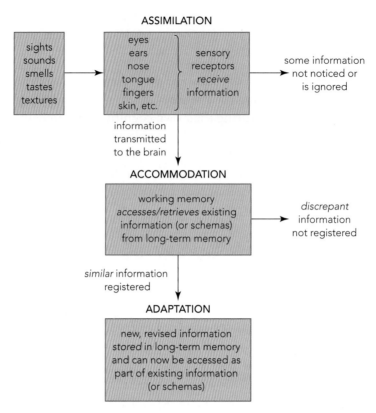

Figure 6.1: Understanding assimilation, accommodation and adaptation

there needs to be some connection between them. *Similar* information can be stored as it relates to existing information. *Discrepant* information cannot be stored because it is not related to existing information. Piaget described internal mental processes as schemas and the ways in which they are used when thinking as operations. Mental processes or schemas do not remain static; they continually develop as we acquire new information and extend our understanding of the world.

Research by people such as Margaret Donaldson suggests Piaget underestimated young children's cognitive abilities – the use of appropriate language within a meaningful context enables 3 and 4 year olds to use logical thinking and to understand concepts such as the conservation of number, volume and weight. For example, the number conservation task, which involves two identical rows of objects. Young children agree that there are the same number of objects in each row until the adult moves the objects in one of the rows, so that it is longer than the other row – although the number of objects remains the same, young children will say the longer row has more objects (see Figure 6.2). However, when this task is done using a 'naughty' teddy bear to upset the arrangement of the objects, then young children can state that the number of objects remains the same. The task has to *make sense* to the young child and the adult needs to use language which the child can understand.

Donaldson also challenged Piaget's claim that children under 7 years old are highly egocentric – that is, they could not see things from another person's point of view. Piaget's evidence for this claim included the 'mountains' task in which young children had to indicate what a doll would see but instead would state their *own* view of the situation (see Figure 6.3). Piaget described this as *egocentric illusion*.

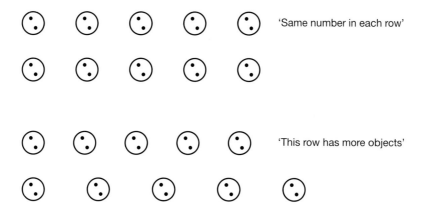

'Same number in each row'

'This row has more objects'

Figure 6.2: Conservation of number task

Donaldson states that there is evidence which strongly suggests that Piaget's claim was incorrect. For example, 'the policeman and little boy' task devised by Martin Hughes, which showed that even 3 and 4 year olds could assess the policeman's viewpoint and hide the little boy where the policeman would not be able to see him (see Figure 6.4). This was because this task makes sense to young children – they could understand what they are supposed to do as even very young children can understand the motives and intentions of the policeman and the boy. The 'mountains' task is too abstract and the children do not understand what they are supposed to do (Donaldson, 1978).

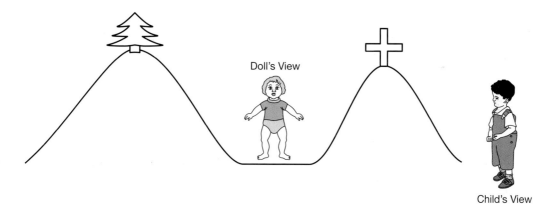

Doll's View

Child's View

Figure 6.3: Piaget's 'mountains' task

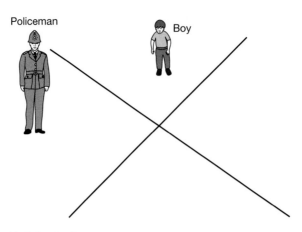

Figure 6.4: The 'policeman and little boy' task

Revisions of Piaget's work demonstrate that young children are very capable thinkers as long as their learning takes place in meaningful contexts where appropriate language is used to facilitate the children's understanding. Language is seen as having a key role in children's development – children use language to develop their understanding of the world around them. In later life Piaget recognised the importance of social development in connection with the development of cognitive skills. Social interaction helps stimulate and formulate intelligence. Prior to this Piaget had concluded that cognitive development progressed parallel to social development but was not influenced by it. In his earlier work Piaget did recognise the role of peers in children's cognitive development – a child on their own might be unable to solve a problem but working with other children could reach a solution. One of the most valuable contributions Piaget makes to our understanding of children's cognitive development is that children's thinking and learning is an active process rather than one of passive absorption (see section below on active learning).

Activity!

- Make a list of the main points of Piaget's theories of cognitive development.
- Which points do you think accurately describe children's thinking and learning? Give examples from your own experiences of working with children.

L. S. Vygotsky, a Russian psychologist, argued that the social interaction between children and other people enables children to develop the intellectual skills necessary for thinking and logical reasoning. Language is the key to this social interaction. Through language and communication children learn to think about their world and modify their actions accordingly.

Like Piaget, Vygotsky was concerned with the active process of cognitive development, but there were also many differences between their viewpoints:

Piaget's viewpoint	Vygotsky's viewpoint
Egocentric young child separate from others for a long period of development (0–7 years) but gradually becomes socialised.	Young child is a social organism who develops awareness of self through interactions with others.
Peer interaction can be helpful. Adults provide rich and stimulating environment but too much adult interference can be harmful. Teaching by adults inhibits young children's 'natural' development.	Social interaction with children and adults is crucial. The adult's role in teaching new skills is very important, e.g. providing assisted learning situations within each child's zone of proximal development (see Figure 6.5)
Thought develops independent of language.	Language is a tool for thought.

Adults support children's learning by assisting the children's own efforts and thus enabling children to acquire the necessary skills, knowledge and understanding. As children develop competent skills through this assisted learning, the adults gradually decrease their support until the children are able to work independently. With appropriate adult assistance children are able to complete tasks and to solve problems that they would not be able to do on their own. It is important for adults to recognise when to provide support towards a child's next step of development and when support is no longer required. Vygotsky used the idea of the zone of proximal development or area of next development to describe this framework of support for learning. Children can be in different zones for different skills or tasks.

The zone of proximal development can be represented in four stages
For example children learning to read may progress in this way:
Stage 1: learning phonic, decoding and comprehension skills with assistance of childcarers, parents, teachers, teaching assistants (assistance from others).
Stage 2: sounding out difficult/unfamiliar words, reading aloud to self, lips moving during silent reading, etc. (self-help).
Stage 3: reading competently using internal prompts (auto-pilot).
Stage 4: new words, complicated texts, learning to read in a different language, etc. require further assistance (relapses to previous steps).

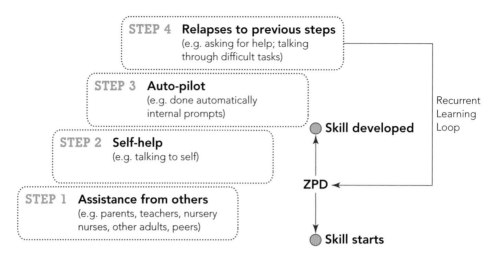

Figure 6.5: *The zone of proximal development* (adapted from Tharp and Gallimore, 1991; p.50)

Activity!

Draw your own diagram showing how the zone of proximal development could apply to:
- Your own learning (for example learning to cook or learning to drive).
- A pupil's learning (for example learning to write or learning a new mathematical skill).

Jerome S. Bruner, an American psychologist, viewed the role of the adult and the role of language as being essential to children's thinking and learning. Like Piaget, Bruner believed in the importance of children discovering things for themselves by exploring the environment and developing ideas in realistic situations, hence the importance of learning through play (see section below on the role of play in children's learning and development).

However, Bruner (like Vygotsky) emphasised the importance of the adult in supporting children's thinking and learning. Bruner used the term scaffolding to describe this adult support. Picture a builder using scaffolding to support a house while it is being built. Without the scaffold the house could not be built; but once the house is finished, the scaffolding can be removed. The adult supports the child's learning until they are ready to stand alone.

Bruner also emphasises the adult's skills of recognising where and when this support is needed and when it should be removed. The structuring of children's learning should be flexible – the adult support or scaffold should not be rigid as it needs to change as the needs of the child change, for example as the child gains knowledge and understanding and/or acquires new skills.

The adult supports children's learning and development by:
- Providing learning experiences within a meaningful context.
- Adapting tasks and learning experiences.

key words

Scaffolding: Bruner's term for adult assistance given to support child's thinking and learning, as the child develops competence the adult decreases support until child works independently.

Zone of proximal development: Vygotsky's description for a child's next area of development where adult assistance is only required until the child has developed the skill and can do it independently.

- Selecting appropriate materials for each child's needs and abilities.
- Encouraging children to make choices about what they want to do and when.

Bruner believed that any subject can be taught to any child at any age as long as it is presented in an appropriate way. Learning does not occur in pre-determined stages, but is dependent on linking knowledge to children's existing knowledge in a holistic way.

Bruner's sequence of cognitive development is divided into three areas:
1. **Enactive**: understanding the world through action (relates to Piaget's sensori-motor stage).
2. **Iconic**: manipulation of images or 'icons' in child's thinking about the world (corresponds to Piaget's pre-operational stage).
3. **Symbolic**: use of language and symbols to make sense of the world (similar to Piaget's operational stage).

Bruner viewed language as central to children's thinking and learning and stresses how language is used to represent experiences and how past experience or knowledge is organised through language in ways which make information more accessible. Language connects a person's understanding of one situation to another. The adult has a particular role in establishing effective communication to encourage and extend children's thinking and learning. Adults use language to: capture children's interest and direct their attention; develop children's problem-solving abilities; assist children's understanding of concepts; encourage and extend children's own ideas and negotiate choices with children.

Figure 6.6: Adult supporting children engaged in writing activity

 **Activity!**

- Summarise the main points of Vygotsky's and Bruner's theories concerning children's thinking and learning.
- Think about how these ideas relate to your experiences of working with pupils.

The nature versus nurture debate in cognitive development

Is children's cognitive development derived from their genetic inheritance (nature) or the result of their upbringing and experiences (nurture)? This is one of the questions concerning children's cognitive (or intellectual) development. If a person's cognitive skills are dependent on heredity (nature) then it is possible to believe that people are born with a predetermined level of intelligence which remains the same all their lives – they can only be as intelligent as those intellectual abilities permit. However, if a person's cognitive skills arise as the result of their environment (nurture) then it is possible to believe that people are as intelligent as their learning experiences allow.

Research indicates that the development of children's cognitive abilities depends on both nature and nurture – babies and young children have a *predisposition* towards learning which is activated by *environmental triggers* such as social interaction, language and learning opportunities. For example, research with twins (separated and raised in different environments) shows that genetics is a key factor because the twins had similar IQ scores despite their different life experiences. While research on children from ethnic minority groups has shown that environment is also important because where there was racial discrimination the children did less well educationally, but when their families moved to areas where there was little or no discrimination these children's IQ scores were the same as non-minority children. Intelligence is not determined by just one factor (see section below on factors affecting learning), similar to the way children's language and communication skills are affected by other factors (see Chapter 11).

 **Activity!**

Having read the information in this chapter about children's cognitive development, what is your own opinion regarding the nature versus nurture debate?

Learning experiences

Every learning experience can be viewed as a journey, travelling along different pathways to reach our destination or learning goal (Drummond, 1994). At different points of a learning experience the learning may be:

- Very easy – speeding along a clear motorway.
- Interesting, but uncertain in parts – taking the scenic route.
- Very difficult and complicated – stuck in a traffic jam on a spaghetti junction.
- Totally confusing – trying to find the correct exit from a big road traffic island.
- Completely beyond us – entering a no-through road or going the wrong way down a one-way street.

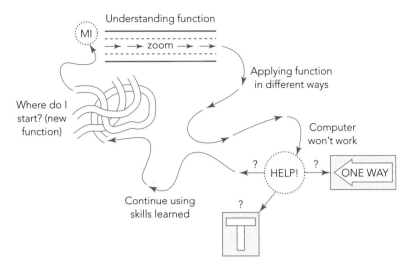

Figure 6.7: Learning pathways

 **Activity!**

Think about your own experiences of learning:
- As an adult (for example learning to drive, cook, study; becoming a teaching assistant).
- As a child (for example learning to tie shoe laces, read, ride a bike, swim).

Draw diagrams to show your learning pathways or journeys. Your pictures might look something like the diagram in Figure 6.7.

Patterns of learning

The experience of learning is a never-ending cycle; learning new skills continues indefinitely. Once one skill is gained in a particular area, further skills can be learned. For example, once pupils have learned basic reading skills, they continue to develop their literacy skills, even as adults by: increasing their vocabulary; improving spelling; decoding unfamiliar words and reading and understanding more complex texts.

 **Activity!**

Think about the learning experiences of the pupils in your school. Select two pupils and draw diagrams of their learning experiences. Compare them with your own experiences of learning. Are there any similarities or differences?

As well as the circular nature of learning experiences, you may also have noticed the importance of *active participation* in all learning experiences. For example, watching someone else use a computer or read a book can only help so much – to develop the relevant skills, people need hands-on experience of using the computer or handling books.

Active learning

Active participation is essential in all effective learning experiences. Active learning is an important part of all learning experiences – not just for children but for adults as well. For example, at college or school you may find that learning situations take the form of workshops, group activities and discussions rather than formal lectures.

It is essential that pupils become actively involved in the learning process. Learning needs to be practical not theoretical. Pupils need concrete learning experiences, that is, using real objects in a meaningful context. Children (and adults) learn by doing. In all learning situations it is important to provide information in small portions with plenty of discussion and activity breaks to maintain interest and concentration. This is because the average attention span of a child is about 5 to 10 minutes and can be as little as 2 to 3 minutes.

Active learning encourages children to be curious, handy at problem-solving, imaginative and creative. You can remember this with the mnemonic CHIC. When providing learning opportunities, you should start from where the child is and build upon the child's experiences and interests. An awareness of children's patterns of learning and their current interests (for example, their favourite objects or hobbies) can help our knowledge and understanding of children's cognitive development. A child's particular interest can provide a strong motivating force for learning.

Activity!

- Think about the pupils in your setting. Focus on two pupils who you know reasonably well. Can you identify their current predominant interest?
- How could you encourage and/or extend their learning using each pupil's particular interest as the starting point? Suggest practical ways to do this.

The role of play in children's learning and development

Play is an essential part of the active learning process. Through active learning, pupils use play opportunities to encourage and extend the problem-solving abilities that are essential to developing their intellectual processes. Play activities provide informal opportunities for pupils to develop ideas and to understand concepts through active learning and communication.

Early learning involves learning through stimulating play activities with appropriate adult support to provide young children with the essential foundations for later learning. Young children who are pushed too hard by being forced to do formal learning activities before they are ready may actually be harmed in terms of their development and they may also be put off literacy, numeracy and other related activities. Young children need a combination of real and imaginary experiences to encourage early learning. This is why play is an important aspect of young children's development and learning. Young children need to handle objects and materials to understand basic concepts. For example, in mathematics using objects for counting and addition such as buttons, cones and plastic cubes. Once children have plenty of practical experiences they can cope more easily with abstract concepts such as written sums or mental arithmetic. Children use play opportunities to encourage and extend the problem-solving abilities that are essential to developing their intellectual processes.

Play activities provide informal opportunities for children to develop ideas and to understand concepts through active learning and communication. Language is a key component in children's thinking and learning. Play is an invaluable way to provide opportunities for language and to make learning more meaningful, especially for young children. It enables children to learn about concepts in a safe and non-threatening environment. Play activities help to promote all aspects of children's development.

✎ Activity!

Describe the planning and provision of play opportunities in your setting.

Figure 6.8: Play provides opportunities for active learning

Learning styles

Pupils have different ways of processing information. Pupils use the skills of looking, listening or touching in varying amounts depending on their individual learning style. For example, some pupils require visual stimulation; some respond well to verbal instructions while others need more 'hands on' experiences. In addition, different times of the day affect individual levels of concentration; some pupils work better in the morning, others in the afternoon. You need to be aware of the individual learning styles of the pupils you work with in order to plan and provide appropriate learning activities. Recognising learning styles will help you to understand the ways pupils learn and to assist them in achieving educational success.

Visual learners gather information through observation and reading. Pupils with this learning style may find it difficult to concentrate on spoken instructions, but respond well to visual aids such as pictures, diagrams and charts. They tend to visualise ideas and remember the visual details of places and objects they have seen. According to research, about 65 per cent of people have this learning style.

Auditory learners process information by listening carefully and then repeating instructions either out loud or mentally in order to remember what they have learned. Research suggests that about 30 per cent of people use this style of learning. Pupils with this learning style tend to be the talkers as well as the listeners in group and/or class situations and benefit from being able to discuss ideas. Auditory learners can be easily distracted by noise and may concentrate better with background music to disguise potentially disruptive noises.

Kinaesthetic learners process information through touch and movement. All young children rely on this learning style to a large extent hence the importance of active learning (see below), especially in the early years. About 5 per cent of people continue to use this style even as adults. Pupils with this learning style will benefit from physical interaction with their environment with plenty of emphasis on learning by doing.

Pupils are not restricted to learning in only one way as they can learn to use different learning styles for different activities within the curriculum. However, research shows that working outside their preferred learning style for extensive periods can be stressful. Providing opportunities for pupils to use their preferred learning style wherever practical increases their chances of educational success (Tobias, 1996).

As well as relying on one particular style of learning, people also tend to use one of two styles of processing information: either analytic or global. Analytic learners process information by dividing it into pieces and organising it in a logical manner, by making lists, putting things in order, following clear instructions or rules, completing/handing in work on time. Analytic learners prefer order and a planned, predictable sequence of events or ideas. Global learners process information by grouping large pieces of information together and focusing on the main ideas rather than details, by drawing spider-grams, using pictures or key words, ignoring or bending rules, including missing deadlines. Global learners prefer spontaneity and activities which allow them creative freedom.

key words

Analytic learner: processes information by dividing it into pieces and organising it in a logical manner, by making lists, putting things in order, and following clear instructions or rules.

Global learner: processes information by grouping large pieces of information together and focusing on the main ideas rather than details, by drawing spider-grams, using pictures or key words.

 Activity!

- Think about how the pupil or pupils you work with gather information. Do they prefer to: work as an individual or in a group; follow step-by-step instructions or have open-ended projects; read and talk about work; engage in practical activities and experiment for themselves?
- Think about how the pupils you work with process information. Are they analytic or global learners?

Factors affecting learning

Intellectual development is affected by other factors besides the pupil's chronological age. Factors affecting learning can include: lack of play opportunities; unrewarding learning activities; lack of opportunities to use language and communication skills; inappropriate learning activities; introduction to formal learning situations at too early an age and English as an additional language. Some pupils may not develop their intellectual processes in line with the expected pattern of development for their age due to special needs such as: communication and/or interaction difficulties; learning difficulties; behavioural, social or emotional difficulties (see Chapter 13).

Others factors affecting learning include:

- **Low self-esteem**: The lack of opportunities to explore, experiment and create within a stimulating learning environment can result in pupils having no sense of purpose or achievement. A pupil's emotional well-being is based on positive interactions with others and the world around them.
- **Lack of concentration**: Poor concentration leads to poor listening skills and difficulty in following instructions. Play opportunities are an effective way to motivate younger pupils' learning, as children are more likely to concentrate on self-chosen activities they enjoy. If they have not had play opportunities they will find it especially difficult to concentrate in more formal learning situations.
- **Boredom**: Lack of concentration can lead to boredom. If pupils have not had discovery opportunities they will often lack interest in others and the world around them. This can lead to disruptive and/or attention-seeking behaviour.
- **Reluctance to participate**: Some pupils may have a tendency to withdraw from activities (especially those involving problem-solving skills) for fear of 'failing'. Pupils who have lacked play opportunities will have missed out on learning in safe, non-threatening situations.
- **Over-dependency on adult support**: Some pupils may be reluctant to do things for themselves if they have not had opportunities to engage in play and independent learning activities. Dependency on adults can also be linked to a pupil's fear of 'failing'.

The inability to concentrate, to work independently or to use investigative skills may make it very difficult for some pupils to participate fully in learning activities. This may lead to subsequent learning difficulties in curriculum areas such as English, Mathematics, Science, Technology, and so on. Some pupils may be inaccurately thought to have learning difficulties, when they are really experiencing a lack of appropriate intellectual stimulation. Children with little or no intellectual stimulation cannot develop their own thinking skills or formulate new ideas. It is vital that all pupils have access to a stimulating learning environment that enables them to learn in exciting and challenging ways. Intellectual stimulation through appropriate learning activities allows pupils to develop their intellectual abilities and to fulfil their potential as individuals.

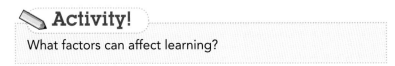

Activity!

What factors can affect learning?

Curriculum frameworks

As appropriate to your particular role, you will need to support learning activities within the curriculum frameworks for education for your home country: England, Northern Ireland, Scotland or Wales. For example in England the curriculum frameworks for education are the Early Years Foundation Stage (0 to 5 years) and the National Curriculum Key Stages 1 to 4 (5 to 16 years).

The Early Years Foundation Stage

Orders and regulations under section 39 of the Childcare Act 2006 brought the Early Years Foundation Stage (EYFS) into force in September 2008. All early years providers are required to use the EYFS to ensure a coherent and flexible approach to children's care, learning and development that will enable young children to achieve the five *Every Child Matters* outcomes: staying safe; being healthy; enjoying and achieving; making a positive contribution; and achieving economic well-being (see Chapter 8).

There are six areas covered by the early learning goals and educational programmes. None of these areas can be delivered in isolation from the others. They are equally important and depend on each other to support a rounded approach to child development. All the areas must be delivered through planned, purposeful play, with a balance of adult-led and child-initiated activities. The six areas of learning and development are:

- Personal, Social and Emotional Development
- Communication, Language and Literacy
- Problem Solving, Reasoning and Numeracy
- Knowledge and Understanding of the World
- Physical Development
- Creative Development.

For more information on EYFS see: **http://nationalstrategies.standards.dcsf.gov.uk/earlyyears**.

The National Curriculum

The National Curriculum sets out the statutory requirements for the knowledge and skills that every child is expected to learn in schools. The National Curriculum framework enables teachers to provide all school-aged children with challenging learning experiences, taught in ways that are both balanced and manageable. The National Curriculum sets out the standards to be used to measure the progress and performance of pupils in each subject to help teachers plan and implement learning activities that meet the individual learning needs of pupils.

The National Curriculum applies to children of compulsory school age in schools in England. The National Curriculum sets out what pupils should study, what they should be taught and the standards that they should achieve. It is divided into four key stages:

- **Key Stage 1**: 5 to 7 year olds (Year groups: 1 and 2)
- **Key Stage 2**: 7 to 11 year olds (Year groups: 3, 4, 5 and 6)
- **Key Stage 3**: 11 to 14 year olds (Year groups: 7, 8 and 9)
- **Key Stage 4**: 14 to 16 year olds (Year groups: 10 and 11)

The primary curriculum

In Key Stages 1 and 2 of the National Curriculum the compulsory subjects consist of: English; Mathematics; Science; Information and Communication Technology; Design and Technology; History; Geography; Art and Design; Music; and Physical Education. In addition there is a non-statutory framework for Personal, Social and Health Education (PSHE) and Citizenship. Primary schools must also provide Religious Education although parents may withdraw their children from this if they wish to do so. Primary schools must also provide sex education, but again parents can withdraw their children from these lessons. From September 2010, the teaching of Modern Foreign Languages will be statutory in Key Stage 2.

For more information see: **http://nationalstrategies.standards.dcsf.gov.uk/primary**.

The secondary curriculum

In Key Stage 3 of the National Curriculum the compulsory subjects are: English; Mathematics; Science; Information and Communication Technology; Design and Technology; History; Geography; Art and Design; Music; Physical Education, Citizenship; and Modern Foreign Languages.

In Key Stage 4 the compulsory subjects are English, Mathematics, Science, Information and Communication Technology, Physical Education and Citizenship. Secondary schools must make entitlement curriculum areas (the arts, design and technology, the humanities and modern foreign languages) available to all students who wish to study them. In addition, there is a new statutory requirement for work-related learning and a non-statutory framework setting out the minimum experience that schools should provide for work-related learning. For more information see *The Work-related Learning Guide* at **http://www.dcsf.gov.uk/14-19/ documents/work-relatedlearningguide_2.pdf**

In Key Stages 3 and 4 there is a non-statutory framework for Personal, Social and Health and Economic Education as well as Religious Education, which is a statutory subject with a non-statutory programme of study. As in primary schools, parents may withdraw their children from Religious Education and sex education lessons if they wish to do so, except for the aspects of sex education (such as human reproduction) included as part of the Science programme of study. For more information see: **http://nationalstrategies.standards.dcsf.gov.uk/secondary**

The Diploma is a new qualification for 14 to 19 year olds which offers a mix of academic and practical skills within one of these broad sector-related subject areas: Construction and the Built Environment; Creative and Media; Engineering; Information Technology; Society, Health and Development; Environmental and Land-based Studies; Business, Administration and Finance; Manufacturing and Product Design; Hospitality; and Hair and Beauty Studies. From September 2010 the following areas will also be available: Travel and Tourism; Public Services; Sport and Active Leisure; and Retail Business. Three more areas will be available from September 2011: Humanities and Social Sciences; Languages and International Communication; and Science.

The Diploma does not replace GCSEs or A levels but will be studied alongside compulsory subjects such as English, Mathematics, Science and ICT. The Diploma has three levels of study: Foundation Diploma (equivalent to 5 GCSEs at grades D to G); Higher Diploma (equivalent to 7 GCSEs at grades A* to C); Advanced Diploma (equivalent to 3.5 A levels). For more information see: **http://www.qcda.gov.uk/qualifications/28.aspx**

Curriculum frameworks in Northern Ireland, Scotland and Wales

You should know the relevant national curriculum guidelines for teaching and learning relevant to the pupils you work with. The above curriculum information relates to England. The revised school curriculum for Northern Ireland was put in place in 2006 with new requirements being phased in from September 2007. Information about the statutory curriculum in Northern Ireland can be accessed from: **http://www.nicurriculum.org.uk/**.

The curriculum in Scotland has been under review and from August 2010 all schools will be expected to adopt the new 'Curriculum for Excellence'. Information about this new curriculum for 3 to 18 year olds can be found at: **http://www.ltscotland.org.uk/ curriculumforexcellence/curriculumoverview/index.asp**.

The school curriculum for 3 to 19 year olds in Wales has been implemented since September 2008. Information about this revised curriculum in Wales is available at: **http://wales.gov.uk/ topics/educationandskills/curriculumassessment/arevisedcurriculumforwales/?lang=en**.

 **Activity!**

What is the curriculum framework for the pupils you work with?

Curriculum plans

Schools should be able to explain their approach to the curriculum and to show how they meet the statutory requirements for all learners, including any variations to meet the needs of individual pupils. Detailed information about a school's curriculum plans can be found in: policy statements for the whole curriculum and for each subject of the curriculum; schemes of work and teaching plans for pupils in each key stage; class or group timetables and Individual Education Plans.

Developing curriculum plans involves planning learning activities that will provide all pupils with appropriate opportunities to learn which reflect the range of needs, interests and the past achievements of pupils in each year group at each key stage. Curriculum plans include:

- **Policy statements** showing the balance between different parts of the curriculum at each key stage.
- **Practical guidelines** for staff assisting the delivery of each curriculum subject, for example general information about resources and important teaching points.
- **Long-term plans** showing the content and skills in the programmes of study for every subject at each key stage and how these are covered, including links between subjects as well as progression, consolidation and diversification for pupils across units (such as between units in the DfES/QCA schemes of work).
- **Medium-term plans** defining the intended learning outcomes for units of work, including information on learning activities, recording and assessment methods.
- **Short-term plans** setting out detailed information on learning activities for pupils in each class on a weekly and daily basis, including lesson plans and/or activity plans with details of specific targets, organisation, resources and strategies to support learning.

(QCA, 2001)

Subject:	Completed by:	Time:	Location:	Duration:
Date:	Class:	Year:	Number:	Term:

Curriculum/strategy links:
Children's previous experiences:
Learning objectives:

Differentiation:	Support needs:
Resources:	Health and safety:
Key Questions:	Key Vocabulary:

Organisation/Content Introduction:	Teaching Assistant Activity:	Pupil Activity:
Organisation/Content Main:	Teaching Assistant Activity:	Pupil Activity:
Organisation/Content Plenary:	Teaching Assistant Activity:	Pupil Activity:

Assessment: Who?	Criteria:	Strategies:	Evidence/recording:
Notes			

Figure 6.10: Planning sheet for a teaching assistant

Activity!

Give examples of how you plan activities.

Supporting the teacher in the delivery of learning activities

The teaching assistant supports the delivery of learning activities as directed by the teacher. To provide effective support the teaching assistant must know and understand the objectives of the learning activities and the strategies to support pupils' learning.

As a teaching assistant, you should be aware of your experience and expertise in relation to supporting learning activities and how this relates to the planned activities. You should ensure that you are adequately prepared for your contribution to the learning activities, such as understanding the relevant subject knowledge and support strategies as well as obtaining appropriate resources. This may mean discussing development opportunities to improve your skills in areas where you currently lack experience or expertise (see Chapter 9).

When supporting learning activities you should remember these important points:

1. **Develop an effective partnership with the class teacher**: know and understand your exact role; know and understand the teacher's role; contribute to the planning of learning activities; use the same strategies as the teacher to support learning; share the same goals as the teacher for pupils' learning and establish good communication with the teacher.
2. **Follow agreed class rules and class routines**: how the pupils enter and exit the classroom; classroom organisation; the storage and use of materials and equipment; discipline – approaches to pupil behaviour; rewards and sanctions and marking work.
3. **Understand the teaching methods for learning activities**: class teaching; question time; group work and individual tasks.
4. **Provide effective support during learning activities**: understand requirements of the lesson; know the intended learning outcomes for pupils; prepare and organise resources as directed by the teacher; know the group (their character, ability, strengths, individual needs, etc); know what support individuals within the group may need; use appropriate support strategies; give the teacher feedback on the pupils' responses, including their achievements and any difficulties experienced during the learning activity.

(Balshaw and Farrell, 2002)

The teaching assistant's role in delivering learning activities

Your role will depend on the school and your own experience and/or qualifications. As a teaching assistant you may have a general role working with different classes in a year group/key stage, or specific responsibilities for a pupil, subject area or age group. When working with a specific pupil or pupils you should have information regarding their special educational needs and any special provision including details of statements of special educational needs, Individual Education Plans and/or Behaviour Support Plans. You may be involved in implementing a structured programme designed by a specialist such as a speech and language therapist (see Chapter 13).

When delivering learning activities you should ensure that you make accurate and detailed records of what has been planned and delivered in order to: clarify the aims and learning objectives of activity plans; avoid contradictory strategies/unnecessary duplication of work; use the time available more effectively; evaluate the success of plans/activities and provide continuity and progression for future planning.

Preparing for learning activities

The teacher's short-term plans (individual lesson plans and/or activity plans) should include information about your role in delivering learning activities. These plans should include the learning objectives and the teacher's expectations of what the learning outcomes for the pupils might be. Use your personal timetable, the class timetable and the available systems of communication within the school to help you know and understand: what you have to do before you deliver the learning activity; where, when and with whom the learning activity will take place; and why the learning activity is being implemented.

You need the relevant lesson plans at least the day before so that you have time to prepare what you need for the learning activities. This preparation may involve: finding resources; doing some photocopying; checking equipment and its availability; reading up on a subject; finding artefacts or reference books for the pupils or asking the teacher for further information.

You need time and the opportunity to discuss the teacher's plans beforehand. If you do not understand any aspect of the learning activities you are expected to support, than you must ask the teacher for further information. You will not be able to provide effective support for the pupils unless you are absolutely clear about the requirements of each learning activity (Watkinson, 2003).

Your role in delivering learning activities involves assisting the teacher by:

- Preparing the learning environment to meet the individual learning needs of each pupil in the class.
- Providing appropriate learning activities for individuals and groups of pupils.
- Selecting and using appropriate learning materials.
- Supervising an individual or small group of pupils.
- Maintaining pupil safety during the learning activity.
- Interacting with the pupils in ways that focus their attention on the learning potential of the learning materials, for example by asking questions such as 'What happens if you do…?'.
- Using praise and encouragement to help pupils participate fully in learning activities.
- Observing pupil responses during the learning activity (see below).

 **Activity!**

Describe your role in delivering learning activities.

Organising learning resources

The learning resources in the school should support learning activities across the full range of the curriculum. A wide variety of learning resources will help to maintain interest in the subject area and help to support individual learning needs. The school should decide on spending priorities when allocating resources, as some areas of the curriculum may require more substantial or expensive learning materials than others. Careful criteria should be set for selecting and using learning resources. For example: health and safety; ages/ability levels of the pupils; quality and durability; versatility and value for money; special educational needs (specialist or modified learning materials) and equal opportunities (resources reflecting positive images of cultural diversity, gender roles and people with disabilities).

Figure 6.11: Teaching assistant supporting a pupil during a learning activity

The organisation of learning resources is also an important consideration. For example, to encourage independent learning, classroom resources should be organised in ways that allow pupils to locate the learning resources they need and to put them away afterwards. Learning resources should be clearly labelled and stored where they are accessible to the pupils. Learning resources must be regularly maintained, cleaned and checked for damage. Items that are incomplete, unhygienic or past repair should be appropriately discarded.

Providing support for learning activities

When supporting learning activities you will need to: deliver learning activities as directed by the teacher; use appropriate resources and support strategies for each pupil's needs and abilities; adapt learning activities to meet the learning objectives and assist each pupil at an appropriate level; promote independent learning (see below).

The strategies to support learning should ensure that each pupil participates fully in every lesson. As a teaching assistant you should:

- Ensure that pupils in your group(s) concentrate and behave responsibly.
- Ensure that pupils understand and follow the teacher's instructions.
- Remind pupils of teaching points made by the teacher.
- Translate or explain words and phrases used by the teacher.
- Use the correct language and vocabulary for the learning activity.
- Question pupils and encourage their participation.
- Organise and participate in appropriate play activities or games.
- Help pupils to use equipment and resources relevant to the learning activity.
- Use visual or practical aids, or a computer with suitable software, especially when supporting pupils with special educational needs.
- Look for and note any common problems that pupils have, or mistakes that they make, so that the teacher can address these in future learning activities.

Figure 6.12: Supporting children's learning

Promoting independent learning

You need to arrange with the teacher the strategies and resources to be used to promote independent learning. To promote independent learning you can: encourage and support pupils in making decisions about their own learning; provide appropriate levels of assistance for individual pupils; use technology to enable pupils to work more independently; provide challenges to promote independent learning and encourage pupils to review their own learning strategies, achievements and future learning needs. All pupils should be encouraged to develop independent learning in preparation for the next key stage, college, work and adult life.

Younger pupils should be encouraged to develop these independent learning skills:

- Take turns to speak and listen.
- Respond appropriately to other pupils and adults.
- Know, understand and apply class/school rules.
- Ask an appropriate adult for help.
- Make choices about books.
- Listen carefully and follow verbal instructions.
- Use pre-selected learning materials for independent learning.
- Select resources independently.
- Follow simple written instructions.
- Work with a partner to check or review work.
- Use spelling aids such as individual wordbooks, topic word banks and simple dictionaries.
- Use the school library with support.
- Access information from pictures, artefacts, simple charts and diagrams with support.

Older pupils should be encouraged to continue using the skills listed above and also to develop these independent learning skills:

- Start work independently.
- Interpret written instructions independently.
- Work cooperatively with other pupils.

- Manage own reading book and help keep reading record up-to-date.
- Put name on any loose paperwork.
- Put correct date on all work.
- Aim to complete all tasks set in a given time.
- Carefully organise and keep own work.
- Be able to make notes during lessons.
- Use the school library independently.
- Use computers independently.
- Access information from artefacts, simple charts, diagrams and text with increasing independence.
- Use information from various sources and include references.

 **Activity!**

- What strategies have you used to support pupils' learning?
- Give examples of how you have promoted independent learning, for example by using ICT skills.

Pupil responses and preferences

Pupil responses should also be considered when providing support for learning activities. Take notice of non-verbal responses and preferences demonstrated by the pupils; these are just as important as what the pupil says. You should be sensitive to pupil needs and desires. Despite careful planning, you may find that when you are delivering a learning activity it is not appropriate for all the pupils you are working with. You will need to monitor pupils' responses to learning activities and take appropriate action to modify or adapt activities to achieve the intended learning objectives or provide additional activities to extend their learning.

You can use pupils' positive or negative responses to modify or extend activities to meet each pupil's needs more effectively. For example, if the learning objectives prove too easy or too difficult, you may have to set new goals. By breaking down learning activities into smaller tasks, you may help individual pupils to achieve success more quickly. You may need to provide an alternative version of the activity or you might be able to present the learning materials in different ways or offer a greater/lesser level of assistance.

You may need to modify or adapt activities for the following reasons: the pupil lacks concentration; the pupil is bored or uninterested; the pupil finds the activity too difficult or too easy; the pupil is upset or unwell (if so, you may need to abandon/postpone the activity). In modifying plans you are continuing a cycle of planning and implementing activities. Remember to give the pupils positive encouragement and feedback to reinforce and sustain their interest and efforts in the learning process. (See section on the importance of praise and encouragement in Chapter 3.)

Dealing with problems and difficulties

Regular observations and evaluations of learning activities are helpful in identifying any potential problems pupils may have in their development, learning or behaviour. By carefully observing pupils during learning activities you can identify: the ways in which individual pupils learn; how pupils interact with each other (behaviour and social skills); any difficulties pupils may have during the learning activity, such as following the instructions, performing the necessary skills or understanding concepts.

A continuous record of a pupil's learning difficulties can help identify specific problems. Working with parents, colleagues and specialist advisors (if necessary) the teacher can then plan a suitable programme to enable the pupil to overcome these difficulties. Observations can provide a check that the pupil's learning is progressing in the expected ways.

You will need to be able to resolve any difficulties you may have in supporting the learning activities as planned. For example: modifying or adapting an inappropriate activity; coping with insufficient materials or equipment breakdown or dealing with uncooperative or disruptive pupils. You must report any problems you are unable to resolve to the teacher.

Supporting the teacher in the evaluation of learning activities

After you have planned and/or delivered a learning activity, you will need to evaluate it. Some evaluation also occurs during the learning activity, providing continuous assessment of a pupil's performance. It is important to evaluate the learning activity so that you can: identify if the learning activity has been successful, that the aims and learning objectives or outcomes have been met; consider the ways in which the learning activity might be modified/adapted to meet the individual learning needs of the pupil or pupils; provide information on learner responses and whether or not a particular learning activity has been successful to the teacher, SENCO or other professionals.

Evaluating learning activities

When involved in evaluating learning activities for an individual pupil or group of pupils, remember these important points:

- How do the pupil or pupils respond to the learning activity?
- Do you need to adapt the original plan, perhaps through changing the resources or the timing of the learning activity?
- Did the pupil(s) achieve the intended learning objectives?
- How effective was the preparation and delivery of the learning activity?
- Make a note of pupil achievements and/or any difficulties.
- Record these using methods as appropriate to your role.
- Report achievements, difficulties or concerns to the teacher.
- Have you identified any future learning needs for the pupil(s) as a result of pupil responses during this learning activity?
- Are there any possible modifications you could make for future learning activities?
- Discuss your ideas with the teacher.

Providing information on pupil progress and responses

You will need to keep accurate records of pupil progress and responses to learning activities in order to feed back information to the teacher and other relevant people. You can record significant aspects of pupil participation and progress during the learning activity (if possible) or shortly afterwards so that you remember important points.

After the activity, use all the available relevant information to evaluate the effectiveness of your planning and implementation of the activity, gather information from parents, colleagues and other professionals. You must provide feedback about the pupils' learning achievements to the teacher. Any suggested changes to future activity plans should be agreed with the teacher and other relevant staff.

You can provide information on pupil progress and responses by considering these questions:

1. Did the pupil(s) achieve the objectives/outcomes set? If not, why not?
2. If the pupil(s) has achieved the objectives, what effect has it had (e.g. on behaviour, learning or any special need)?
3. Were the objectives too easy or too hard for the pupil(s)?
4. How did any staff involvement affect pupil(s) achievement?
5. Was the lesson or activity plan successful? If not, why not?

 **Key Task**

Describe *two* learning activities you have helped to plan, deliver and evaluate. Include information on: a brief description of each learning activity; the objectives of each learning activity; a list of materials and/ or equipment used; your contribution to the learning activities; the type and level of support for the pupils; the specific strategies for supporting learning activities and an evaluation of each learning activity.

Include copies of planning and evaluation sheets.

NOS Links:

Level 3:   **STL 18.1**   **STL 18.2**   **STL 23.1**   **STL 23.2**   **STL 23.3**   **STL 24.1**   **STL 24.2**

Summary of key points in this chapter:

- **Understanding pupil development and learning** including: how children think and learn; cognitive approaches to how children think and learn; the nature versus nurture debate in cognitive development; learning experiences; patterns of learning; active learning; the role of play in children's learning and development; learning styles; factors affecting learning.

- **Curriculum frameworks** including: the Early Years Foundation Stage; The National Curriculum in England; curriculum frameworks in Northern Ireland, Scotland and Wales.

- **Curriculum plans** including: long-term plans; medium-term plans; short-term plans.

- **Supporting the teacher in the planning of learning activities** including: planning learning activities; the teaching assistant's role in planning learning activities.

- **Supporting the teacher in the delivery of learning activities** including: the teaching assistant's role in delivering learning activities; preparing for learning activities; organising learning resources; providing support for learning activities; promoting independent learning; pupil responses and preferences; dealing with problems and difficulties.

- **Supporting the teacher in the evaluation of learning activities** including: evaluating learning activities; providing information on pupil progress and responses.

Further reading

Alfrey, C. (2004) *Understanding Children's Learning: A Text for Teaching Assistants*. David Fulton Publishers.

Balshaw, M. and Farrell, P. (2002) *Teaching Assistants: Practical Strategies for Effective Classroom Support*. David Fulton Publishers.

Bentham, S. (2003) *A Teaching Assistant's Guide to Child Development and Psychology in the Classroom*. Routledge.

Brookes, G. (2008) *The Complete Guide for Teaching Assistants in Secondary Education*. Continuum International Publishing Group Ltd.

Bruce, T. (2001) *Helping Young Children Learn Through Play*. Hodder & Stoughton.

Cheminais, R. (2008) *Every Child Matters: A Practical Guide for Teaching Assistants*. David Fulton Publishers.

Dean, J. (2005) *The Teaching Assistant's Guide to Primary Education*. Routledge Falmer.

Dupree, J. (2005) *Help Students Improve Their Study Skills: A Handbook for Teaching Assistants in Secondary Schools*. David Fulton Publishers Ltd.

Graf, M. (2009) *The Teaching Assistant's Guide to Understanding and Supporting Learning*. Continuum International Publishing Group Ltd.

Hutchin, V. (2007) *Supporting Every Child's Learning Across the Early Years Foundation Stage*. Hodder Murray.

Lindon, J. (2001) *Understanding Children's Play*. Nelson Thornes.

Overall, L. (2007) *Supporting Children's Learning: A Guide for Teaching Assistants*. Sage Publications.

QCDA (2010) *The National Curriculum: Primary Handbook*. Qualifications and Curriculum Development Agency.

7. Promoting positive behaviour

This chapter relates to QCF unit:

TDA 3.4 Promote children and young people's positive behaviour

Expectations for behaviour

Pupil behaviour can be defined as a pupil's actions and reactions or a pupil's treatment of others. Behaviour involves children *learning to conform* to parental expectations for behaviour, school expectations for behaviour and society's expectations for behaviour.

Parental expectations for behaviour

Parents have expectations for their children's behaviour based on: the media; cultural or religious beliefs; individual variations in child-rearing practices; adherence to traditional child-rearing practices; comparisons to other children (of relatives, friends and neighbours) and perceptions of their own childhood and *their* parents' attitudes to behaviour.

Many parents may have idealised or unrealistic expectations concerning their children's behaviour because some childcare/education books and the media promote unrealistic age-related expectations so that many children do not seem to 'measure up' to what the experts say. Smaller families (often with few or no relatives nearby) mean many parents lack first-hand experience of caring for children *before* they have their own children and may feel less confident about their parenting skills. Parents of children with special needs may be unsure of what to expect from their children in terms of behaviour; they may over compensate for their child's special needs by being over protective or by letting the child get away with behaviour that would not be appropriate in a child of similar age/level of development.

In the past children did not dare challenge parental authority for fear of physical punishment. Today some parents still feel that if they were brought up this way, then this is how they expect their children to behave. In the twenty-first century, society recognises the rights of the child and has the expectation that all parents should be more caring and responsive to their children's needs by using positive methods such as praise, encouragement, negotiation and rewards to achieve appropriate behaviour. Children learn what their parents consider to be appropriate behaviour and will bring these expectations to the setting. Children also observe their parents' behaviour that may be:

- Assertive: sensitive to their own *and* other people's needs.
- Passive: too sensitive to other people's needs so *ignores own needs.*
- Aggressive: obsessed with own needs so *ignores other people's needs.*

The school's expectations for pupil behaviour

Children who are not prepared (or are unable) to conform have to accept the consequences, such as sanctions or punishments for unacceptable behaviour. Learning about behaviour (as with all learning) always takes place within a social context. Certain types of behaviour may be acceptable in one context but not in another (for example families may make allowances for their child's behaviour), however different rules apply in school because adults must consider the needs of all pupils. What is acceptable in one situation may not be acceptable in another, even within the same school, for example loud, boisterous behaviour is acceptable in the playground but not in the classroom. Conforming brings limitations to pupils' behaviour, for example following school rules and participating in all curriculum areas even those they do not like.

 **key words**

Behaviour: a person's actions, reactions and treatment of others.

Social context: *any* situation or environment where social interaction occurs, e.g. home, nursery, school, local community.

 **Activity!**

What are *your* expectations regarding what is acceptable behaviour for yourself, for the pupils in your school and for the individual in society?

Other influences on pupil behaviour

The media (television, magazines and comics) and computer games can have positive or negative influences on pupil behaviour, depending on what the children see and how they are affected by it. Children exposed to violent images may see aggressive behaviour as an acceptable way to deal with others. Children who observe more assertive behaviour (with its emphasis on negotiation and compromise) are likely to demonstrate similar positive behaviour. Television programmes, characters and personalities provide powerful role models for children's behaviour. Just consider the effectiveness of advertising!

Peer pressure may have a negative influence on pupil behaviour as other children may: persuade them to participate in dangerous activities including 'dares'; pressure them into socially unacceptable behaviour, such as lying, stealing or bullying; exclude or threaten them if they do not conform; or encourage them to act in ways they never would as an individual, 'mob rule'. However, you can sometimes use peer pressure to encourage positive behaviour by highlighting the positive benefits of certain behaviour for the group, class or school.

 **key words**

Peer pressure: feeling compelled by people of about the same age to behave in a manner similar or acceptable to them.

Providing positive role models

Children model their attitudes and actions on the behaviour of others. They imitate the actions and speech of those they are closest to, for example acting at being 'mum', 'dad', 'nursery nurse', 'play worker' or 'teacher'; copying the actions and mannerisms of adults around the home, childcare setting or school. All adults working with children need to be aware of the significant impact they make to children's social (and emotional) development by providing positive role models. When working with pupils you should strike a balance between allowing for the children's increasing need for independence and providing adequate supervision with appropriate guidelines for socially acceptable behaviour. Observing the behaviour of parents and other significant adults (such as childcarers, teachers and teaching assistants) affects children's own behaviour, how children deal with their own feelings and how children relate to others. This is why it is so important for adults to provide positive role models for children's behaviour.

 Activity!

- Who were your role models when you were younger? How do you think these early role models influenced your own behaviour?
- How could a teaching assistant model positive behaviour? Give examples from your experiences of working with pupils.

Promoting positive behaviour

Creating an environment that promotes positive behaviour helps to shape the school's ethos and reflect the setting's values. Positive behaviour is an essential building block for creating a welcoming and pleasant learning environment in which all members of the school feel respected, safe and secure. When helping teachers to create an environment that promotes positive behaviour, you should remember that pupils are more likely to behave in positive ways if they are: in a welcoming and stimulating learning environment; engaged in interesting and challenging learning activities that are appropriate to their ages and levels of development; given clear and realistic guidelines on behaviour; and work with adults who have positive expectations for pupil behaviour.

Examples of positive pupil behaviour:	Examples of negative pupil behaviour:
Sharing resources and adult's attention; taking turns.	Not sharing; attention-seeking; jealousy.
Working cooperatively.	Disrupting activities, e.g. taking things without asking, fighting or arguing.
Being friendly; helping/comforting others.	Being aggressive/abusive, e.g. upsetting or hurting others, bullying.
Concentrating on activities, e.g. remaining on task.	Not concentrating on activities, e.g. being easily frustrated or distracted.
Complying with adult requests.	Being defiant and refusing reasonable adult requests.
Contributing creative ideas.	Overriding or ridiculing other people's ideas.
Expressing self effectively.	Expressing self inappropriately, e.g. emotional outbursts, whining or nagging.
Being aware of danger.	Having no sense of danger; being too compulsive.
Being polite.	Being rude, cheeky or interrupting others.
Being responsible for own actions.	Blaming others or lying about own actions.
Being independent.	Being easily led or too dependent on others.
Being flexible.	Resisting change or overly upset by change.

What is considered to be positive or acceptable children's behaviour depends on each adult's tolerance levels. Adult tolerance for different kinds of children's behaviour may depend on: their expectations for children's behaviour in relation to age/level of development; the social context in which the behaviour is demonstrated and how the adult feels at that particular time.

The benefits of positive behaviour

Promoting positive behaviour can bring many benefits to pupils, staff and schools. These benefits include: creating a positive framework with realistic expectations for pupils' behaviour; providing consistent care/education for pupils with clear rules and boundaries; the security and stability of a welcoming and structured environment; positive motivation through praise, encouragement and rewards; positive social interaction between pupils and staff; encouraging pupils' self-reliance, self-confidence and positive self-esteem; encouraging

The school behaviour management policy

Section 61 of the School Standards and Framework Act 1998 requires a governing body to ensure that its school pursues policies designed to promote positive behaviour. This includes making and reviewing a written statement of principles to guide the head teacher in determining measures for promoting positive behaviour in the school. The school's behaviour policy should cover how the school promotes high standards of behaviour as well as promoting excellent attendance and tackling poor attendance. School policies for behaviour include a behaviour policy, attendance policy and an anti-bullying policy. These policies can be combined into one document to form an overall school behaviour management policy.

The behaviour management policy should include:

- The school's aims and underlying principles for behaviour.
- The roles and responsibilities of staff members.
- A code of conduct for pupils.
- How positive behaviour will be promoted.
- How regular attendance will be encouraged.
- Strategies to combat bullying.
- How the policy will be implemented.
- The use of rewards and sanctions.
- The arrangements for supporting pupils and staff.
- Monitoring and reviewing procedures for the policy.

The policy should ensure consistency by providing clear guidelines for all staff on its implementation as well as practical advice to parents and carers on how they can help. This information could be included in documents such as the staff handbook and the home-school agreement.

The behaviour management policy should be an integral part of the school curriculum. The policy must be based on clear values (such as respect, fairness and inclusion) that are also reflected in the school's aims, equal opportunities policy and special educational needs policy. To promote positive behaviour, the expectations in the behaviour management policy need to be taught explicitly as part of the curriculum. For example, pupils' moral, social, emotional and behavioural development could be encouraged through the religious education programme and designated PSHE lessons. Pupils should have regular explicit opportunities for learning about how to behave in accordance with the school's values and beliefs. In promoting positive behaviour schools should implement practical strategies for intervention including using support available from the LEA, Education Welfare Service, Police, Connexions Service, multi-agency teams, complementary schools etc. (DfES, 2003). On 31 March 2010 the Department for Children, Schools and Families (DCSF) published revised guidance about behaviour and attendance partnerships for secondary schools – *Guidance on School Behaviour and Attendance Partnerships*. This revised guidance takes account of the Apprenticeships, Skills, Children and Learning Act 2009 which requires all maintained secondary schools and Academies to cooperate and form behaviour and attendance partnerships to improve behaviour and tackle persistent absence among pupils. The guidance came into effect on 1 September 2010.

Staff responsibilities for managing pupil behaviour

Staff members are responsible for the behaviour of *all* pupils and not only those that they have been assigned to. Adults should always act as good role models for positive behaviour. Parents and pupils need to be informed of school expectations for behaviour. School and classroom rules need to be displayed and referred to. Pupils need to be encouraged to become self-disciplined, to be responsible for their own actions, in order to develop their confidence and independence. Pupils need to know the consequences of negative behaviour. Pupils need to understand that they can improve their behaviour and make a new start. Work within classrooms must take account of individual ability. Poor behaviour needs to be monitored with notes and dates put in social records. The class teacher should inform the parent(s) at an early stage if any problems occur with their child.

The Education and Inspections Act 2006 gives all staff in maintained schools in England and Wales new legal rights to discipline pupils. The Act gives all staff in lawful charge of pupils the power to discipline them for inappropriate behaviour or for not following instruction. This means that head teachers can delegate the responsibility of discipline to support staff as well as teaching staff. Every head teacher is required to draw up and publicise a discipline policy for their school and bring it to the attention of pupils, parents and staff at least once a year. The policy should set out strategies to prevent all forms of bullying and state what measures will be determined by the head teacher to ensure pupils complete any tasks that have been reasonably assigned to them in connection with their education. (ATL, 2007; p.2) Guidance on school discipline and pupil behaviour policies can be downloaded from: **www.teachernet.gov.uk/ wholeschool/behaviour/schooldisciplinepupilbehaviourpolicies**

The teaching assistant's role for managing pupil behaviour

When managing pupil behaviour, you need to recognise and respond promptly and appropriately to anti-social behaviour; remember to follow school policies. For example, you may need to remind pupils about the school/class rules or protect other pupils and yourself from harm when challenging behaviour is demonstrated by a pupil. You will need to report any problems in dealing with unacceptable or challenging behaviour to the class or subject teacher. You should also be able to identify and report any pupil's uncharacteristic behaviour patterns to the appropriate person, such as the class or form teacher (see below).

Supporting behaviour management strategies

Many pupils find it difficult to settle in school and to concentrate on their work because of behaviour problems. These pupils often challenge the authority of the teacher and the teaching assistant as well as their parents. Teachers and teaching assistants need to help these pupils learn how to behave in class because difficult behaviour makes it hard for teaching and learning to take place. In addition, disruptive behaviour demonstrated by one or two pupils can affect the learning opportunities for other pupils. Improving the behaviour of individual pupils helps schools to raise the educational standards for all pupils.

Most behaviour problems in class are of a low level type that can be easily managed when teachers and teaching assistants use the correct strategies (see below). However, if this low level of behaviour is incorrectly managed then challenging confrontations can result. Learning to behave appropriately in school is essential because unless pupils can settle to learn they will not reach their full academic potential.

When supporting the management of pupil behaviour, you should consistently and effectively implement agreed behaviour management strategies. You will also need to provide constructive feedback on the effectiveness of the behaviour management strategies including the improvements or setbacks of pupils with Behaviour Support Plans. You may also be asked to contribute to ideas for improvements to behaviour management strategies.

 **Activity!**

- What are staff members' general responsibilities for managing pupil behaviour?
- Summarise the role and responsibilities of the teaching assistant for managing pupil behaviour.

School code of conduct for pupils

A school's behaviour management policy must set explicit standards of behaviour and attendance, including a code of conduct for pupils. The purpose of the code should be to promote positive behaviour, so rules should be expressed in positive terms. The code should outline the school's expectations for pupil behaviour in the classroom and around the school. A system of rewards and sanctions should be used to support the code of conduct. Positive behaviour and regular attendance should not be taken for granted – they should be actively encouraged and reinforced (DfES, 2003).

Example of a school code of conduct for pupils

1. Treat everyone and everything with respect.
2. Try to understand other people's point of view.
3. Make it as easy as possible for everyone to learn and for the teacher to teach by: arriving on time with everything you need for the day; listening carefully, following instructions, not interrupting when your teacher is talking; helping each other when you can; and working quietly and sensibly without distracting or annoying your classmates.
4. Move sensibly and quietly around the school. This means: never running, barging or shouting; opening doors or standing back to let people pass; and helping to carry things.
5. Always speak politely to everyone, children and adults alike. Never shout.
6. Be silent whenever you are required to be. If the class is asked a question, put up your hand and answer. Do not call out.
7. Take pride in your personal appearance, attending school clean and dressed appropriately.

8. Keep the school clean and tidy so that it is a welcoming place we can all be proud of by: putting all litter in bins; keeping walls and furniture clean and unmarked; and taking great care of displays, particularly of other people's work.

9. Leave toys, jewellery, etc. at home as these can get lost or damaged or can cause arguments.

10. Always remember when out of school, walking locally or with a school group that the school's reputation depends on the way you behave.

✎ Activity!

Find out about the code of conduct for the pupils in your school.

Setting goals and boundaries

As well as helping pupils to follow the school code of conduct, you will also help them work towards specific goals and within certain boundaries as set by the teacher including individual, group or class targets for behaviour. Goals are the *expectations* for behaviour; usually starting with 'Do…'. Boundaries are the *limitations* to behaviour, often starting with 'Don't…'. Working with the teacher you should set goals and boundaries for the pupils that take into account: their ages and levels of development; their individual needs and abilities in different areas of the curriculum and the social context, for example the learning activity and group size.

Figure 7.2: Pupil in a praise assembly

Pupils are more likely to keep to goals and boundaries if they have some say about them. Pupils need to be active participants, not only in following rules, but in establishing them. Having a feeling of ownership makes rules more real and gives pupils a sense of control. Tutorials or 'circle time' with pupils can provide opportunities for you to support the teacher in establishing and maintaining class rules as well as encouraging pupils to work co-operatively with each other.

🔑 key words

Boundaries: the limitations to behaviour, often starting with 'Don't…'. For example: 'Don't run in the corridors because you could hurt yourself or others'.

Goals: the expectations for behaviour, usually starting with 'Do…'. For example: 'Do remember to keep the school tidy by putting rubbish in the bins provided'.

When supporting the teacher in setting goals and boundaries consider the following:

1. *What* **is the goal or boundary?** Focus on the behaviour staff would like to change. Encourage pupils to talk about, draw a picture or write down what they would like to change. Remember to be positive.

2. *Why* **is the goal necessary?** To improve behaviour, to provide happier atmosphere or to encourage cooperation or for safety reasons.

3. *Who* **does the goal or boundary apply to?** Does it apply to everyone in the school, just the group/class, or one particular individual?

4. ***Where* does the goal or boundary apply?** Does it apply everywhere in school, in a particular room/class, or indoors or outdoors?

5. ***When* will the pupils start working towards the goal?** *When* will the boundary apply? Will it apply at all times in the classroom or school or only at certain times?

6. ***How* will the goal or boundary be implemented?** *How* will the pupils be encouraged to keep to the goal or boundary? Include positive incentives such as smiley faces, stickers or merit/house points.

7. ***What* happens when the goal is achieved?** Ask the pupils what *they* would like. Rewards might include a badge, certificate, assembly praise or a special treat.

8. **Set new goal.** Start with the next goal or boundary which needs changing.

Example cover

Example page

Figure 7.3: Example of individual pupil record of rewards

Key Task

- Think about the goals and boundaries that might be appropriate to the pupil or pupils you work with in your school.
- If possible, encourage the pupil or pupils to draw up their own list of rules that promote positive behaviour.

NOS Links:

Level 3:   STL 3.4   STL19.2   STL20.1   STL20.2   STL20.3   STL37.1

Rewards and sanctions

The school behaviour policy should state how the school establishes a climate where praise and encouragement have precedence over the use of sanctions. A wide range of rewards should be available, especially the frequent use of praise during lessons and around the school to show instant recognition for positive behaviour, punctuality and regular attendance. You must know which rewards and sanctions you are free to use and those which you would have to negotiate with, or leave to the teacher, to apply.

Formal reward systems including credits, merits and prizes can also be used to recognise and congratulate pupils who are good role models for behaviour. Rewards should not be given just to the same 'good' pupils but also to pupils who demonstrate improvement in their own behaviour or attendance (DfES, 2003).

Rewards can provide positive incentives for positive behaviour. Pupils can be motivated by rewards such as: choice of favourite activity; special responsibility; smiley faces, stars or stamps; stickers or badges; merit points and certificates; mention in praise assembly; mention in head teacher's praise book; or a letter from the head teacher to the pupil's parents.

Rewards are most effective when they are:

- Immediate and clearly linked to the pupil's behaviour, effort or achievement so that the pupil connects the reward with the behaviour.
- Meaningful and appropriate to the pupil's age/level of development, for example smiley faces and stickers are more real to younger pupils than merit or house points.
- Related to an individual's behaviour, effort or achievement rather than a group; every pupil needs the chance to obtain rewards for some positive aspect of their own behaviour.
- Recognised and consistently applied by all the staff in the school. Some adults hand out rewards like confetti (making them meaningless), while others strictly ration them (making rewards virtually unobtainable) – either way pupils will not be motivated.

The difficulty with some school reward systems is that pupils who find it easier to behave appropriately may do very well, but those with emotional or behavioural difficulties may not. Reward systems that display stars or points for the whole group can be particularly damaging to pupils' self-esteem and often they do not indicate what the reward was for. An individual chart or book for each pupil can be better as they are then clearly competing against their own past efforts or improving their own behaviour.

For example, each pupil could have a small exercise book with a page a week for stickers, smiley faces or merit points which are clearly linked to the pupil's behaviour and/or learning. The teacher can negotiate with each pupil the targets they are expected to achieve that particular week. If the pupil achieves this target they receive an appropriate reward such as a certificate or the choice of a favourite activity. This makes it easier for pupils to see their individual efforts and achievements and can also help to set future goals for behaviour and learning.

While the emphasis should be on promoting positive behaviour through encouragement, praise and rewards, there may be times when these do not work. Sometimes it is necessary to impose sanctions for pupils whose behaviour goes beyond acceptable boundaries or who break the school/class/playground rules.

Schools should have a scale of sanctions for inappropriate behaviour. The school behaviour management policy should explain why these sanctions are necessary. Effective sanctions should be designed to discourage inappropriate behaviour rather than to punish pupils who break the rules. Consistency in the application of sanctions is essential and staff should use reprimands sparingly and fairly. Sanctions are more likely to discourage inappropriate behaviour if pupils see them as fair.

The school behaviour management policy should be supported with a range of sanctions for pupils who break the rules, ranging from letters to parents/carers, loss of privileges and detention right up to exclusion for the most serious or persistent inappropriate behaviour (DfES, 2003).

Sanctions for inappropriate behaviour may include: staff registering disapproval and explaining why to the pupil(s); staff warnings to pupils that their behaviour is unacceptable; 'time out' involving isolation of the pupil for a short period; extra or alternative tasks for the pupil; pupil losing a privilege, for example loss of playtime; pupil writing a letter of apology or writing about what happened during an incident; parents being told at the end of the day or a letter being sent home outlining a serious incident; parents being invited into school to discuss a serious incident or when a pupil appears to be developing a pattern of poor behaviour; and a pupil being referred to their key stage coordinator, the SENCO, the deputy or head teacher.

Sanctions are most effective when they:

- Balance against appropriate rewards.
- Are reasonable and appropriate to the pupil's action so that major sanctions do not apply to minor lapses in acceptable behaviour.
- Apply only to the pupils responsible and not the whole group/class.
- Discourage unwanted/unacceptable behaviour without damaging pupils' self-esteem.
- Are used as a last resort; every effort should be made to be positive and to encourage acceptable behaviour through positive rather than negative reinforcement.

 **Activity!**

- What is the school's policy for rewards and sanctions relating to pupil behaviour? What rewards and sanctions have you seen in action? Which were the most effective and why?
- Get a copy of the school policy for rewards and sanctions relating to behaviour. Highlight which rewards and sanctions can be applied by the teaching assistant.

The use of reasonable force to control or restrain pupils

The UN Convention on the Rights of the Child states that 'children have the right to be protected from all forms of physical and mental violence and deliberate humiliation' (Article 19). Where parental expectations concerning punishment conflict with those of the school, staff should point out to parents the school's legal requirements under the Children Act 1989, which is no physical punishment. Physical or corporal punishment is not allowed in maintained schools, day nurseries and play settings:

> 'Corporal punishment (smacking, slapping or shaking) is illegal in maintained schools and should not be used by any other parties within the scope of this guidance. It is permissible to take necessary physical action to prevent personal injury either to the child, other children or an adult or serious damage to property.' (DH, 1991, The Children Act 1989; Volume 2, Section 6.22.)

In addition, using physical punishment is never acceptable because it teaches children and young people that violence is an acceptable means for getting your own way. Shouting and verbal abuse are also totally unacceptable. Smacking and shouting do not work; adults end up having to smack harder and shout louder to get the desired behaviour. Children and young people do not learn how to behave better by being smacked or shouted at; they are just hurt and humiliated, which can have lasting damage on their self-esteem.

However, all school staff members have a legal power to use reasonable force to prevent pupils committing a criminal offence, injuring themselves or others or damaging property, and to maintain good order and discipline. In schools force is generally used for two different purposes – to control pupils and to restrain them.

- Control can mean either passive physical contact (such as standing between pupils or blocking a pupil's path) or active physical contact (such as leading a pupil by the hand or arm, or ushering a pupil away by placing a hand in the centre of the back).
- When members of staff use 'restraint' they physically prevent a pupil from continuing what they were doing after they have been told to stop. Restraint techniques are usually used in more extreme circumstances, such as when two pupils are involved in a fight and physical intervention is needed to separate them.

(DCSF, 2010; p.4)

Some examples of situations where reasonable force might be used are to:

- Prevent a pupil from attacking a member of staff, or another pupil, or to stop a fight between two or more pupils.
- Prevent a pupil causing deliberate damage to property.
- Prevent a pupil causing injury or damage by accident, by rough play, or by misuse of dangerous materials or objects.
- Ensure that a pupil leaves a classroom where the pupil persistently refuses to follow an instruction to do so.
- Prevent a pupil behaving in a way that seriously disrupts a lesson.
- Prevent a pupil behaving in a way that seriously disrupts a school sporting event or school visit.

(DCSF, 2010; p.4)

From September 2010, governing bodies must ensure that a procedure is in place for recording each significant incident in which a member of staff uses force on a pupil, and for reporting these incidents to the pupil's parents as soon as practicable after the incident. Governing bodies must take all reasonable steps to ensure that staff follow the procedure. Members of staff should not put themselves at risk. An individual would not be seen to be failing in their duty of care by not using force to prevent injury, if doing so threatened their own safety. Remember that it is always unlawful to use force as a punishment. This is because it would fall within the definition of corporal punishment, which is illegal (DCSF, 2010; p.5).

 Key Task

- Working with the teacher, set goals and boundaries for a pupil or group of pupils as part of a framework for positive behaviour.
- Outline how you would implement this framework. Remember to emphasise the positive aspects of behaviour.
- Devise a system of rewards for encouraging the pupils to demonstrate the targeted positive behaviour. If appropriate, include possible sanctions for unwanted/unacceptable behaviour.

NOS Links:

Level 3: STL 3.4   STL 19.1   STL 19.2   STL 20.1   STL 20.2   STL 20.3
          STL 37.1   STL 37.3

Supporting pupils with difficult behaviour

You should be able to identify the sorts of behaviour patterns that might indicate problems such as child abuse, substance abuse or bullying. You should also know who to report these to, for example the class teacher or the person responsible for child protection in the school.

Recognising behaviour patterns

Behaviour patterns that might indicate problems in younger pupils include:

- Unusually aggressive behaviour towards people and/or property.
- Regression to earlier level of development, such as emotional outbursts, wetting or soiling.
- Defiance, for example refusing to comply with adult requests.
- Lack of cooperation during learning activities.
- Attention-seeking behaviour such as excessive swearing.
- Being very passive or withdrawn.
- Wandering around the classroom aimlessly or staring into space.
- Repetitive or self-damaging behaviour, such as rocking, thumb-sucking, frequent masturbation, picking own skin, pulling out own hair, head-banging.
- Appearing very nervous and anxious.
- Inability to concentrate at usual level.
- Deterioration of school work.
- Refusing to eat and/or drink while at school.

> **key words**
>
> **Regression:** demonstrating behaviour characteristic of previous level of development.

Behaviour patterns that might indicate problems in older pupils include:

- Deterioration in the pupil's academic work.
- Gradual changes in their appearance or behaviour over period of time.
- Rapid or acute increase in behavioural or emotional changes.
- Emotional instability and mood swings; irritability.
- Loss of confidence and heightened levels of anxiety.
- Unexplained, persistent lateness and absenteeism.
- Tiredness due to disturbed sleep.
- Signs of substance abuse, such as slurred speech, memory impairment, lack of coordination, poor concentration, irritability.
- Withdrawal from social contact.
- Inappropriate responses to normal situations.
- Noticeable changes in eating habits.

Concerns about a pupil's behaviour patterns should be discussed with colleagues, but remember confidentiality. Adults in schools have a legal duty to report serious concerns about a pupil's welfare, for example the possible signs and symptoms of abuse – each school has guidelines about this. (See section on responding to concerns about possible abuse in Chapter 2.)

In practice

Frankie is working with pupils aged 14 to 15 years and has noticed over the last few days that one of the pupils has slurred speech, memory impairment, lack of coordination and poor concentration as well as being very irritable. What would you do in this situation?

Reporting concerns about pupil behaviour

You will need to recognise and respond promptly and appropriately to anti-social behaviour, remembering to always follow the school's agreed policies for managing pupil behaviour. You will need to report any problems in dealing with unacceptable or challenging behaviour to the class teacher.

Concerns about behaviour or discipline problems should be discussed with colleagues and sometimes with other professionals, but remember confidentiality. You may need specialist advice, guidance or support to provide the best possible approaches to responding to some pupils' behavioural and/or emotional difficulties. Every school has clear structures for reporting concerns about pupil behaviour to colleagues/other professionals and appropriate ways to deal with these concerns. Be aware of your own role and responsibilities within these structures.

key words

Colleagues: the pupil's class, form or subject teacher; key stage/year group coordinator; special educational needs coordinator (SENCO); deputy head teacher; head teacher.

Other professionals: health visitor; paediatrician; clinical psychologist; educational psychologist; social worker; education welfare officer; play therapist; music therapist.

 Key Task

- What sorts of behaviour patterns might indicate problems such as child abuse, substance abuse or bullying?
- When and to who should you report concerns relating to a pupil's welfare?

NOS Links:

Level 3:   **STL 3.3**

Managing pupils' challenging behaviour

As part of your role as a teaching assistant you will be promoting the school's policies regarding pupil behaviour by consistently and effectively implementing agreed behaviour strategies as directed by the class teacher, SENCO or other professional. Teaching assistants need to be familiar with the ways teachers deal with pupils who demonstrate difficult behaviour to avoid giving conflicting messages to pupils.

Approaches to responding to persistent challenging or unwanted behaviour

1. **Think approaches not solutions.** There are no easy answers or quick solutions to dealing with challenging or unwanted behaviour. You may need to use a variety of approaches.

2. **Consider past experiences.** Children learn about behaviour through their early relationships and experiences; the effects these have depend on individual personality (see Chapter 3). No one's behaviour is static; they can acquire new behaviour patterns and discard behaviour which is ineffective or inappropriate.

3. **Remember adult influences on children's behaviour.** Adults working in schools have major influences on pupils' behaviour. Adult responses to pupil behaviour can make things better or worse. You may need to modify your own behaviour and responses.

4. **Be patient**. Changing pupil behaviour takes time, so do not expect too much all at once – take things one step at a time. Remember that behaviour may get worse before it gets better because some pupils will resist attempts to change their behaviour (particularly if they have behaved this way for some time) and will demonstrate even more challenging behaviour, especially if minor irritations are being ignored.

5. **Establish clear rules, boundaries and routines**. Pupils need to understand rules and the consequences if they do not follow the rules. Pupils need clear boundaries as to what is or is not acceptable behaviour, including frequent reminders about what these are.

6. **Be consistent**. Staff need to be consistent when responding to pupils with persistent unwanted behaviour or the pupils become confused. Adults need to discuss and agree on responses to the pupil's behaviour. Adults in schools need to work with the child's parents so the child sees that both are working together to provide a consistent framework for behaviour.

7. **Use diversionary tactics**. You can sometimes divert the pupil from an emotional or aggressive outburst or self-damaging behaviour. This does not always work, but often does. Be aware of possible triggers to unwanted behaviour and intervene or divert the pupil's attention *before* difficulties begin. Pupils can also be diverted by being offered alternative choices or being involved in decision making.

8. **Encourage positive social interaction**. Help pupils to develop their social skills so they can join in activities with other pupils. Start off with one to one, then small groups and then larger groups. Play tutoring can help, that is, using adult involvement to develop and extend social play. Encourage older pupils to join school clubs.

9. **Help pupils find alternative ways to gain attention**. Most children want adult attention; it is the way they behave to gain attention that may need changing. Instead of being disruptive, pupils need to be encouraged to use more acceptable ways to get adult attention by asking or showing the adult that they have something to share.

10. **Help pupils to express their feelings**. Encourage pupils to express strong feelings such as anger, frustration or fear in positive ways – through play and communication. Older pupils need opportunities to express their grievances.

11. **Look at the environment**. Identify and, where possible, change aspects of the environment and routines within the classroom/school which may be contributing towards the pupil's unwanted behaviour.

12. **Label the behaviour not the pupil**. Make sure any response to unwanted behaviour allows the pupil to still feel valued without any loss of self-esteem, say 'I like you, Tom, but I don't like it when you …'.

13. **Be positive**. Emphasise the positive and encourage pupils to be positive too. Phrase rules in positive ways, say 'do' rather than 'don't'. Think about which unwanted behaviour must be stopped and which can simply be ignored so that pupils are not being told 'No' or 'Don't do …' all the time. Encourage pupils to focus on positive aspects of school, such as friends, favourite subjects, school clubs.

14. **Remember punishments rarely work**. Punishments may satisfy the people giving them, but they are often of little value in changing pupil behaviour. Pupils may become devious or blame others in order to avoid being punished. Quiet reprimands are more effective than a public 'telling off', which only causes humiliation in front of other pupils and increases the pupil's resentment towards the adult. Rewarding positive behaviour is more effective than punishing unacceptable behaviour.

15. **Use praise, encouragement and rewards**. Set realistic and achievable goals and use pupils' interests to motivate them. Use regular positive feedback to encourage pupils to behave in acceptable ways and raise their self-esteem. Praise pupils' efforts as well as achievements. Find out which kinds of rewards matter to the pupils and use them.

16. **Avoid confrontation if at all possible**. Use eye contact and the pupil's name to gain/ hold their attention. Keep calm, sound confident and in control. If the pupil is too wound up to listen, give them a chance to calm down, perhaps through 'time out'.

17. **Give individual attention and support**. This encourages pupils to share their worries or concerns with a trusted adult. Time in involves giving pupils special individual attention to reinforce positive behaviour and decreases the need for them to gain adult attention through unwanted behaviour. It involves pupils talking one to one (or in a small group) with an adult about their day including reviewing positive aspects of the day.

18. **Use behaviour modification**. Using positive reinforcement to encourage acceptable behaviour; ignoring all but harmful unwanted behaviour. Work on one aspect of behaviour at a time and reward the pupil for any progress no matter how small.

 Key Task

Observe a pupil who regularly demonstrates challenging or unwanted behaviour during group activities. In your assessment include information on:

- The pupil's behaviour during the activity.
- The pupil's communication skills.
- How the adult responds.
- How the other pupils respond to the pupil's behaviour.
- Suggest ways to monitor the pupil's future behaviour.
- Suggest ways to encourage the pupil's positive behaviour.

NOS Links:

Level 3:	STL18.1	STL19.1	STL19.2	STL20.1	STL20.2	STL29.1	STL29.2
	STL37.1	STL37.2	STL37.3	STL41.1	STL41.2		

Behaviour modification

Ivan Petrovich Pavlov was a Russian biologist who studied animal behaviour. His experiments involved teaching dogs to salivate in response to the sound of a bell. Before giving the dogs their food, Pavlov rang a bell. Eventually the dogs began to salivate when the bell rang even when there was no food. The dogs had learned to respond to the bell sound with their salivating reflex. This type of learned response or behaviour is called a *conditioned reflex*. Pavlov extended his ideas concerning conditioning to human psychology; he believed that human behaviour consists of many conditioned reflexes that are triggered by external influences.

B.F. Skinner was an American psychologist who discovered that the behaviour of rats could be controlled by food rewards. This idea of *operant conditioning* can be applied to any situation where the required behaviour is reinforced with a reward. Skinner believed that positive reinforcement (rewards) and negative reinforcement (sanctions) both contribute towards an individual's motivation for learning and behaviour.

The basic principles of behaviour modification are:

- **P**raise and reward acceptable behaviour.
- **R**educe the opportunities for unwanted behaviour.
- **A**void confrontations.
- **I**gnore minor unwanted behaviour.
- **S**tructure appropriate sanctions.
- **E**stablish clear rules, boundaries and routines.

 Key Task

- Think about the basic principles of behaviour modification.
- Look back at your behaviour observation on page 165 and focus on one aspect of that pupil's behaviour.
- Outline a step-by-step approach to encourage the pupil to behave in more acceptable ways. Remember to include appropriate rewards (and sanctions).

NOS Links:

Level 3: **STL18.1   STL19.1   STL19.2   STL20.1   STL20.2   STL29.2   STL37.1
STL37.2   STL37.3   STL41.1**

Behaviour Support Plans

Persistent behavioural difficulties are recognised as special educational needs (SEN) and pupils with behavioural difficulties will require additional support in school. Teaching assistants are often used to provide this additional support. Providing support for pupils with behavioural difficulties is one of the most challenging roles that teaching assistants undertake. When supporting these pupils you may sometimes feel hopeless, annoyed or helpless. However, working with pupils with behavioural problems can also be very rewarding, as by providing support, you are helping them to develop the life skills and coping strategies they need.

You should always remember that a teaching assistant is not a teacher and that the teaching assistant's responsibilities are set within clear boundaries. The teacher who manages your work has the responsibility to ensure that appropriate behaviour and learning programmes are planned, followed and monitored. The teacher also has the responsibility to ensure that you are well supported in your role of supporting pupils who have behavioural difficulties.

Pupils with persistent behavioural difficulties usually have an Individual Education Plan (IEP) and/or an individual Behaviour Support Plan (BSP). A pupil's BSP should include the following information:

- the short-term targets for the pupil
- the strategies to be used
- the support to be put in place
- when the plan is to be reviewed
- the outcome of any action taken.

These plans will give you information about the support being provided to help the pupil and will often include details of your role in giving behaviour support. You may sometimes be involved in drawing up these plans, along with the teacher, the pupil and the parents or carers. You need to be clear about your exact role in implementing Behaviour Support Plans. For example:

- Helping the pupil to follow specific routines in particular lessons.
- Being vigilant at lesson changes, break times and lunchtimes that can provide stress points for pupils with difficult behaviour, as there is not as much structure as in lesson times.
- Fostering the participation of pupils in social and academic processes of a school.
- Helping the pupils to take a real part in school life both through positive friendships and achievement in learning.
- Providing support to enable the pupil to remain as a part of the full class group for as much time as possible.

Support systems for pupils and staff

The school should have a range of strategies for responding to pupils who demonstrate challenging behaviour including:

- Regular pastoral reviews to identify pupils most at risk.
- Contact with parents in the early stages of any problem.
- Advice or support from senior colleagues and training in behaviour management.
- Referrals for specialist advice from agencies linked to the school (such as the LEA Behaviour Support Team or Educational Psychology Service).
- Referrals to a Learning Support Unit for a short period of additional support outside the classroom environment.
- Parent/carer consultations and family sessions.
- One to one counselling with a trained specialist.
- Support from Learning Mentors or specially trained Teaching Assistants.
- Strategies for responding to pupils with persistent unwanted behaviour.

(DfES, 2003)

 **Activity!**

- What strategies may the school use when responding to pupils who demonstrate challenging behaviour?
- What specialist advice on behaviour management is available within the school?

Summary of key points in this chapter:

- **Expectations for behaviour** including: parental expectations for behaviour; the school's expectations for pupil behaviour; other influences on pupil behaviour; providing positive role models.
- **Promoting positive behaviour** including ways to encourage children's positive behaviour.
- **The school behaviour management policy** including: staff responsibilities for managing pupil behaviour; the teaching assistant's role for managing pupil behaviour.

- **Supporting behaviour management strategies** including: school code of conduct for pupils; setting goals and boundaries; rewards and sanctions; the use of reasonable force to control or restrain pupils.

- **Supporting pupils with difficult behaviour** including: recognising behaviour patterns; reporting concerns about pupil behaviour; managing pupils' challenging behaviour; approaches to responding to persistent challenging or unwanted behaviour; behaviour modification; Behaviour Support Plans; support systems for pupils and staff.

Further reading

Bentham, S. (2005) *Teaching Assistant's Guide to Managing Behaviour in the Classroom*. Routledge.

Blandford, S. (1998) *Managing Discipline in Schools*. Routledge Falmer.

Chaplain, R. (2003) *Teaching Without Disruption in Secondary Schools: A Model for Managing Behaviour*. Routledge Falmer.

DCSF (2007) *School Discipline and Pupil-Behaviour Policies: Guidance for Schools*. DCSF. (Available free at: **http://www.teachernet.gov.uk/wholeschool/behaviour/ schooldisciplinepupilbehaviourpolicies/**)

DCSF (2010) *The Use of Force to Control or Restrain Pupils: Guidance for Schools in England*. DCSF. **http://www.teachernet.gov.uk/wholeschool/familyandcommunity/childprotection/ usefulinformation/useofforceguidance/**

Dix, P. (2008) *Taking Care of Behaviour: Practical Skills for Learning Support and Teaching Assistants*. Longman.

Docking, J.W. and MacGrath, M. (2002) *Managing Behaviour in the Primary School*. David Fulton Publishers.

Glenn, A. et al (2003) *Behaviour in the Early Years*. David Fulton Publishers.

Kay, J. (2006) *Managing Behaviour in the Early Years*. Continuum International Publishing Group.

Lee, C. (2010) *The Complete Guide to Behaviour for Teaching Assistants and Support Staff*. Sage Publications Ltd.

Morgan, J. (2007) *The Teaching Assistant's Guide to Managing Behaviour*. Continuum International Publishing Group.

Mortimer, H. (2002) *Behavioural and Emotional Difficulties*. Scholastic.

Rogers, B. (2000) *Behaviour Management: A Whole School Approach*. Paul Chapman Publishing.

Train, A. (2004) *ADHD: How to Deal with Very Difficult Children*. Souvenir Press Ltd.

8. Promoting equality, diversity and inclusion

This chapter relates to QCF unit:

TDA 3.6 Promoting equality, diversity and inclusion

Understanding children's needs and rights

The principles and values of equality, diversity and inclusion should underpin all work with children. Article 2 of the United Nations Convention on the Rights of the Child requires that children are 'protected from all forms of discrimination'. The Common Core of Skills and Knowledge for the children's workforce sets out common values for those working with children, young people and families that promote equality, respect diversity and challenge stereotypes (Griffin, 2008).

In the past decade there has been a major shift in attitude toward children's rights. Previously children's rights were mainly concerned with children's basic welfare needs. Now as well as their basic rights to life, health and education, children are viewed as having a much wider range of rights, including the right to engage in play activities, to express their views and to participate in making decisions that affect them directly.

Children's rights, as stated in the UN Convention on the Rights of the Child, are clear and universal: they apply to all children. Also, while children's individual needs may differ, they all have the same rights. Children's rights are based on their needs, but emphasising rights rather than needs demonstrates a commitment to viewing and respecting children as valued citizens. (The Children's Rights Alliance for England: **www.crae.org.uk/**.)

All children are special and unique; all children have individual needs because they perceive the world differently and interact with others in different ways. All children (including identical twins) have different life experiences which affect their view of the world. Children experience different social and environmental factors which along with their genetic differences shape their personalities, knowledge

 key words

Children's rights: the universal entitlements to life, health, education, play and consultation which applies to *all* children aged 0 to 18 years.

Children's needs: these include basic welfare needs such as food, shelter and physical care as well as communication and interaction with others; in addition, educational needs are also important, for example opportunities for play and learning which are appropriate for each child's age/level of development.

Figure 8.1: Example of child's poster about children's rights

Legislation relating to children's rights

As a teaching assistant you should know and understand the basic requirements of the national legislation relating to children's rights in your home country. For example, The Children Act 1989 came into force on 14 October 1991 and is concerned with families and the care of children, local authority support for children and their families, fostering, childminding and day care provision. The Children Act 1989 is particularly important because it emphasises the importance of putting the child first.

In summary, the Act states that:

- What is best for the child must always be the first consideration.
- Whenever possible children should be brought up in their own family.
- Unless the child is at risk of harm, a child should not be taken away from their family without the family's agreement.
- Local authorities must help families with children in need.
- Local authorities must work with parents and children.
- Courts must put children first when making decisions.
- Children being looked after by local authorities have rights, as do their parents.

The Children Act 1989 provides the legislative framework for the child protection system in England and Wales. The Children (Northern Ireland) Order 1995 and The Children (Scotland) Act 1995 share the same principles as The Children Act 1989 but contain their own guidance. The Children Act 2004 introduced changes to the structure and organisation of the child protection system in England and Wales. For information about the 2004 Act see: **www.everychildmatters.gov.uk/strategy/guidance/**.

for the public sector including actively promoting race equality. Under a new European Union Directive the grounds for discrimination go beyond the three main areas of race, gender and disability (which are discussed in this chapter) to include age, religious belief and sexual orientation. Individual rights are also protected by The Data Protection Act 1998, Human Rights Act 1998 and Freedom of Information Act 2000.

The Equality Act 2010 received royal assent on 8 April 2010. This Act will provide a single legal framework with clearer legislation to effectively tackle disadvantage and discrimination.

The Act came into force for employment and education in October 2010. A draft code of practice for schools should be available in May 2011. See the Equality and Human Rights Commission website for guidance which explains the Act and how the law has changed: **http://www.equalityhumanrights.com/legislative-framework/equality-bill/equality-act-2010-guidance/**.

 **Activity!**

Find out about the legislation covering equality, diversity and inclusion and how it relates to your school, for example the school's equal opportunities policy, inclusion policy and/or special educational needs policy.

Anti-discriminatory and inclusive practice

Anti-discriminatory practice in the school can be defined as words and actions which prevent discrimination and prejudice towards any individual or group of people and actively promote equal opportunities. This means ensuring that all pupils, parents, colleagues and other professionals are treated in an unbiased, fair and non-prejudiced way. This includes ensuring that all the school's policies, procedures and strategies demonstrate a positive and inclusive attitude towards all individuals regardless of age, gender, race, culture or disability.

Inclusive practice in the school can be defined as words and actions which encourage the participation of *all* pupils (including those with disabilities or from other minority groups) within a mainstream setting. This means ensuring that all pupils are valued as individuals and are given appropriate support to enable them to participate fully in the play and learning activities provided by the school.

> **key words**
>
> **Anti-discriminatory practice:** taking positive action to counter discrimination and prejudice.
>
> **Inclusive practice:** identifying barriers to participation and taking positive action to eliminate those barriers and encourage participation in the full range of activities provide by the setting.

As a teaching assistant you should know how to judge whether the school is inclusive and supportive of diversity. You should be able to demonstrate that you support inclusion and diversity through your words, actions and behaviours in the school. Inclusion is about the child's right to: attend the local mainstream setting; be valued as an individual and be provided with all the support needed to thrive in a mainstream setting. Inclusive provision should be seen as an extension of the school's equal opportunities policy and practice. It requires a commitment from the whole staff, parents and pupils to include the full diversity of children in the local community. This may require planned restructuring of the whole school environment to ensure equality of access.

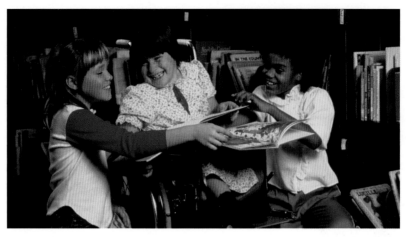

Figure 8.2: An inclusive learning environment

 **Key Task**

Find out about your school's policies and practices for inclusion, including equal opportunities and special educational needs.

Briefly outline the school's procedures for inclusion and anti-discriminatory practice including your role in implementing these procedures.

NOS Links:

Level 3:	STL 20.1	STL 34.2	STL 35.2	STL 36.2	STL 36.3	STL 38.1	
	STL 38.2	STL 39.1	STL 40.1	STL 41.1	STL 42.1	STL 44.1	STL 47.1

Positive attitudes towards cultural diversity, gender and disability

Children are influenced by images, ideas and attitudes that create prejudice and lead to discrimination or disadvantage. Children are not born with these attitudes; they learn them. You have an important role to play in promoting children's positive attitudes towards themselves and other people. In addition, you must not have stereotyped views of children's potential nor have low expectations of children based on culture, gender or disability.

As a teaching assistant you should:

- Recognise and eliminate racial discrimination.
- Have high but realistic expectations for all children.
- Maximise each child's motivation and potential.
- Encourage each child to feel a positive sense of identity.
- Ensure the learning environment reflects positive images.
- Challenge stereotypes in the media, literature and everyday life.
- Give all children the opportunities to play with a wide variety of toys, games and play equipment.
- Ensure that children do not think they are superior to others.
- Expect the same standards of behaviour from all children regardless of culture, gender or disability.

- Recognise children with disabilities as individuals not by their condition or impairment (for example 'the child *with* autistic tendencies' not 'the autistic child').
- Encourage the 'able' world to adapt to those with disabilities, not the other way round.

Figure 8.3: Promoting positive images

Twelve ways to promote positive images of children, young people and the community

You can help the teacher to provide an environment, activities and experiences that promote positive images of children and reflect the wider community in the following ways:

1. Sharing books and stories about real-life situations with people the children can identify with.

2. Using posters, pictures, photographs, displays, jigsaws, puzzles, toys and other play materials which reflect positive images of race, culture, gender and disability.

3. Providing activities that encourage children to look at their physical appearance in a positive light, for example games looking in mirrors; self-portraits (ensuring paints provided for all skin tones); drawing round each other to create life-size portraits.

4. Providing activities that encourage children to focus on their abilities in positive ways, for example the 'I can ...' tree with positive statements about what each child can do.

5. Providing activities which encourage children to express their likes and dislikes, plus confidence in their own name and who they are, for example circle games such as 'The name game' where each child takes it in turn to say 'My name is ...and I like to ... because ...' or 'Circle jump' where child takes a turn at jumping into the circle, making an action that they feel expresses them and saying 'Hello, I'm ...'; then the rest of the children copy the action and reply 'Hello ...[repeating the child's name]'.

6. Sharing experiences about themselves and their families through topics like 'All about me' and by inviting family members such as parents/grandparents to come into the setting to talk about themselves and their backgrounds.

7. Providing opportunities for imaginative/role play which encourages children to explore different roles in positive ways, such as through dressing-up clothes, cooking utensils, dolls and puppets that reflect different cultures.

8. Visiting local shops, businesses and community groups that reflect the cultural diversity of the setting and the local community.

9. Inviting visitors into the setting to talk positively about their roles and lives, invite a (female) police officer or fire fighter, (male) nurse, people with disabilities or from different ethnic groups. (Avoid tokenism; include these visitors as part of on-going topics.)

10. Celebrating cultural diversity through the festivals of the faiths in the local community, such as Diwali (Hindu), Channuka (Jewish), Christmas (Christian) and Eid (Muslim).

11. Valuing language diversity by displaying welcome signs and other information in community languages.

12. Providing positive examples of:
    - Black and Asian people and women from all ethnic groups in prominent roles in society, such as politicians, doctors, lawyers, teachers, entrepreneurs.
    - Black and Asian people's past contributions to politics, medicine, science, education, etc. Look at important historical figures like Martin Luther King, Mahatma Gandhi and Mary Seacole.
    - People with disabilities participating fully in modern society, such as Stephen Hawking, Marlee Matlin and the late Christopher Reeve, as well as famous people from the past like Louis Braille, Helen Keller and Franklin D. Roosevelt.

 **Key Task**

Compile a resource pack with positive images of children, young people and the wider community that promotes positive attitudes towards cultural diversity, gender and disability. You could include the following information and resources:

- posters, wall charts, photographs and pictures
- booklets and leaflets
- suggested activities to promote positive images
- book list of relevant children's books and stories
- list of useful organisations and addresses.

Plan, implement and evaluate at least one activity suggested in your resource pack.

NOS Links:

Level 3:   STL 20.1   STL 35.1   STL 36.2   STL 38.1   STL 38.2   STL 47.1

Summary of key points in this chapter:

- **Understanding children's needs and rights** including: the United Nations Convention on the Rights of the Child; legislation relating to children's rights; *Every Child Matters*.
- **Promoting equality, diversity and inclusion** including: legislation relating to equality, diversity and inclusion; anti-discriminatory and inclusive practice; positive attitudes towards cultural diversity, gender and disability;

Further reading

ACCAC (2001) *Equal Opportunities and Diversity in The School Curriculum In Wales*. Qualifications, Curriculum and Assessment Authority for Wales. (Available at: **http://wales.gov.uk/docs/dcells/pu blications/090902guidanceresourcesequalopportunitiesen.pdf**)

Alderson, P. (2000) *Young Children's Rights: Exploring Beliefs, Principles and Practice*. Jessica Kingsley Publishers.

Cheminais, R. (2008) *Every Child Matters: A Practical Guide for Teaching Assistants*. David Fulton Publishers.

DCSF (2010) *Breaking the Link Between Disadvantage and Low Attainment – One Year On*. DCSF.

DfES (2001) *Inclusive Schooling*. DfES. (Available free online from: **http://www.teachernet.gov.uk/_doc/4621/InclusiveSchooling.pdf**.)

DfES (2004) *Every Child Matters: Change for Children*. DfES (Available free online at: **http://www.dcsf.gov.uk/everychildmatters/**.)

Griffin, S. (2008) *Inclusion, Equality & Diversity in Working with Children*. Heinemann.

Hodkinson, A. and Vickerman, P. (2009) *Key Issues in Special Educational Needs and Inclusion*. Sage Publications.

Johnstone, D. (2001) *An Introduction to Disability Studies*. David Fulton Publishers.

Knowles, G. (2009) *Ensuring Every Child Matters*. Sage Publications.

Lindon, J. (2006) *Equality in Early Childhood: Linking Theory and Practice*. Hodder Arnold.

Richards, G. and Armstrong, F. (eds) (2000) *Key Issues for Teaching Assistants: Working in Diverse and Inclusive Classrooms*. Routledge.

9. Engaging in team work and personal development

This chapter relates to QCF unit:

SHC 32 Engage in personal development in health, social care or children's and young people's settings

TW 3 Team working

Effective teamwork

When working with others to support teaching and learning in schools, you need to understand your role in contributing to effective teamwork and working effectively with colleagues. Much of adult life involves working with other people, usually in a group or team. Individuals within a team affect each other in various ways. Within the team there will be complex interactions involving different personalities, roles and expectations as well as hidden agendas that may influence the behaviour of individual members of the team. Teamwork is essential when working closely and regularly with other people over a period of time.

Effective teamwork is important because it helps all members of the team to:

- **T**ake effective action when planning and/or assigning agreed work tasks.
- **E**fficiently implement the agreed work tasks.
- **A**gree aims and values which set standards of good practice.
- **M**otivate and support each other.
- **W**elcome feedback about their work.
- **O**ffer additional support in times of stress.
- **R**eflect on and evaluate their own working practices.
- **K**now and use each person's strengths and skills.

As a team leader, you must know and understand: your exact role and responsibilities; the exact roles and responsibilities of each member of your team; how to contribute to effective team practice; and how to participate in team meetings (see below).

Stages in team development

As a team leader, you should also know and understand how group dynamics affect the various stages of team development; that is, people's social interaction and their behaviour within social groups. Each individual has different personal characteristics that affect their ability to communicate effectively and work comfortably alongside others. From your experiences of working with colleagues you may have identified their differing characteristics that influence their willingness or reluctance to interact within the team. You also need to be aware of the stages in the development of a team and how these affect group dynamics. Research suggests that groups and teams grow and develop through a four-stage cycle:

1. **The forming stage**: A team starts by learning about others in the team. First impressions are important and the team leader should assist colleagues in this early stage by providing appropriate introductions, 'ice breaking' activities and an induction programme. The team leader should also ensure participation by all team members.

2. **The storming stage**: Team members establish their positions within the team and decide on group functions. There may be arguments and personality clashes between certain members of the team. The team leader can assist by providing opportunities for group discussion which tackle these matters in an open and positive manner, helping colleagues to sort minor disagreements between themselves and acting as an impartial referee if necessary. This can be a difficult stage but it is essential to the healthy development of the team as more serious conflicts may emerge later on if the team does not work through this stage.

3. **The norming stage**: Team members reach agreement on how to work together, including establishing ground rules for the team and their individual responsibilities. They plan and organise the setting's working practices, for example ground rules for the children using the setting, the timetable/provision of activities and the rota for routine tasks such as tidying up, providing refreshments, etc.

4. **The performing stage**: Group trust is established and the team works well together. At this stage the team is usually positive, enthusiastic, cooperative and energetic with team members supporting each other. There is a positive atmosphere within the setting.

(Houghton and McColgan, 1995)

Remember that colleagues will need to work through these stages again when changes arise, such as a person leaving or joining the team. You also need to be aware of the possible problems that can arise within a team and how to identify any signs of tension. These include: frequent arguments about differing views and ideas; uncertainty concerning team objectives or activities; confusion over roles and responsibilities within the team; lack of participation by some team members; and lack of support for team members. (See sections on handling disagreements with other adults in Chapter 3 and grievances and disciplinary procedures in Chapter 4.)

Team objectives

You must also know and understand the purpose, objectives and plans of your team including: how to set and achieve team objectives which are SMART (Specific, Measurable, Achievable, Realistic and Time-bound) in consultation with team members and demonstrate to team members how their personal work objectives contribute to team objectives (see section below on developing your personal development objectives).

Working as part of a team

As a teaching assistant, you need to know and understand the different roles of the team members in your school and the process of decision-making within the team. A teaching assistant in a primary, secondary or special school is part of a team which will include some or all of the following: other teaching assistants; class or subject teachers; deputy head teacher; head teacher; special educational needs coordinator (SENCO); specialist teachers, to support pupils with sensory or physical impairment; parent helpers and/or other volunteers; students on placement from college; pupils on work experience from secondary school.

 **Activity!**

Outline the role and main responsibility of each member of your particular team.

Effective communication with colleagues

You should know how to communicate effectively with members of your team. Effective communication is essential for developing effective team practice. Look back at the list of inter-personal skills needed for effective communication with children (and adults) in Chapter 3. Effective lines of communication are also important to ensure that all members of the team receive the necessary up-to date information to enable them to make a full contribution to the life of the school.

As a teaching assistant you may feel particularly isolated if you work only part time, work in only one class or support an individual pupil with special educational needs. Make sure you check school notice boards, newsletters and/or staff bulletins for important information. You can also use informal opportunities, such as break or lunch times, to share information, experiences and ideas with the SENCO, teachers or other teaching assistants. Regular lines of communication are particularly important if more than one teaching assistant works with the same pupil or pupils. You might find a communications book or file may be useful, as well as regular meetings with other teaching assistants. If you are a new (or student) teaching assistant you may benefit from the knowledge and understanding of existing teaching assistants; if you are an experienced teaching assistant you can make a valuable contribution to the induction or on-going training of new teaching assistants, possibly acting as a mentor.

Participating in team meetings

Staff meetings are essential for effective planning and organisation within the education setting. Such meetings also provide regular opportunities to share day-to-day information and to solve any problems. Staff meetings should be held regularly – about once every 4 to 6 weeks. There should be an agenda for the meeting and the minutes of the meeting should be recorded and be easily accessed by staff. Colleagues should be encouraged to share best practice, knowledge and ideas on developing appropriate play and learning activities in the setting. As well as general staff meetings there should also be regular team meetings for the more detailed planning of routines, play and learning activities, as well as the allocation of work within your area of responsibility.

As a teaching assistant you will also be involved in regular team meetings with the teacher (or teachers) in whose class you work and/or the SENCO. These meetings will enable you to make relevant contributions to provide more effective support for both the teacher and pupils. You may discuss specific plans the teacher has made relating to the pupils' learning, the progress made by pupils, including their achievements and any difficulties, plus the appropriate resources and support approaches.

You may also be invited to more general staff meetings. Where there are logistical problems in all teaching assistants being able to attend all staff meetings, you may be welcome to attend any meeting but be specifically invited to attend meetings where issues are to be discussed that are directly relevant to your work in schools.

You need to prepare for meetings carefully, especially if you have been asked to provide information, for example, on the progress of a pupil with whom you work. Even if you are not required to make a specific contribution, you still need to look at the meeting agenda and any relevant reports in advance so that you can participate in discussions during the meeting. At team meetings, participate in ways which are consistent with your role as a teaching assistant. Ensure your contributions are relevant and helpful to the work of the team. Express your

Figure 9.1: Team meeting

opinions in a clear, concise manner and demonstrate respect for the contributions made by other team members. Make notes during the meeting to remind yourself of any action you need to take as a result of the issues discussed and decisions made by the team.

Key Task

- Participate in a team meeting relevant to your role in school; for example, a planning meeting to discuss a week's or half term's learning activities for the pupils. (When doing this task, for reasons of confidentiality, avoid meetings where problems concerning specific pupils are referred to in detail.)
- Make notes on the key points discussed at the meeting. With the team leader's permission include a copy of the agenda.
- Then consider the following points:
  - What preparation did you need to make before the meeting?
  - What was your contribution to the meeting?
  - What action did you need to take as a result of the meeting (were you set specific tasks and if so, what were they)?

NOS Links:

Level 3:   STL 18.1   STL 20.4   STL 21.1   STL 23.1   STL 24.1   STL 27.1
            STL 52.3   STL 61.1   STL 62.1   STL 62.2

The allocation of work in your team

Work and responsibilities for your team may be allocated in a variety of ways. For example:

- **Responsibility for an area**: Each team member (or group) is responsible for a specific area of the setting and promoting the learning and development of pupils within that area, for example the year group, key stage or curriculum area. The team members will plan and provide appropriate support for the individual needs of the pupils in that area, including appropriate adult supervision or intervention as and when necessary.

- **Responsibility for an activity**: Each team member is responsible for a specific activity, such as literacy, numeracy, science, ICT or arts and crafts. The adult stays with the same activity throughout the day/week and is responsible for: selecting and setting out materials or helping the pupils to access these for themselves; encouraging the children's interest and participation in the activity; providing appropriate adult supervision or intervention as required and helping children to clear away afterwards.

- **Responsibility for a group of children**: Each team member is responsible for a small group of children as their key person or key worker. The adult helps them to settle into the setting. The adult is responsible for: greeting their group of children on arrival; encouraging the children's care, learning and development in the setting; establishing and maintaining a special relationship with each child and their family.

- **Responsibility for an individual child**: A team member (such as a teaching assistant) may have special responsibility for a pupil with a disability. The adult will be responsible for: ensuring that child's particular needs are met in an inclusive way within the setting; ensuring they have the necessary materials to participate in routines and activities including any specialist equipment; establishing and maintaining a special relationship with the child and their family.

Monitoring the work of the team

When monitoring the progress and quality of work of individuals or teams within your area of responsibility, you should encourage your colleagues to take responsibility for their own work tasks and to use existing feedback systems to keep you informed of work progress. When establishing procedures for monitoring work in the setting include the following: formal procedures (reports, formal meetings, mentoring, staff appraisals, supervision); informal procedures (observations, informal meetings, conversations); the type of information required (checklists, evaluation sheets, progress reports); when the information will be delivered to you or others in the team (daily, weekly, monthly, half-termly, termly, annually); the form of the information (verbal, written, email, audio-visual); where and how the information will be delivered (meeting, face-to-face, presentation, electronic) and the amount of detail required (Wandsworth EYDCP).

Key Task

- Give examples of effective planning and fair allocation of work within your area of responsibility. You could include copies of planning sheets, minutes from a staff or team meeting and a work rota.
- Outline the ways in which you monitor work in your team.

NOS Links:

Level 3: STL 20.4 STL 21.1 STL 21.1 STL 23.1 STL 23.2 STL 23.3
STL 24.1 STL 24.2 STL 62.1 STL 62.2 STL 63 STL 64
STL 65 (single element units)

Making an effective contribution to your team

In order to make a more effective contribution to your team you need to: develop and maintain confidence in your own abilities; maintain or improve your self-esteem; practise assertiveness techniques and take care of your emotional well-being.

Self-esteem is developed from childhood; some children and adults have feelings of low self-esteem which have negative effects on their confidence in their own abilities. You may need to develop your own feelings of self worth to improve your self-esteem (see suggestions for Further Reading at the end of this chapter).

Assertive people gain control over their lives by expressing personal feelings and exerting their rights in such a way that other people listen. Assertive individuals also show respect for other people's feelings. Practising assertiveness techniques involves:

1. Being aware of your own feelings.
2. Putting your feelings into words.
3. Connecting how you feel with the actions of others.
4. Being aware of the other person's feelings.
5. Arranging a specific time and place for a discussion.
6. Making a statement showing you are aware of their feelings.
7. Listening actively to their feedback.

(Houghton and McColgan, 1995)

Working with children or young people is a rewarding but often challenging, or even stressful, occupation. You need to take responsibility for your own emotional well-being and take the necessary action to tackle or reduce stress in your life. For example: develop assertiveness techniques; take regular exercise including relaxation; have a healthy diet and manage time effectively.

Time management

Effective time management involves being clear about what you need to do and that you are able to do it. Unrealistic work goals lead to: work tasks piling up; unnecessary stress; feeling overwhelmed and time being wasted in unnecessary disagreements due to tempers flaring.

Ten essential steps to effective time management

1. Decide to use time more effectively.
2. Check what you need to do, then prioritise: urgent/essential down to unimportant.
3. Make 'to do' lists in order of priority.
4. Estimate the time needed for tasks realistically.
5. Say 'No' or delegate if you cannot do a task in the time specified.
6. Forward plan using a good diary.
7. Organise how you intend to do each task.
8. Do it!
9. Monitor or revise plans if necessary.
10. Value other people's time by being punctual for meetings and appointments.

Efficient organisation of the learning environment can also contribute to more effective time management. For example:

- A chalk or white board may be used to indicate where people are.
- Check that cupboards, desk drawers, filing cabinets, etc. are clearly labelled.
- Remember 'A place for everything and everything in its place'!
- Keep everything you need for specific tasks in one place.
- Store items you use regularly in accessible places.
- Throw away rubbish!
- Find out if there is a quiet room/area for undisturbed work or discussions.

 ## Activity!

- How do you plan your time to include work duties, study requirements and home/family commitments?
- Make a list of the ways you could manage your time more effectively.

Ten ways to provide effective support for colleagues

You can provide effective support for your colleagues by:

1. Working with other members of staff as part of a team.
2. Working in partnership with them to prepare and maintain the learning environment.
3. Working in partnership with parents and carers.
4. Knowing and following relevant school policies and procedures.
5. Attending staff or team meetings.
6. Helping to monitor and evaluate children's participation and developmental progress.
7. Providing feedback about children's play, learning and behaviour.
8. Helping with resources and school administration.
9. Recognising and using personal strengths and abilities.
10. Developing skills through work-based training and other courses.

 **Key Task**

- Describe how you have asked for help, information or support from your colleagues.
- Give examples of how you have offered support to colleagues including:
  - teaching assistants working at the same level as you
  - your line manager (for example the class teacher or SENCO)
  - staff for whom you are responsible (such as new teaching assistants, students, parent helpers, volunteers).

NOS Links:

Level 3: **STL 20.4   STL 21.1   STL 21.2   STL 62.1   STL 62.2   STL 63   STL 64 STL 66 (single element units)**

Identifying effective practice

Effective practice requires committed, enthusiastic and reflective practitioners with a breadth and depth of knowledge, skills and understanding. To be an effective, reflective practitioner, you should use your own learning to improve your work with pupils and their families in ways which are sensitive, positive and non-judgemental. Through initial and on-going training and development, you can develop, demonstrate and continuously improve your:

- relationships with both children and adults
- understanding of the individual and diverse ways that children develop and learn
- knowledge and understanding in order to actively support and extend children's learning in and across all areas and aspects of learning
- practice in meeting all children's needs, learning styles and interests
- work with parents, carers and the wider community
- work with other professionals.

(DfES, 2005b)

The Key Elements of Effective Practice (KEEP) provides a framework for early years practitioners to: reflect on their work; understand what effective practice looks like; record their qualifications; formulate their self-development plan; and allow managers to understand staff experience/ qualifications and training needs to support the development of the setting. KEEP supports self-appraisal, appraisal, quality assurance, self-evaluation and performance management as it links the needs of children, parents, the setting and practitioners. (DfES, 2005b) See: **http:// nationalstrategies.standards.dcsf.gov.uk/node/88576**.

KEEP has been developed alongside and is consistent with *The Common Core of Skills and Knowledge for the Children's Workforce* which sets out the six areas of expertise that everyone working with children, young people and families should be able to demonstrate. For details see: **http://www.dcsf.gov.uk/everychildmatters/strategy/deliveringservices1/ commoncore/commoncoreofskillsandknowledge/**.

 **Key Task**

Outline the standards of professional practice expected from you and your colleagues.
(This information may be included in a code of practice for staff which may be in the staff
handbook and/or set out in best practice benchmarks such as KEEP.)

NOS Links:

Level 3:   **STL 22.1**

Evaluating your personal effectiveness

You need to know and understand clearly the exact role and responsibilities of your work as
a teaching assistant (see Chapter 4). Review your professional practice by making regular and
realistic assessments of how well your working practices match your role and responsibilities.
Share your self-assessments with those responsible for managing and reviewing your work
performance, for example during your regular discussions/meetings with your colleagues
or with your line manager. You should also ask other people for feedback about how well
you fulfil the requirements and expectations of your role. You can also reflect on your own
professional practice by making comparisons with appropriate models of good practice, for
example the work of more experienced teaching assistants within the school.

Self-evaluation

Self-evaluation is needed to improve your own professional practice and to develop your ability
to reflect upon activities and modify plans to meet the individual needs of the pupils you work
with. When evaluating your own practice you should consider:

- Was your own particular contribution appropriate?
- Did you choose the right time, place and resources?
- Did you intervene enough or too much?
- Did you achieve your goals (the objectives/outcomes for the pupil or pupils and yourself)? If
  not, why not? Were the goals too ambitious or unrealistic?
- What other strategies/methods could have been used? Suggest possible modifications.
- Who to ask for further advice (for example class teacher, SENCO, head teacher, other
  professional)?

 Key Task

- How do you monitor the processes, practices and outcomes from your work?
- Give examples of how you evaluate your own practice including: self-evaluation; reflections
  on your interactions with others; sharing your reflections with others and using feedback
  from others to improve your own evaluation.
- Describe how you have used reflection to solve problems and improve practice.

NOS Links:

Level 3:   **STL 18.1   STL 20.4   STL 21.1   STL 21.2   STL 22.1   STL 23.3**
            STL 24.2   STL 27.3   STL 29.1   STL 61.1   STL 61.2   STL 62.2

Developing personal development objectives

You should take part in continuing professional development by identifying areas in your knowledge, understanding and skills where you could develop further. This involves being able to identify your own SMART personal development objectives:

- **S**pecific: identify exactly what you want to develop, such as the particular skills you need to update or new skills you need to acquire, for example first aid or ICT skills.
- **M**easurable: define criteria that can be used to measure whether or not your objectives have been achieved, such as best practice benchmarks, course certificate of attendance or qualification.
- **A**chievable: avoid being too ambitious; set objectives which you know are attainable.
- **R**ealistic: be realistic about what you want to develop.
- **T**ime-bound: plan a realistic time frame within which to achieve your objectives.

 **Activity!**

Identify your own SMART personal development objectives.

You should discuss and agree these objectives with those responsible for supporting your professional development, that is, your line manager. This includes developing and negotiating a plan to develop your knowledge, skills and understanding further, through a Personal Development Plan. For example, you may consider that some of your work tasks require modification or improvement and discuss possible changes with your line manager. Or you may feel that you lack sufficient knowledge and skills to implement particular activities and need to discuss opportunities for you to undertake the relevant training. To achieve your personal development objectives you should make effective use of the people, resources (such as the internet, libraries, journals) and other professional development or training opportunities available to you (see below).

 **key words**

Personal Development Plan: a document relating to your on-going or continuous professional development that includes your individual training and personal development goals and how these relate to the aims of the school, the requirements of your specific job role and the particular needs of the pupils you work with.

When assessing your personal development and training needs you need to consider:

- Your existing experience and skills.
- The needs of the pupils you work with.
- Any problems with how you currently work.
- Any new or changing expectations for your role.
- Information and/or learning needed to meet best practice, quality schemes or regulatory requirements.

A professional portfolio highlighting your existing experience and qualifications can form the basis for assessing your training needs. This portfolio will also be a tangible record of your professional development and will help to boost your self-esteem.

Staff appraisals can also help you to identify your training needs. Once your training needs have been identified, you need to agree with your line manager on an appropriate training course or qualification that will help to meet these training needs.

Key Task

Describe how you assess your personal development and training needs. Include information on:

- your existing strengths and skills
- skills and knowledge you need to improve
- plans for improving your work
- preparing for future responsibilities.

NOS Links:

Level 3:   STL 21.1   STL 21.2   STL 22.1   STL 28.1   STL 28.2

Professional development and training opportunities

Good quality and appropriate professional development and training opportunities can have a huge, positive impact on workplace performance which in turn can greatly enhance the learning experiences of the pupils within the school. To be effective, staff development should take into account the needs of individual staff members and the needs of the school as a whole. You should have a Personal Development Plan or Continuing Professional Development Plan that includes training and personal development goals and how these relate to the aims of the school.

When considering professional development you may have a choice of training options including: attending training courses at the local educational development centre or local college, such as literacy and numeracy seminars or ICT courses; attending sessions run by outside providers, such as first aid training; or attending in-house training such as INSET days.

Another aspect of professional development involves sharing knowledge, skills and experience with others, perhaps through acting as a mentor (see above) or training as an NVQ assessor. Training opportunities should also be offered to parents and carers as well as staff members, including meetings with speakers, discussion groups, reading materials such as books, fact sheets and information packs.

Figure 9.2: First aid training

The areas of training and development identified by teaching assistants include: knowledge of curriculum subject content; supporting literacy activities; supporting numeracy activities; behaviour management; supporting specific special needs; working with parents and developing ICT skills. Teaching assistants indicate that they prefer practical training opportunities and many of the courses available are skills or competency-based. Research shows that some of the most effective training for teaching assistants takes place in schools as part of their INSET provision. However, it is not always possible to teach the necessary skills in schools, especially those relating to specific special needs. Many LEAs provide training courses for teaching assistants employed directly by them or those recruited by individual schools.

Specific training and recognised qualifications for the professional development of teaching assistants are also available:

- Level 3 Award in Supporting Teaching and Learning in Schools
- Level 3 Certificate in Supporting Teaching and Learning in Schools
- Level 3 Certificate in Cover Supervision
- Level 3 Diploma in Specialist Support for Teaching and Learning in Schools
- Higher Level Teaching Assistant (HLTA) training and assessment
- Foundation Degree.

Training courses and qualifications can have a positive influence on improving the status of teaching assistants as well as enabling them to share examples of good practice with others who support teaching and learning. Schools also benefit from having teaching assistants who are able to improve their expertise and increase their job satisfaction.

 Key Task

- Find out about the professional development and training opportunities for teaching assistants in your local area.
- Give examples of how you have accessed professional development and training opportunities.

NOS Links:

Level 3:   **STL 21.2   STL 22.2   STL 28.1   STL 28.2**

Summary of key points in this chapter:

- **Effective teamwork** including: stages in team development; team objectives; working as part of a team; effective communication with colleagues; participating in team meetings; the allocation of work in your team; monitoring the work of your team.
- **Making an effective contribution to your team** including: time management; ways to provide effective support for colleagues.
- **Identifying effective practice**.
- **Evaluating your personal effectiveness** including self-evaluation.
- **Developing personal development objectives**.
- **Professional development and training opportunities**.

Further reading

Hartley, M. (2005) *The Assertiveness Handbook*. Sheldon Press.

Harvey, N. (2006) *Effective Communication*. Second revised edition. Gill & MacMillan Ltd.

Kerry, T. (2001) *Working with Support Staff: Their Roles and Effective Management in Schools*. Pearson Education.

Lindenfield, G. (2000) *Self Esteem: Simple Steps to Developing Self-Reliance and Perseverance*. Harper Collins.

Miller, L. et al (2005) *Developing Early Years Practice*. David Fulton Publishers.

Morgan, J. (2007) *How to be a Successful Teaching Assistant*. Continuum Publishing.

Ramsey, R. D. (2002) *How to Say the Right Thing Every Time: Communicating Well with Students, Staff, Parents and the Public*. Corwin Press.

Roet, B. (1998) *The Confidence to be Yourself*. Piatkus.

Watkinson, A. (2009) *The Essential Guide for Experienced Teaching Assistants*. David Fulton Publishers.

10. Supporting assessment for learning

This chapter relates to QCF units:

TDA 3.7 Support assessment for learning

TDA 3.9 Invigilate tests and examinations

TDA 3.26 Maintain learner records

Assessment for learning

As well as being able to observe children's development (see Chapter 1) you also need to help the teacher assess children's development based on observational findings and other reliable information from pupils, parents, carers, colleagues and other appropriate adults. You must be able to make formative and summative assessments (see below) and record your assessments as appropriate to the policies and procedures of your school. You should share your findings with pupils and their parents as appropriate to your role. You should also refer any concerns about pupils to the teacher, senior colleagues and/or relevant external agencies when required. Always remember to follow the school's confidentiality and record keeping requirements (see section below on maintaining pupil records).

Assessment for learning involves using assessment, as part of teaching and learning, in ways that will raise pupils' achievement. The characteristics of assessment for learning are that it:

- is embedded in a view of teaching and learning of which it is an essential part
- involves sharing learning goals with pupils
- aims to help pupils to know and to recognise the standards they are aiming for
- involves pupils in self-assessment
- provides feedback which leads to pupils recognising their next steps and how to take them
- is underpinned by confidence that every pupil can improve
- involves both teacher and pupils reviewing and reflecting on assessment information.

(TDA, 2007)

Assessment strategies are the approaches and techniques used for on-going assessment during lessons or learning activities, such as: using open-ended questions; observing pupils; listening to how pupils describe their work and their reasoning; checking pupils' understanding and engaging pupils in reviewing progress.

Formative and summative assessments

Formative assessments are initial and on-going assessments. Formative assessments identify learning goals for individuals and groups as appropriate to the ages, developmental needs and abilities of pupils *and* the requirements of the school. Formative assessments are continuous and inform planning provision to promote children's development and learning. Examples of formative assessments include: pupil observations; tick charts/lists; reading records; maths records and daily target records for pupils with Individual Education Plans.

Formative assessment involves observing pupils, monitoring pupils' work, providing oral feedback and informative and critical marking.

Critical marking allows pupils to:

- appreciate their own performance
- find and correct their own mistakes
- identify their own strengths and weaknesses
- receive praise and rewards for their efforts
- be motivated by seeing that their work is valued.

Critical marking allows teachers and teaching assistants to:

- respond consistently in acknowledging pupils' work
- recognise effort and progress as well as attainment
- respond positively, constructively and sympathetically
- involve pupils in the marking process, whenever possible
- monitor the performance of individuals and groups of pupils
- set targets as and when appropriate
- tell the pupils what they need to do next to progress
- make an assessment of pupils' achievement
- develop their curriculum planning
- inform parents about their children's progress.

 key words

Formative assessments: are initial and on-going assessments that identify future targets for pupils as appropriate to their ages, developmental needs and abilities.

Summative assessments: are assessments that summarise findings and involve more formal monitoring of pupil progress that allow judgements to be made about each pupil's level of achievement.

Learning goals: are the personalised learning targets for individual pupils. Learning goals relate to learning objectives (what the teacher intends the pupils to learn) and take account of the past achievements and current learning needs of the pupil.

Summative assessments are assessments that summarise findings. Summative assessments involve more formal monitoring of pupil progress. Summative assessments should be used appropriately and allow judgements to be made about each pupil's achievement. Summative assessments are usually in the form of criterion based tests or tasks. Examples of summative assessments include: Early Years Foundation Stage Profile; Standard Assessment Tasks (SATs); teacher assessments; annual school reports and reviews of pupils with special educational needs. (See also the section on providing information on pupil progress and responses in Chapter 6.)

Curriculum frameworks and assessment requirements

You need to know the relevant school curriculum and age-related expectations of pupils in the subject/curriculum area and age range of the pupils with whom you are working. For example, in England the relevant curricula are The Early Years Foundation Stage and the National Curriculum. (Information about curriculum frameworks is in Chapter 6.)

The Practice Guidance for the Early Years Foundation Stage provides detailed formative assessment suggestions in the 'Look, listen and note' sections of the areas of learning and development.

Early years practitioners should: make systematic observations and assessments of each child's achievements, interests and learning styles; use these observations and assessments to identify learning priorities and plan relevant and motivating learning experiences for each child; and match their observations to the expectations of the early learning goals. *The Early Years Foundation Stage Profile* is a way of summing up each child's development and learning achievements at the end of the EYFS. It is based on practitioners' ongoing observation and assessments in all six areas of learning and development. Each child's level of development must be recorded against the 13 assessment scales derived from the early learning goals. Judgements against these scales, which are set out in Appendix 1 of the *Statutory Framework for the Early Years Foundation Stage*, should be made from observation of consistent and independent behaviour, predominantly children's self-initiated activities (**www.standards.dfes.gov.uk/eyfs**).

During Key Stages 1 to 3, pupil progress in most National Curriculum subjects is assessed against eight levels. At the end of Key Stage 1 each pupil's level of attainment is based on the teacher's assessment of reading, writing, speaking and listening, mathematics and science which take into account the pupil's performance in several tasks and tests in reading, writing (including handwriting and spelling) and mathematics. By the age of seven years most pupils are expected to reach Level 2. At the end of Key Stage 2 each pupil's level of attainment is based on the teacher's assessment and the pupil's performance in the national tests in English, Mathematics and Science. By the age of eleven years most pupils are expected to reach Level 4. In Key Stage 3, each pupil's level of attainment is based on the teacher's assessment of: English; Mathematics; Science; Information and Communication Technology; Design and Technology; History; Geography; Art and Design; Music; Physical Education, Citizenship; Modern Foreign Languages; Religious Education. By the age of fourteen most pupils are expected to achieve Level 5. In Key Stage 4, each pupil's attainment is assessed by GCSE levels of achievement at age 16 (Year 11) in the compulsory subjects English, Mathematics, Science, Information and Communication Technology, Physical Education and Citizenship as well as the pupil's chosen subjects in the entitlement curriculum areas (the arts, design and technology, the humanities and modern foreign languages). At the end of Key Stage 4 most pupils are expected to attain at least 5 GCSEs at Grades A–D.

Further information about curriculum assessment in England is available at: **http://www. qcda.gov.uk/assessment/82.aspx**.

Information about curriculum assessment in Northern Ireland is available at: **http://www. nicurriculum.org.uk/foundation_stage/assessment/assessment_for_learning.asp**

Information about curriculum assessment in Scotland is available at: **http://www.ltscotland. org.uk/curriculumforexcellence/assessmentandachievement/index.asp**

Information about curriculum assessment in Wales is available at: **http://wales.gov.uk/ topics/educationandskills/curriculumassessment/?lang=en**

 Activity!

Find out about the curriculum framework and assessment requirements applicable to the pupils you work with.

Ashwood Park Primary School

CHILD'S RESULTS

End of key stage 2 assessment results 2003

Name: Thomas Jennings   Class: 6B

ENGLISH

Teachers assessment results

Speaking and listening	level 4
Reading	level 5
Writing	level 5
English result	**level 5**

Test results

Reading	level 5
Writing	level 5
English result	**level 5**

MATHEMATICS

Teacher assessment result	level 4
Test result	level 4

SCIENCE

Teacher assessment result	level 4
Test result	level 5

Level 3 and below represent achievement below the nationally expected standard for most 11-year-olds. Level 4 represents achievement at the nationally expected standard for most 11-year-olds. Levels 5 and 6 represent achievement above the nationally expected standards for most 11-year-olds.

Figure 10.1: Example of assessment sheet

Supporting pupils to review their own learning

When supporting assessment for learning you need to support pupils to review their own learning and identify their own emerging learning needs. You can do this by:

- Using information gained from monitoring pupil participation and progress to help pupils to review their learning strategies, achievements and future learning needs.
- Providing time for pupils to reflect upon what they have learnt and to identify where they still have difficulties.
- Listening carefully to pupils and positively encouraging them to communicate their needs and ideas for future learning.
- Supporting pupils in using peer assessment and self-assessment to evaluate their learning achievements.
- Supporting pupils to reflect on their learning, identify the progress they have made and identify their emerging learning needs.
- Supporting pupils to identify the strengths and weaknesses of their learning strategies and plan how to improve them.

(TDA, 2007)

Key Task

- What is the curriculum framework applicable to the pupils you work with?
- What are the assessment requirements applicable to the pupils you work with? Provide examples of any assessment sheets you use.
- What are your role and responsibilities in the assessment process?
- List examples of how you support pupils to review their own learning and identify their own emerging learning needs.

NOS Links:

Level 3: STL 18.1   STL 20.4   STL 23.3   STL 24.2   STL 27.3   STL 29.1
STL 30.1   STL 30.2   STL 36.1   STL 55.1   STL 55.2   STL 60.2

School reports

In education settings it is a legal requirement that parents receive a written report at least once a year detailing the progress of their children in the National Curriculum subjects plus RE. General comments should also be made concerning the child's general progress and behaviour along with other achievements in the school including extra-curricular activities. All relevant personnel should be encouraged to contribute to these reports. School reports also contain teacher assessment and test level or examination results at the end of each key stage according to current statutory requirements. Each report must also detail the number of authorised and unauthorised absences since the last report.

A pupil's annual report should:

- Be written clearly and concisely without too much jargon.
- Summarise the pupil's performance since the last report.
- Outline the pupil's level of attainment in the National Curriculum subjects. National Curriculum levels of attainment are required only in the core subjects in Years 2, 6 and 9. However, parents are informed if their child is working below, at or above National Curriculum levels in the remaining year groups. For pupils in Key Stage 4, the school report will outline the pupil's expected GCSE results (Year 10) and actual GCSE results (Year 11).
- Set out what the pupil has actually learned, not just what they have been taught during the school year.
- Highlight positive achievements and progress made by the pupil.
- Identify the pupil's weaknesses and suggests positive future action.
- Set realistic targets to motivate the pupil for the coming school year.

Each report should be shared with the pupil, who should be encouraged to comment on their own progress in writing where possible. Reports are usually given to parents in July, and staff should be available to discuss pupil reports by appointment at a special parents' evening arranged for this purpose. Parents should be invited to write comments about their children's reports on a separate slip that is returned to and kept by the school along with a copy of each report.

Pupil's Name _Thomas Jennings_ **Class** _IN_

Teacher _MRS C.A. NICKLIN_

Attendance:	Sessions School Open	342
	Attendance	99 %
	Unauthorised Absence	0 %

General Progress and Attitude:

Tom has made steady progress in all aspects of the curriculum. He is developing self-confidence and will now ask if unsure of the task set. On occasions progress has been hampered by Tom's tendency to chatter! Tom is always polite and has a keen sense of humour! Tom prefers to play with a couple of special friends.

Target:

Tom has tried hard to listen more carefully.

I have read what my teacher has written about me.

Child's Signature _Tom Jennings_

Teacher's Signature _CA Nicklin_

Headteacher's Signature

C:\serif\pp30\report.ppp

Figure 10.2: Example of school report

Activity!

- Outline your school's policy and procedures for reporting pupil progress to their parents.
- What are your responsibilities for reporting pupil progress to their parents?

Maintaining pupil records

As a teaching assistant, you will help with classroom records under the close supervision of the teacher responsible for maintaining them. This includes helping with the range of written records used within the school to monitor individual pupils, learning activities, classroom resources and requisitions.

The range of pupil records

All schools keep records of essential personal information for each pupil including: home address and telephone number; emergency information such as the names and contact telephone numbers for parents/guardians/carers, GP; medical history and conditions such as allergies; cultural or religious practices which may have implications for the care and education of the pupil such as special diets, exclusion from RE and assemblies; and who collects the pupil (if applicable) including the transport arrangements (such as taxi or minibus) for a pupil with special educational needs. Schools also have records relating to administrative duties, for example, permission slips for educational visits and requisition forms for school supplies.

Schools also have education records relating to the assessment of pupil progress and their achievements within the National Curriculum framework. Formative assessments include: reading records; maths records; tick charts/lists; observation sheets and daily target records for pupils with Individual Education Plans. Summative assessments include: class teacher assessments; SATs results; pupils' annual school reports and reviews of pupils with SEN.

Activity!

What is the range of pupil records? Give examples of the types of pupil records used for the pupils with whom you work.

Record keeping systems and procedures

Record keeping systems and procedures are essential to: monitor pupil progress; provide accurate and detailed information regarding pupils' learning and behaviour; determine the effectiveness of an activity or target; determine the effectiveness of adult support or intervention; give constructive feedback to the pupil; share information with the teacher, other professionals and parents; and identify and plan for new learning objectives or behaviour targets.

The record keeping systems and procedures you need to follow will depend on the planning and assessment requirements of the school, the class/subject teacher, SENCO and any other professionals involved in meeting the pupils' educational needs. It is important to update records on a regular basis; the frequency of updating depends on the different types of records that you make a contribution towards. Records that may indicate potential problems with individual pupils should be shown to the class teacher (for example observations of unacceptable behaviour or daily records which show poor performance).

 **Activity!**

Find out about the record keeping systems and procedures used within the school.

The roles and responsibilities for record keeping

As a teaching assistant, most of your work with pupils will be planned by others, for example, the class/subject teacher, SENCO or relevant specialists. They will need regular information about your work such as updates about a particular pupil's progress. Where, when and how to record pupil information should be as directed by the teacher. For example, when recording a pupil's behaviour using time or event sampling, you will need to agree on specific dates and times on which observations will take place. Some information may be given orally, for example outlining a pupil's progress on a particular activity or commenting on a pupil's behaviour.

Spoken information needs to be given in a professional manner, that is: to the appropriate person (class or subject teacher or SENCO); in the right place (not in a corridor where confidential information could be overheard); at the right time (urgent matters need to be discussed with the class or subject teacher immediately while others may wait until a team meeting).

Requests for records or reports should be dealt with professionally and handed in on time. This is particularly important if the information is needed for a meeting or review as any delay may stop others from performing their responsibilities effectively. Always remember to maintain confidentiality as appropriate to the school's requirements (see below).

 Key Task

- Find out about the school's record keeping policy. Highlight the responsibilities of the teaching assistant as set out in this policy.
- What is your role and your responsibilities in maintaining pupil records? With the teacher's permission include: copies of individual pupil records, such as literacy and numeracy records, Early Years Foundation Stage profile, Individual Education Plans (IEPs), Behaviour Support Plans/logs, copies of school or class records such as registers, and educational visit documentation with your comments about your involvement.

NOS Links:

Level 3:	STL 18.1	STL 20.4	STL 21.1	STL 23.3	STL 24.2	STL 27.3
	STL 29.1	STL 30.1	STL 30.2	STL 36.1	STL 40.3	STL 44.3
	STL 50.4	STL 51.1	STL 51.2	STL 55.1	STL 55.2	STL 58.1
	STL 60.2	STL 61.1	STL 61.2	STL 69.1	STL 69.2	

Storing records

You need to know the exact policy and procedures for storing records in the school. You should also know what your own role and responsibilities are regarding the storage of records. Most pupil and staff records are stored and locked away in a central location such as the school office. Some formative records that need to be accessed or updated on a regular basis may be kept in the pupils' classrooms.

You must maintain the safe and secure storage of school records at all times. You should not leave important documents lying around; always put them back in storage after use. As well as the physical security of records, you need to be aware of the levels of staff access to information. You should never give out the passwords to school equipment (such as computers) unless you have permission from the member of staff responsible for the record keeping systems.

 **Activity!**

What is the school policy for the storage and security of pupil records?

Record keeping and confidentiality

Confidentiality is important with regard to record keeping and the storing of information; only the appropriate people should have access to confidential records. Except where a pupil is potentially at risk, information should not be given to other agencies unless previously agreed. Where the passing of confidential information is acceptable then it should be given in the agreed format. Always follow the school policy and procedures regarding confidentiality and the sharing of information; check with the teacher (or your line manager) if you have any concerns about these matters.

Legal implications and restrictions

You should be aware of any legal requirements with regard to record keeping in the school. These include: the Data Protection Act 1998; the Children Act 1989; the Education Act 2002; the Race Relations Act 1976; the SEN Code of Practice 2001. In particular, you need to be aware of the basic legal requirements concerning the recording and filing of personal information under the Data Protection Act 1998 (see section on confidentiality matters in Chapter 3).

There are some circumstances where access to educational records may be restricted:

> '*The Secretary of State may by order exempt from the subject information provisions, or modify those provisions in relation to personal data in respect of which the data controller is the proprietor of, or a teacher at, a school, and which consist of information relating to persons who are or have been pupils at the school...*'. (Section 30 (2) Data Protection Act, 1998.)

 **Activity!**

- What are the basic legal requirements concerning the recording and filing of personal information under the Data Protection Act 1998?
- What are the school's confidentiality requirements with regard to record keeping? Highlight the responsibilities of the teaching assistant as set out in this policy.
- Outline your main responsibilities for maintaining the confidentiality of pupil information.

Invigilating tests and examinations

Part of your role may include invigilating external or internal tests and examinations, including module tests and practical and oral examinations, under formal conditions. This involves running tests and examinations in the presence of the candidates and includes: preparing the examination room and resources; bringing candidates into the room and running the test or examination session according to the centre's procedures. You will also need to know how to deal with specific situations such as: access arrangements for pupils with special needs, for example reading assistance, scribe, sign interpreter; emergencies such as illness or fire evacuation; and suspicion of malpractice such as cheating.

Figure 10.3: Adult invigilating school examination

In practice

Francesca is working with pupils aged 15 to 16 who are sitting a module test for mathematics that includes a non-calculator paper. How would you deal with each of the following situations: a pupil with dyslexia; a pupil who is taken ill during the test; a pupil who appears to be using a calculator?

Invigilating tests and examinations may involve:

- Assisting with making public examinations entries and receiving and processing results.
- Assisting with the organisation of public examinations before, during and after each session.
- Assisting with the administration of school examinations.
- Ensuring the requirements for the conduct of tests and examinations are met, for example the required number and positioning of desks/work stations, display of notices, seating plan, clock, centre number, instructions for candidates and attendance register.
- Considering health and safety arrangements and environmental conditions such as heating, lighting, ventilation and the level of outside noise.
- Meeting specific requirements, such as additional requirements in relation to further guidance, erratum notices, and supervision of individual candidates between tests or examinations, and access arrangements for candidates with additional needs.
- Being responsible for the issue of certificates and archives.
- Producing the school's examination statistics.

 **Key Task**

Outline your role and responsibilities for invigilating tests and examinations. Include information on the following: the policy, procedures and regulations applicable to tests and examinations in your school; how you prepare to run tests and examinations; how you implement and maintain invigilation requirements.

NOS Links:
Level 3:   **STL 17.1**   **STL 17.2**

Summary of key points in this chapter:

- **Assessment for learning including**: formative and summative assessments; curriculum frameworks and assessment requirements; supporting pupils to review their own learning; school reports.

- **Maintaining pupil records**: the range of pupil records; record keeping systems and procedures; the roles and responsibilities for record keeping; storing records; record keeping and confidentiality; legal implications and restrictions

- **Invigilating tests and examinations** including running tests and examinations in the presence of the candidates under formal conditions.

Further reading

Balshaw, M. and Farrell, P. (2002) *Teaching Assistants: Practical Strategies for Effective Classroom Support*. David Fulton Publishers.

CCEA (2009) *Assessment for Learning: A Practical Guide*. Council for the Curriculum Examinations and Assessment. (**http://www.nicurriculum.org.uk/docs/assessment_for_learning/AfL_A%20 Practical%20Guide.pdf** .)

Dean, J. (2005) *The Teaching Assistant's Guide to Primary Education*. Routledge Falmer.

DfES (2005) *Working Together: Teaching Assistants and Assessment For Learning*. DfES.

DfES (2007) *Primary and Secondary National Strategies: Pedagogy and Personalisation*. DfES.

Dupree, J. (2005) *Help Students Improve Their Study Skills: A Handbook for Teaching Assistants in Secondary Schools*. David Fulton Publishers Ltd.

Galloway, J. (2004) *ICT for Teaching Assistants*. David Fulton Publishers Ltd.

Hutchin, V. (2007) *Supporting Every Child's Learning Across the Early Years Foundation Stage*. Hodder Murray.

Lindon, J. (2005) *Understanding Child Development: Linking Theory and Practice*. Hodder Arnold.

QCA (2008) *Assessing Pupils' Progress: Assessment at the Heart Of Learning*. Qualifications and Curriculum Authority.

The Scottish Government (2010) *Curriculum for Excellence: Building the Curriculum 5 – A Framework for Assessment*. The Scottish Government.
(**http://www.scotland.gov.uk/Publications/2010/01/14141415/0**.)

Welsh Assembly Government (2007) *How to Develop Thinking and Assessment for Learning in The Classroom.* Welsh Assembly Government. **(http://wales.gov.uk/docs/dcells/publications/100507howdevthinkingen.pdf)**

Wyse, D. and Hawtin, A. (1999) *Children: A Multi-professional Perspective.* Arnold. (Covers child development and learning from birth to 18 years.)

[Note: the DfES publications are available free online at: **www.standards.dfes.gov.uk**]

11. Supporting speech, language and communication

> ### This chapter relates to QCF unit:
> **EYMP 5** Support children's speech, language and communication
>
> **TDA 3.17** Support bilingual learners
>
> **TDA 3.18** Provide bilingual support for teaching and learning

Defining speech, language and communication

The word language is often used to describe the process of speaking and listening, but it is much more than just communication. Language is what makes humans different from all other animals. All animals, including humans, communicate through the use of signals. For example, a cat hisses and its tail bristles when it feels threatened and a dog may bark to indicate that there is an intruder. Humans also communicate using signals such as body language and gesture; what makes us different is the use of symbols (such as words) to indicate more complex needs and feelings. While animals are only able to deal with the here and now, humans can use language to store and later recall ideas, feelings and past experiences, and to look forward to the future.

Humans have the ability to utilise language by use of a recognised system of symbols, which includes a common understanding of what those symbols mean. Anyone could make up their own language system, but they would not be able to communicate with others unless they shared this system or code with them. For example, in Britain the majority of people use the language system 'English' so that they can communicate effectively in an English-speaking society. There are many other language systems as indicated by the many languages and alphabet systems used around the world.

 **key words**

Language: a recognised system of gestures, signs and symbols used to communicate.

Communication: the transmission of thoughts, feelings or information via body language, signals, speech or writing.

Speech: verbal communication; the act of speaking; the articulation of words to express thoughts, feelings or ideas.

Language acquisition theories

There are different ideas about how babies and young children acquire language and communication skills. Here we look at the nurture, nature and social interaction theories. (Information about the sequence of children's communication and language development is in Chapter 1.)

The nurture theory

This theory originates from the work of the philosopher John Locke (1600s) and was developed by behavioural psychologists such as Pavlov (1950s). This theory suggests that a baby is born with a mind like a *tabula rasa*, a 'clean slate'. This means that babies have to learn *everything*, including language, from scratch. Language has to be learned in the same way as any other skill. Children's parents and carers shape the way in which children learn language by encouraging the required sounds (and then words) while ignoring others. Children learn language by copying sounds, words and phrases around them, and through the positive reinforcement of their attempts to communicate.

The nature theory

This theory, put forward mainly by the linguist Noam Chomsky (1960s), states that babies are born with *some* knowledge of language. He argues that language systems are too complex to be acquired solely from being copied from and/or taught by adults. Language is innate and all humans have a genetic pre-disposition towards using language. Chomsky concludes that humans have a 'language acquisition device' (LAD) which allows them to process and to use language. To reinforce this argument, Chomsky points to how all children appear to learn language in the same way and that the early stages of language are the same for all children. For example, all children (whatever their community language) first learn to speak using holophrases: one word utterances to convey whole sentences; followed by telegraphic speech: two or three word sentences to convey meaning.

key words

Holophrases: one word utterances to convey whole sentences.

Telegraphic speech: two or three word sentences to convey meaning.

The social interaction theory

This theory from the psychologists Vygotsky (1930s) and Jerome Bruner (1970s) suggests that young children acquire language as a means to communicate more effectively with others than can be done through non-verbal communication alone. This theory is similar to the behaviourist tradition in that children learn language through their interactions with others. However, this theory differs in that even very young children are seen as active participants in their language development. For example, research has shown that babies can *initiate and control* pre-verbal 'conversations' with their parents/carers rather than the other way round; babies make adults pay attention to them through body language, crying and babbling and end 'conversations' with adults by breaking off eye contact or simply falling asleep! The role of the adult in children's language development is to provide the social context in which meaningful communication can take place. This theory also stresses the strong link between language acquisition and children's cognitive or intellectual development (see information about intellectual development in Chapter 1). Language arises from the need to understand the environment and from social interactions with others.

Activity!

- What is your own view of how young children acquire language?
- Give a detailed account using examples from your own experiences.

Factors that may affect language development

To participate fully in all aspects of education (and society), children need to successfully develop a wide range of language and communication skills. Adults working with young children need an awareness of the wide variety of language experiences which young children bring to the early years setting and the environmental/social factors or special needs which may affect language development. Depending on their individual language experiences, some young children may not have reached the same level of language development as their peers, or they may lack effective communication skills while some children may even be ahead of what is usually expected for children their age (for example, already have some reading skills).

Language development is affected by many factors not just a child's chronological age. Some children may have special needs which affect their ability to communicate effectively with others (see sections on supporting pupils with communication and interaction needs, supporting pupils with behavioural, social and emotional development needs, and supporting pupils with sensory and/or physical needs in Chapter 13).

Other factors which affect children's speech, language and communication include: poverty, race/culture, parental expectations and language experiences at home and in education settings (see below). Another important factor to remember is that physical maturity also plays a part in children's language development. Babies need to have physical control over their vocal chords, tongue, lips and jaw muscles to be able to articulate the sounds necessary to form their first words.

In addition, children (and adults) have two important areas of vocabulary usage: passive vocabulary – the language used by others which they can *understand*; active vocabulary – the words which they actually *use* themselves. Children (and adults) can recognise and understand a larger number of words than they can speak (or write) themselves, whatever their level of development. The size of an individual's vocabulary (like all aspects of language development) depends on their language experiences, especially access to books and reading.

 key words

Passive vocabulary: the language used by others which children can *understand*.

Active vocabulary: the words which children actually *use* themselves.

Environmental factors and social/cultural factors

It has been suggested (for example, by Laing and Chazan in Fontana, 1984) that some children grow up within environmental and social circumstances which may restrict the children's opportunities to explore their environment and to develop language and communication skills through positive and stimulating interactions with others. For example, circumstances such as: poverty; race and culture; family size and parental background/low expectations.

Certainly society and current social trends contribute to the nature and practices of family life and this in turn affects the opportunity for, and quality of, the social interactions experienced by children. Society and work patterns have changed greatly, for example: the rise of family breakdown and the increase in divorce; remarriage and step-families; unemployment and redundancy; both parents working; and the difficulties facing single parent families. These changes all affect family life, the quality of children's lives and their social skills.

Poverty

Some people believe that poverty is a crucial factor affecting all aspects of children's development (Leach, 1994). No matter what level of importance parents place on language and learning, it may be very difficult to provide books and activities to stimulate children's interest in language and reading in some circumstances. For example: no local library; travel costs to the nearest library being too high; local parks/play areas that are not safe due to crime; financial worries/unemployment that make providing stimulating language opportunities more difficult.

Research indicates that poverty and related problems, such as poor housing, can affect children's educational success (National Commission on Education, 1993). One of the reasons for this lack of success is due to problems involving language and communication; without appropriate language and communication skills, it is impossible to access and process the information that is essential to learning.

Race and culture

We live in a multiracial and multicultural society. Some children coming into early years settings may not speak English at home. Social interaction depends on cultural patterns. How adults and children communicate with each other depends on how a culture or society views children and child development.

Not so long ago, British society considered that 'children should be seen and not heard' and also that 'children should not speak until spoken to'. Children develop communication skills in line with the expectations of their culture and race. For example, English-speaking children may be used to adults who modify their speech or adults who simplify their language to help their children's comprehension; while children from many non-English speaking backgrounds may be used to more adult patterns of speech and more direct language instructions from adults in their social interactions.

Children may find communicating within the early years setting difficult at first because they find it hard to relate to staff or other children from different races and/or cultures. The lack of ethnic role models is a particular problem in educational settings. For example, in England 17 per cent of pupils are from minority ethnic backgrounds while the percentage of teachers from minority ethnic backgrounds is only 9 per cent, although this figure increases to 31 per cent in London (DfES, 2005c). However, it is dangerous to make assumptions about children's language abilities based solely on their culture or race. You should always look at each child as an *individual*.

Family size

In the past some researchers were concerned that children in large families lacked the opportunities to interact in a meaningful way with adults, as their parents were too busy coping with so many children (Rutter in Leach, 1994). The presence of brothers and sisters was seen as a negative factor in children's development. There is little evidence to support this idea.

It has been suggested that children who are the first (or only) child in their family develop language at a faster rate and have a larger vocabulary than other children (Cunningham, 1993). This assumption should not be made as it depends on the interaction and communication the child has with his/her parent(s). The important factor is not family size, but the quality of adult and child interactions. We will look at the importance of this aspect later on in this chapter.

Parental background and/or expectations

In the past, researchers such as Bernstein suggested that 'working class' children were at a disadvantage in school because of their inability to use language in the same way as 'middle class' children. More recently it has been realised that it is the social context of language which is the important factor in children's language development rather than any notions related to 'class'. It depends on how individual families use language: some families see language and learning as very important and pass this attitude onto their children (Foster-Cohen, 1999); some families may have other priorities.

Some parents may be unaware of the ways they can assist their children's language development and communication skills. Some children may have various experiences of language and literacy which are not the same as the linguistic experiences provided in education settings.

By the time most children attend an early years/education setting they have already developed many aspects of language and will have a wide variety of communication skills. Depending on their home experiences some children will feel at ease talking with both adults and children, while some children will be shy and make only limited responses to others. Children who are poor communicators may come from backgrounds dissimilar to the adults in the setting, but this does not mean that they are incapable of communicating in meaningful ways in other contexts, for example with other children or their own family (Meadows, 1993).

Parents who encourage their children's interest in language and literacy through general conversation, talking about everyday/children's activities and sharing stories/books will be providing their children with a distinct advantage in terms of communication and education.

The language environment

The various ideas concerning the effects of children's very early experiences on their language development may be too simplistic. While there are differences between children's language experiences, it is often staff attitudes towards children from differing circumstances which can create problems. Adults in education settings may come from different backgrounds/cultures compared to the children they are working with and so may have lower expectations of these children. This in turn can lead to low achievement by these children with regard to their language and learning (Bruce and Meggitt, 1999).

In fact later experiences also affect children's language development, hence the importance of providing a quality, language-rich learning environment. For example, the education setting could actually have a negative effect if it limits the opportunities for language.

Remember that while you may sometimes have limited control over the environmental/social factors outside the setting, but you can and should help to maximise opportunities within your setting for enabling language development and encouraging communication skills by providing a stimulating, language-rich environment.

Group organisation

Following the more intimate interactions which most children experience in the home, many children find the prospect of communicating within the larger education setting extremely daunting. Even as adults it can be difficult to communicate with others in situations such as parents' evenings/open days, staff meetings, on courses at college or presentations.

Shy or less confident children may be reluctant to talk, particularly in large group situations. It is important to be flexible, and to provide a variety of groupings: one-to-one; pairs/small groups; large groups and whole class. This allows for individual differences within the setting and gives every child opportunities to develop many different communication skills in a variety of meaningful ways.

Each individual, whether adult or child, has different personal characteristics which affect their ability to communicate effectively and comfortably with others. From your experiences of working with children you may have identified children's differing characteristics which influence their willingness or reluctance to communicate within a group. For this reason, ability groups are not always the best way for young children to work, particularly when you want to encourage communication skills.

Ability groups are used to organise children according to academic ability, especially for literacy or numeracy, making it easier to plan activities at an appropriate level for each child's or group's ability. The difficulty with ability groups is that even very young children know if they are in the 'clever' group or the 'not-so-clever' group, no matter how the adults try to disguise the fact. This can have serious consequences for children's future development: if the child *believes* they are not good at reading then they may give up trying to read.

Friendship or temperament groups involve children with similar characteristics being encouraged to work together and/or children being free to choose who they work with. Friendship groups are often a better way for children to work because children feel more at ease socially and so *all* the children have the opportunity to communicate comfortably within the group, without the more articulate or confident children tending to dominate group discussions and activities. New children coming into the setting can fit in more easily too; by using the 'buddy' system where one child befriends the newcomer until they are established and can make their own choice as to which group they would like to join. This way of grouping children even works with very shy children or those who are extremely reluctant to communicate, as every child usually has at least one special friend who can be included in their group.

 **Key Task**

- Observe a small group of children involved in a language activity.
- In your assessment comment on each child's language and communication skills:
  - Use of verbal language (such as vocabulary, sentence structure, babbling, imitating sounds).
  - Use of non-verbal communication (such as body language, gestures, facial expressions, signing).
  - Level of participation in the group situation (for example the frequency of language, need for prompts from other children/adults).
  - Level of social interaction (such as their ability to take turns in speaking and listening, following instructions for the activity or rules of a game).
- Suggest practical ideas to assist the children's language and communication skills in future activities.

NOS Links:

Level 3: **STL 20.2** **STL 25.3** **STL 29.1** **STL 29.2**

Links with social and emotional development

Children's social and emotional development is closely linked with their language development as communication involves social interaction with at least one other person. Confidence, self-esteem and self-image affect the way we all interact with other people, so this will necessarily affect the development of communication skills. (See sections on self-esteem and self-image in Chapter 14.)

 Key Task

- Plan, implement and evaluate a language activity for a small group of children such as news time, circle time, discussion, story time or a phonics session.
- You could use your suggestions from the above observation as the starting point for planning this activity.
- The activity should encourage the children's active participation, including attentive listening and communicating with others during the activity as well as supervising and maintaining the children's interest throughout the activity.

NOS Links:

Level 3: **STL 20.2** **STL 23.1** **STL 23.2** **STL 23.3** **STL 24.1** **STL 24.2** **STL 25.3**

Communicating with children

It is essential to communicate with children in a manner that is clear and concise and appropriate to their ages, needs and abilities. (See section on communicating with children and young people in Chapter 3.)

Adults working with children need to spend time listening carefully to individual children and to what children have to communicate, in small or large group situations such as news time or story sessions. In order to do this effectively, education settings should be well-staffed with a high adult to child ratio. Many communications in education settings relate to giving information or instructions, for example setting children on to activities and discussions in preparation for tasks.

However, informal 'conversations' are an important part of communicating with children. When adults are not actively involved in the children's activities, perhaps because they are putting up displays or preparing materials for later activities, they should always be willing to listen to the children who will undoubtedly approach them to start up a conversation. Children can learn a great deal about language and the world around them from the spontaneous, unplanned communications that occur during everyday activities such as break/playtime, milk/juice time, meal times, setting up/clearing away play and learning activities.

Providing opportunities for conversation

Many of the following activities allow children the opportunity to talk and listen in more relaxed, informal situations. They allow children and adults to share their experiences in a more natural way through situations which may be similar to their home experiences such as meal times. Activities which can encourage conversations include:

- **Natural materials**: sand, water, play dough, clay.
- **Domestic activities**: milk/juice times, meal times, tidy up times, cooking and washing up, washing clothes. (Remember children's safety.)
- **Books**: sharing books and stories with individual or small group.
- **Special occasions**: birthdays, festivals, preparing for visits or visitors.
- **Displays**: interest tables, wall displays, posters.
- **Animals**: pets (in the setting or in the home), visits to farms, animal sanctuaries, safari parks.
- **Toys/hobbies**: special days/times for 'show and tell' when children can talk about their special interests/favourite objects.

 Activity!

Think of examples of informal communication from your own experiences of working with children.

Figure 11.2: Promoting language diversity

The language of learning

Effective communication is not just about conversations with young children. It also involves children being able to understand and use the language of learning. That is, the language needed to: understand concepts; participate in problem-solving and develop ideas and opinions.

Adults need to be able to utilise language effectively themselves in order to encourage and extend children's communication skills. A sound knowledge of children's language development plus the realistic organisation of the setting, activities and time are essential components for effective communication with children.

Helping children to understand the structure of language

As well as enabling children to use language, adults can also help children to understand the rules of language. Once children start to combine words to make sentences, they progress through various stages through which the structure and organisation of language becomes gradually more systematic. This systematic structuring of language is called grammar. For example:

- **Stage 1**: Children use simple two/three word phrases or sentences. Grammatical indicators are not present at this stage: no plurals, for example 'Many car' ; no possessive 's', for example 'Tom teddy'; no tense markers ('ed', 'ing'), for example 'It rain'; no auxiliary verbs ('is', 'do'), for example 'No like cake'. Children only use nouns, verbs, adjectives and adverbs such as 'now' or 'soon'.
- **Stage 2**: Children begin to use grammatical indicators previously missing. Note the irregular use of past-tense forms, such as 'comed' (came), 'goed' (went) and plurals, such as 'sheeps'. Gradually children begin to use grammar in increasingly adult forms.

Children do not learn grammar through imitation alone; children need opportunities to discover the rules of language for themselves by experimenting and being creative with words in a variety of situations. Adults can also help children with grammar by repeating back the correct form of language when the child makes a grammatical error. Some examples are:

- **Possessive pronouns** – the child says: 'This Tom hat and that Teena hat'; the adult replies: 'Yes, that is *your* hat and this is *my* hat'.
- **Possessive's'** – the child says: 'Here Marley boots and teacher boots'; the adult replies: 'Yes, these are Marley*'s* boots and those are Ms Kamen*'s* boots'.
- **Plurals** – the child says: 'We saw sheeps'; the adult replies: 'Yes, we saw *some sheep* at the farm'.
- **Tense markers** – the child says: 'The cat goed out'; the adult replies: 'Yes, the cat *went* outside'. Or the child says: 'Mummy come!'; the adult replies: 'Yes, your mummy is com*ing* into the nursery now'.
- **Auxiliary verbs** – the child says: 'We done play dough': the adult replies: 'Yes, we *did* make play dough this morning'. Or the child says: 'We is walking to the park'; The adult replies: 'Yes, we *are* walking to the park'.
- **Negatives** – the child says: 'I not eat 'nana'; the adult replies: 'I see you *haven't* eaten your banana'.
- **Questions** – the child asks: 'More?'; the adult asks: 'Would you like some more milk?'.

The importance of labelling

Very young children respond to labels even before they can read them; they will ask adults what labels say. Using pictures or objects as well as written words helps children to make sense of labels and to develop their own literacy skills. Labelling introduces young children to one of the important purposes of written language: providing information or directions. Labels encourage children's independence in reading and writing. A special place for children to keep their belongings (whether on a hook, in a drawer, tray or basket) clearly labelled with each child's name, is an essential part of the effective language-rich environment. With very young children, a picture on the left-hand side of the label helps them to remember to work from left to right in reading and writing activities:

Labels on important everyday objects in the setting assist children's early literacy skills and help to extend their vocabulary within a meaningful context. Where possible use sentences rather than single words:

Please put the **crayons** back here.

> # Please close the **door.**

Clearly labelled areas and storage can help extend children's language as well as aiding the development of their social skills and independence:

> # 4 Four children can play with the sand.

Effective communication is also promoted by encouraging children to take responsibility for everyday tasks within the setting. Young children are quite capable of making their own decisions and this helps to develop their independence and extends their communication skills even further. For example, children as young as four years old can: be responsible for tidying up their own activities, getting equipment out (under adult supervision for safety reasons, of course); choose their own activities; follow written and/or pictorial instructions for tasks/activities to be done that day and record weather and other data.

In practice

Nathan (aged 6 years) is a quiet and shy pupil who needs lots of encouragement to participate in group and class discussions. He enjoys books and ICT activities. Suggest ways to encourage his communication skills.

The role of the adult

Adults need to organise appropriate opportunities for language and to ask the right type of questions to stimulate communication. (See section on asking and answering questions in Chapter 3.) Adults can do this by providing a wide range of materials and by encouraging children to talk about their interests, what they are doing and what is happening around them. (See section on the teaching assistant's role in promoting children's language development in Chapter 1.)

The adult needs to act as a facilitator by providing appropriate activities and experiences to enable children to develop their speech, language and communication skills in meaningful situations. To do this the adult needs to:

 key words

Facilitator: person who makes things easier by providing the appropriate environment and resources for learning.

- **Provide opportunities for play which are appropriate to the children's ages/levels of development** especially activities which encourage language and communication, such as imaginative and creative play.
- **Provide opportunities for children's self-expression and self-evaluation** through discussion, news time, circle time, painting, drawing, writing, music making, drama and dance.
- **Be positive towards each child's attempts at language and communication** by considering children's individual interest and abilities, valuing children's home or community language(s), and being aware of children's special language needs (see below)
- **Give positive feedback, praise and encouragement to all children** by commenting positively on children's efforts at communicating in different ways. (See section on the importance of praise and encouragement in Chapter 3.)

 **Activity!**

Describe how you have provided appropriate activities and experiences to enable children to develop their speech, language and communication.

Activities to encourage children's speech, language and communication

All children need activities and materials which encourage language and help to develop communication skills. These activities can be divided into five basic categories:

1. **Exploration**
   - Toys and other interesting objects to look at and play with, such as household objects (remember safety).
   - Sounds to listen to including voices, music, songs and rhymes.
   - Noise makers, such as commercial and home-made musical instruments.
   - Bath toys and books.
   - Construction materials including wooden bricks, plastic bricks and 'junk' modelling.
   - Natural materials such as water, sand, clay, dough and cooking ingredients.
   - Creative materials such as paint, paper and glue.
   - Outdoor activities and outings including gardening, visits to parks and museums, swimming.
   - Animals including visits to farms and wildlife centres, looking after small pets.
2. **Description**
   - News time, circle time.
   - Recording events, outings, visits and visitors.
   - Books and stories appropriate to age/level of development including cloth books, board books, activity books, pop-up books, picture books, audio books, textbooks, novels and encyclopaedias.
3. **Conversation**
   - Talking about their day, experiences and interests in a variety of settings with other children and adults, such as play group, nursery, school, after school clubs and youth clubs.
   - Talking during imaginative play activities, such as playing with pretend/role play equipment such as dressing up clothes, home corner, play shop, puppets; playing with dolls, teddies and other cuddly toys; playing with small scale toys such as toy cars, garages and road systems, train set and dolls' houses.

- Talking about special events such as birthdays, new baby or religious festivals.
- Talking while doing activities – not necessarily related to the task!

4. **Discussion**
   - Problem solving during activities such as mathematics, science and technology.
   - Follow up discussion after an activity or event such as watching DVD/television or live performance, listening to a story or recorded music.
   - Cooperative group work.
   - Games and puzzles.

5. **Instruction**
   - Preparation before an activity.
   - Explanation of what to do – verbal and/or written on a board.
   - Instructions during an activity to keep the children on task.
   - Extra support for individuals.
   - Introducing or extending knowledge on a specific skill.
   - Step-by-step instructions.
   - Worksheets, workbooks and work cards.
   - Delivering verbal and/or written messages, carrying out errands.

 **Activity!**

Describe an example activity for each of the five categories based on your own experiences of working with children.

Supporting pupils with special language needs

All pupils have *individual* language needs, but some pupils may have *additional* or *special language needs* that affect their ability to communicate effectively with others. Being able to structure and use language is an enormous task for everyone; it takes the first seven to eight years of life to learn how to form all the different sounds correctly. Some sounds are more difficult to pronounce than others, for example: s, sh, scr, br, cr, gr and th. Most children have problems with these sounds at first, but eventually are able to pronounce them properly.

Some pupils may have difficulties with structuring language, for example problems with:

- Phonology: the articulation of sounds, syllables and words (as mentioned above).
- Grammar or syntax: words, phrases or sentence structure.
- Semantics: *understanding* language (receptive difficulties): and/or using language (expressive difficulties).

Many of the activities already suggested in this chapter will be suitable for *all* pupils including those with special language needs. Some pupils, especially those with severely delayed or disordered language development, may need specialist help from a speech and language therapist. (For more detailed information, see the section on supporting pupils with communication and interaction needs in Chapter 13.)

Key Task

Describe how you have (or could have) provided support for pupils with special language needs in your school. Include examples for pupils with additional communication and/or interaction needs.

NOS Links:

Level 3: STL 18.1   STL 20.2   STL 25.1   STL 25.2   STL 25.3
STL 27.2 (early years) STL 33.1   STL 38.1   STL 38.2   STL 39.1
STL 39.2   STL 40.1   STL 42.1   STL 42.2

Supporting bilingual pupils

Bilingual means 'speaking two languages' which applies to some pupils (and staff) in schools in the United Kingdom. 'Multilingual' is used to describe someone who uses more than two languages. The term 'bilingual' is widely used for all pupils who speak two or more languages.

Promoting language diversity

We live in a multicultural society where a huge variety of languages are used to communicate. We are surrounded by different accents, dialects and other ways of communicating, such as sign language. All pupils should have an awareness and understanding of other people's languages, while still feeling proud of their own community language and being able to share this with others. Pupils in schools where only English (or Welsh) is spoken still need an awareness of other languages to appreciate fully the multicultural society they live in.

You must respect the languages of all the pupils in your school by working with the teacher to provide an environment which promotes language diversity through: welcoming signs in community languages; learning essential greetings in these languages; displaying photographs and pictures reflecting multicultural images; using labels with different languages/writing styles; sharing books, stories and songs in other languages; providing multicultural equipment, such as ethnic dolls, dressing-up clothes, cooking utensils; celebrating festivals; and preparing and sharing food from different cultures.

While promoting language diversity we need to remember that we live in a society where English is the dominant language; developing language and literacy skills in English is essential to all pupils if they are to become effective communicators both in and outside the school. Most children starting nursery or school will speak English even if they have a different cultural background. However, there are some children who do start nursery or school with little or no English because they are new to this country or English is not used much at home.

Key Task

- Give examples of how your school promotes language diversity and encourages pupils to use their community languages.
- How do (or could) you provide support for the communication skills of bilingual pupils?

NOS Links:

Level 3:	STL 18.1	STL 20.2	STL 25.1	STL 25.2	STL 25.3	STL 33.1
	STL 35.1	STL 35.2	STL 36.1	STL 36.2	STL 36.3	

Pupils with English as an additional language

With regard to literacy activities, the term for bilingual pupils is often *pupils with English as an additional language* (EAL). There is a broad range of pupils with EAL including pupils who are: literate in English and do not require extra provision; able to converse in English but need help to use language in their school work; literate in languages other than English but need a little extra support with literacy; learning to speak English as well as learning to read and write it; below the levels of language or literacy expected for their age and require adapted materials to meet their language and/or literacy needs.

There are four important factors to consider when providing support for pupils with EAL:

1. **There are different and changing levels of competence involved in speaking two or more languages**. For example, some pupils are still learning their first language while adding words to their second language. Very young children often do 'language mixing' which involves combining words from two or more languages when involved in conversations or discussions.

2. **Different situations prompt the use of one language over another**. Pupils who are more fluent in English often use whichever language is appropriate to a particular situation. For example: they might speak to one grandparent using Standard English; speak to another grandparent using Mirpuri and Punjabi; conversations with parents and siblings might involve a mixture of Punjabi and English; and language at the setting might involve the use of a local dialect such as that used in the 'Black Country' in the West Midlands.

3. **The range of communication and literacy skills may be different in each language**. Pupils may be aware of different writing systems being used by their families and in the local community. They may be able to speak a particular language and not be able to write in that language. Pupils may have seen writing which went from right to left, as in the Arabic or Hebrew scripts, not just from left to right as with English; or they may be used to vertical rather than horizontal writing systems such as Mandarin Chinese or Japanese. Developing literacy skills can be a confusing experience for some pupils with EAL who could be learning to read and write in English in school while learning the same skills in Punjabi at home or in a community school *and* also learning Arabic when studying the Koran at Saturday school.

4. **Changing circumstances can affect a pupil's use of their community language**. For example, moving to a different area where cultural attitudes may be different so that more or less of the pupil's community language is used.

(Whitehead, 1996)

Pupils with English as an additional language do not see their use of different languages as a difficulty. Adults working in schools need to maintain this attitude and to encourage bilingual pupils to see their linguistic abilities as the *asset* it really is in our multicultural society.

You can support pupils with English as an additional language by:

- Encouraging the pupils to use their community languages some of the time; this promotes security and social acceptance which will make learning English easier.
- Asking the teacher to invite parents/grandparents to read or tell stories in community languages or to be involved with small groups for cooking, sewing or craft activities.
- Using songs and rhymes to help introduce new vocabulary.
- Using other areas of the curriculum to develop language skills in a meaningful context, for example focus on words used when working on the computer or during science experiments.
- Using play activities and/or games to encourage and extend language.

As well as communication, language and literacy activities you can use other areas of the curriculum to develop language skills in a meaningful context, for example use play activities and/or games to encourage and extend language or focus on the words used when working on the computer or during science experiments.

Specialist language support staff can help to ensure that EAL learners are encouraged to apply what they have learnt in the literacy hour across the curriculum. Language support teachers should work with teachers and other staff (such as nursery nurses, teaching assistants) to select resources and texts that meet the needs of EAL learners.

In practice

Paramjit (aged 5 years) is a very quiet pupil who speaks a limited amount of English. She requires lots of extra support for EAL especially during literacy and numeracy activities, but is making steady progress. She likes books and stories. Suggest ways in which to help her continue making progress with EAL.

It is important to distinguish between pupils who have additional language learning needs and those who also have special educational needs (SEN). Some pupils with EAL may also be assessed as having special educational needs. (See section on identification, assessment and provision for pupils with SEN in Chapter 13.)

 ## Key Task

Design and make a booklet about supporting the learning and development of pupils in bilingual or multilingual settings. Include information on the following: the community languages used by the pupils in your school; the school's activities and resources available to support pupils with EAL, such as dual language books; bilingual story sessions; language support staff; multilingual resources from the community centre or local education development centre, etc.

NOS Links:

Level 3:	STL 18.1	STL 20.2	STL 25.1	STL 25.2	STL 25.3	STL 33.1
	STL 35.1	STL 35.2	STL 36.1	STL 36.2	STL 36.3	

Summary of the key points in this chapter:

- **Defining speech, language and communication** including: why we communicate; how we communicate; the modes of language.

- **Language acquisition theories** including: the nurture theory; the nature theory; the social interaction theory.

- **Factors that may affect language development** including: environmental factors and social/cultural factors; poverty; race and culture; family size; parental background and/or expectations; the language environment; group organisation; links with social and emotional development.

- **Communicating with children** including: providing opportunities for conversation; the language of learning; helping children to understand the structure of language; the importance of labelling; the role of the adult; activities to encourage children's speech, language and communication.

- **Supporting pupils with special language needs**.

- **Supporting bilingual pupils** including: promoting language diversity; pupils with English as an additional language.

Further reading

Alcott, M. (2002) *An Introduction to Children with Special Needs*. Hodder & Stoughton.

Bruce, T. and Meggitt, C. (2002) *Child Care and Education*. Third Edition. Hodder & Stoughton.

Conteh, J. (ed) (2006) *Promoting Learning for Bilingual Pupils 3–11: Opening Doors to Success*. Sage Publications Ltd.

Godwin, D. and Perkins, M. (2002) *Teaching Language and Literacy in the Early Years*. David Fulton Publishers.

Harding, J. and Meldon-Smith, L. (2000) *How to Make Observations and Assessments*. Second Edition. Hodder and Stoughton.

Haslam, L. et al. (2004) *English as an Additional Language: Meeting the Challenge in the Classroom*. David Fulton Publishers.

Lindon, J. (2005) *Understanding Child Development: Linking Theory and Practice*. Hodder Arnold.

Palmer, S. and Bayley, R. (2004) *Foundations of Literacy: A Balanced Approach to Language, Listening and Literacy Skills in the Early Years*. Network Educational Press Ltd.

Pim, C. (2010) *How to Support English as an Additional Language*. LDA.

Siraj-Blatchford, J. and Clarke, P. (2000) *Supporting Identity, Diversity and Language in the Early Years*. Open University Press.

Smyth, G. (2003) *Helping Bilingual Pupils to Access the Curriculum*. David Fulton Publishers.

Whitehead, M. R. (2004) *Language and Literacy in the Early Years*. Sage Publications Ltd.

Wilson, A. (2004) *Supporting Speaking and Listening*. David Fulton Publishers.

12. Supporting literacy and numeracy development

This chapter relates to QCF unit:

TDA 3.11 Support literacy development

TDA 3.12 Support numeracy development

TDA 3.15 Provide literacy and numeracy support

National frameworks and curriculum guidelines for English

You should know the relevant national regulatory frameworks and curriculum guidelines for teaching English (or Welsh) relevant to the pupils you work with. (Information about curriculum frameworks is in Chapter 6.)

The Primary Framework for Literacy

In October 2006 the Primary Framework for Literacy replaced The National Literacy Strategy Framework for Teaching YR to Y6 (1998) for pupils aged 3 to 11 years. The renewed Framework builds on the learning that has taken place since the original frameworks for teaching literacy and mathematics were introduced in 1998 and 1999.

The renewed literacy Framework is different from the 1998 framework in the following ways: it is an electronic version and with simplified learning objectives. The online version of the Primary Framework for Literacy can be accessed at:

http://nationalstrategies.standards.dcsf.gov.uk/primary/primaryframework/literacyframework.

The electronic Framework provides a resource that will be added to and expanded with additional support and material as the Framework project develops. Simplified learning objectives give a broad overview of the literacy curriculum in the primary phase. The learning objectives are aligned to twelve strands to demonstrate progression in each strand. These strands link directly to the Early Learning Goals and aspects of English in the National Curriculum. Covering the learning objectives allows pupils to reach the Early Learning

key words

Learning objectives: specific outcomes of the knowledge, skills or attitudes learners should be able to demonstrate following instruction or teaching.

Literacy: the ability to read and write.

Goals for Communication, Language and Literacy and the appropriate National Curriculum levels for Key Stages 1 and 2. The learning objectives are taught through the full range of texts described in the National Curriculum for English. The twelve strands are as follows:

1. Speaking
2. Listening and responding
3. Group discussion and interaction
4. Drama
5. Word recognition: decoding (reading) and encoding (spelling)
6. Word structure and spelling
7. Understanding and interpreting texts
8. Engaging and responding to texts
9. Creating and shaping texts
10. Text struture and organisation
11. Sentence structure and punctuation
12. Presentation.

(DfES, 2006)

The literacy hour

Pupils have daily lessons for literacy where they are taught the knowledge, skills and understanding set out in the National Curriculum for English. The guidance in the renewed Framework still places emphasis on carefully planned, purposeful, well-directed teaching and learning. When the literacy framework was first published the context demanded that attention was given to the structure and organisation of the lesson. Now the challenge is about improving and refining what is in place. The literacy hour has been successful in structuring the pace of learning and planning for progression through Key Stages 1 and 2. The literacy hour provides a structure for teaching in Key Stages 1 and 2, which can be adapted and revised to be sufficiently flexible to meet the learning needs of all pupils, and may sometimes be planned as individual lessons. The renewed Framework promotes planning across a sequence of lessons that offers pupils continuity with a blend of approaches that sustain the challenge and maintain an interest in learning (DfES, 2006).

The Framework for Secondary English

Equipping secondary school pupils with effective literacy skills is the key to raising standards across all curriculum subject areas, to achieving success in their GCSEs and to preparing pupils for adult life.

The renewed Framework builds on the original Framework for teaching English, which was produced in 2001. It is based on the programmes of study for the new secondary curriculum. The Framework is designed to increase pupils' access to excellent teaching and engaging, purposeful learning that will enable them to make good progress through Key Stages 3 and 4.

The Framework for Secondary English identifies yearly learning objectives that encourage ambition and provide challenge for all pupils, showing progression in the subject. The Framework for English learning objectives set out in reasonable detail the knowledge, skills and understanding which need to be acquired in English across a period of time. The objectives are organised across Key Stage 3 and Key Stage 4. These show strands of development in each subject which describe progression in learning, and set out a minimum expectation for the progression in learning of most pupils. The ten strands of progression are as follows:

1. Listening and responding
2. Speaking and presenting
3. Group discussion and interaction
4. Drama, role play and performance
5. Reading for meaning: understanding and responding to print, electronic and multi-modal texts
6. Understanding the author's craft
7. Composition: generating ideas, planning and drafting
8. Composition: Shaping and constructing language for expression and effect
9. Conventions: drawing on conventions and structures
10. Exploring and analysing language.

(DCSF, 2010)

Detailed information about the Framework for Secondary English can be accessed at: **http://nationalstrategies.standards.dcsf.gov.uk/node/16067?uc = force_uj.**

 **Activity!**

What are the national frameworks and curriculum guidelines for teaching English (and Welsh where applicable) relevant to your school?

National Curriculum targets for English

During Key Stage 1 pupils learn how to express their ideas and experiences clearly and creatively using spoken and written forms of language. Pupils listen to and read stories, poems and rhymes from all over the world as well as using books to discover new information.

During Key Stage 2 pupils learn to listen to and discuss the ideas of others in addition to presenting their own ideas. Pupils read for pleasure and to discover new information as well as being able to discuss their opinions about what they have read. Pupils should now be able to put their thoughts into writing more easily due to increased understanding of language structure, spelling and punctuation.

During Key Stage 3 pupils should continue to extend the effective use of the four key English skills by speaking clearly, listening closely, reading carefully and writing fluently. These skills will help pupils to express themselves creatively and increase their confidence about speaking in public and writing for others. Pupils should read classic and contemporary prose and poetry from around the world, examining how writers use language and considering the social/moral issues raised.

During Key Stage 4 pupils learn to use language confidently, both in their academic studies and for the world beyond school. Pupils use and analyse complex features of language; they are keen readers who can read many kinds of text and make articulate and perceptive comments about them.

Key Task

Observe a pupil during a literacy activity in Key Stage 1, 2, 3 or 4. Then answer these questions:

- Did the pupil achieve the learning objectives set? If not, why not?
- If the pupil has achieved the learning objectives, what effect has it had (for example on the pupil's behaviour, learning, any special needs)?
- Were the learning objectives too easy or too hard for the pupil?
- How did any staff involvement affect the pupil's achievement?
- Was the lesson or activity plan successful? If not, why not?

NOS Links:

Level 3:   **STL25.1   STL25.2   STL25.3   STL29.1**

Developing literacy skills

As a teaching assistant you may be involved in helping pupils to develop their literacy skills. Working under the direction of the teacher you should provide support for pupils' literacy development during whole class, group and individual learning activities including: discussing with the teacher how the learning activities will be organised and what your particular role will be; providing the agreed support as appropriate to the different learning needs of pupils; giving feedback to the teacher about the progress of pupils in developing literacy and language skills.

Defining literacy

Literacy means the ability to read and write. The word 'literacy' has only recently been applied as the definitive term for reading and writing, especially since the introduction of the National Literacy Strategy in schools. It makes sense to use the term 'literacy' as the skills of reading and writing do complement one another and are developed together. Reading and writing are forms of communication based on spoken language. Pupils need effective speaking and listening skills in order to develop literacy skills. Literacy unites the important skills of reading, writing, speaking and listening.

The importance of literacy

Developing literacy skills is an essential aspect of development and learning. Without literacy skills individuals are very restricted in their ability to: function effectively in school, college or at work; access information and new ideas; communicate their own ideas to others and participate fully and safely in society. Education depends on individuals being able to read and write. Nearly all jobs and careers require at least basic literacy (and numeracy) skills. Our society also requires people to use literacy skills in everyday life: reading signs such as street names, shop names, traffic signs and warning signs; reading newspapers, magazines, instructions, recipes, food labels; dealing with correspondence such as reading and replying to letters, household bills, bank statements, wage slips and benefits; using computers, the internet and email; and writing shopping lists, memos and notes.

At the centre of all learning are two key skills: literacy and numeracy. Literacy is probably the more important of the two as pupils need literacy to access other areas of the curriculum. For example, to tackle a mathematics problem they might need to read the question accurately before applying the appropriate numeracy skills, or they may need to record the results of a science experiment in a written form.

Developing speaking and listening skills

Speaking and listening are part of the National Curriculum programmes of study for English: Speaking and listening, Reading and Writing. These three areas all focus on language and how it is used in the different modes (see section on supporting communication and language development in Chapter 1). Each mode has its own distinct features but speaking and listening, reading and writing are interdependent. Speaking and listening skills involve:

- Speaking: being able to speak clearly and to develop and sustain ideas in talk.
- Listening: developing active listening strategies and critical skills of analysis.
- Group discussion and interaction: taking different roles in groups, making a range of contributions and working collaboratively.
- Drama: improvising and working in role, scripting and performing, and responding to performances.

(DfES, 2003c)

All areas of the school curriculum provide opportunities for the development of children's speaking and listening skills. The skills used will vary according to the curriculum area. For example, pupils may be involved in learning activities that encourage them to: describe, interpret, predict and hypothesise in Mathematics and Science; express opinions and discuss design ideas in Art, Design and Technology; discuss cause and effect in History and Geography; and discuss social or moral issues in PSHE and RE.

 Key Task

Describe how you have helped pupils to develop their speaking and listening skills in at least one of the following: discussion during news, circle time or tutorials; playing a game with a child or small group of children; sharing a story, poem or rhyme.

NOS Links:

Level 3: **STL18.1**   **STL20.2**   **STL8.2 (ICT)**   **STL23.2**   **STL25.3**   **STL27.2 (early years)**

Developing reading skills

Reading is the process of turning groups of written symbols into speech sounds. In English this means being able to read from left to right, from the top of the page to the bottom and being able to recognise letter symbols plus their combinations as words. Reading is not just one skill; it involves a variety of different abilities: visual and auditory discrimination; language and communication skills; word identification skills; conceptual understanding; comprehension skills; and memory and concentration.

Being able to read does not happen suddenly. Reading is a complex process involving different skills, some of which (such as visual discrimination and communication skills) the individual has been developing since birth. Being able to use and understand spoken language forms the basis for developing reading skills. A child who has a wide variety of early language experiences will have developed many of the skills needed for learning to read. See section on supporting communication and language development in Chapter 1 and supporting speech, language and communication (Chapter 11).

Children who are pushed too hard by being forced to read and write before they are ready may actually be harmed in terms of their literacy development as they can be put off reading, writing and other related activities. The area of learning, communication, language and literacy, included in the early learning goals for the EYFS provides guidelines to help early years staff (and parents) understand the importance of informal approaches to language and literacy.

There is no set age at which children are magically ready to read although most children learn to read between the ages of 4½ and 6 years old. The age at which a child learns to read depends on a number of factors: physical maturity and coordination skills; social and emotional development; language experiences, especially access to books; interest in stories and rhymes; concentration and memory skills; and opportunities for play.

Reading skills checklist:

1. Can the child see and hear properly?
2. Are the child's coordination skills developing within the expected norm?
3. Can the child understand and follow simple verbal instructions?
4. Can the child cooperate with an adult and concentrate on an activity for short periods?
5. Does the child show interest in the details of pictures?
6. Does the child enjoy looking at books plus joining in with rhymes and stories?
7. Can the child retell parts of a story in the right order?
8. Can the child tell a story using pictures?
9. Can the child remember letter sounds and recognise them at the beginning of words?
10. Does the child show pleasure or excitement when able to read words in school?

If the answer is 'yes' to most of these questions, the child is probably ready to read; if the answer is 'no' to any of the questions, the child may need additional support or experiences in those areas before they are ready to read.

Approaches to reading

The whole word, or 'look and say', approach involves teaching pupils to recognise a small set of key words (usually related to a reading scheme) by means of individual words printed on flashcards. Pupils recognise the different words by shape and other visual differences. Once pupils have developed a satisfactory sight vocabulary, they go onto the actual reading scheme. The whole word approach is useful for learning difficult words which do not follow the usual rules of English language. The drawback is that this approach does not help pupils to work out new words for themselves.

4. **Using displays as a stimulus for discussions and to consolidate learning**, for example wall and interactive tabletop displays with interesting objects to talk about, look at and/or play with as well as recorded sounds to listen to including voices, music, songs, rhymes and musical instruments.

5. **Providing opportunities for pupils to follow and give instructions** such as: introducing or extending knowledge on a specific skill; specifying tasks (verbal and/or written on a board); listening to step-by-step instructions; explaining worksheets, work cards or textbooks; verbal instructions during an activity to keep pupils on task or providing extra support for individual pupils; delivering verbal/written messages, errands.

6. **Encouraging pupils to participate in games to develop auditory and visual discrimination** like sound lotto and 'guess the sound' using sounds of everyday objects or musical instruments. Encourage pupils to participate in matching games and memory games to develop visual discrimination and memory, skills such as snap, matching pairs, jigsaws and games like 'I went shopping...'. Provide fun activities to develop letter recognition such as: 'I spy...' using letter sounds; going on a 'letter hunt' (looking around the classroom for things beginning with a particular letter); hang up an 'alphabet washing line'; singing alphabet songs and rhymes.

7. **Providing opportunities for the pupils to write for different purposes and for different audiences** such as: writing about their own experiences as appropriate to their age and level of development, for example news and recording events; creating their own stories and poems as a means of expressing their feelings and ideas; using class or group topics as well as the pupils' own interests to stimulate their ideas for stories and poems; and using storybooks as a starting point for the pupils' own creative writing. Provide pupils with opportunities to write in different styles such as: writing letters; writing reports; writing step-by-step instructions; designing posters, signs and notices. Encourage pupils to use independent spelling techniques such as word banks, personal word books and dictionaries.

8. **Using alternative writing methods** to release younger pupils or those with coordination difficulties (such as dyspraxia) from their physical limitations of writing, for example, allowing them to dictate their ideas while an adult acts as scribe or use a tape recorder or word processor.

9. **Considering the individual interests and abilities of pupils** including valuing children's home experiences/cultural backgrounds and being aware of possible developmental or psychological difficulties that may affect their speaking and listening skills by carefully observing children's development and learning. (See section below on supporting children with special literacy needs.)

10. **Using Information and Communication Technology** (ICT) including television, CD-ROMs and the internet as additional stimuli for discussions and ideas. ICT can also be used to introduce or reinforce information on topics and themes within the setting. Remember that ICT is not a substitute for other forms of communication such as conversation and children's play (see Chapter 11).

Key Task

Give examples of activities you have used to help pupils develop their literacy skills.

NOS Links:

Level 3:   **STL18.1   STL20.2   STL8.2 (ICT)   STL23.2   STL25.1   STL27.2 (early years)**

Resources to support literacy development

The classroom needs to provide the space and opportunities for effective communication to take place and to enable pupils to use the different modes of language (see page 38) while participating in all aspects of the school curriculum. Classroom organisation and groupings will encourage and support active participation by: grouping and regrouping pupils for different activities in order to develop their literacy skills; having supportive pupils in each group, for example competent readers and writers; and using a range of grouping strategies, such as mixed/like ability, language, interest, random, gender and age. The classroom organisation should encourage the practice and development of all four language skills (speaking and listening, reading and writing) through collaborative activities that involve talk, opportunities for feedback to others, activities matched to pupils' needs and abilities and activities that have a clear sense of progression. Suitable areas and resources should be provided to facilitate the development of pupils' literacy skills.

Areas for the primary classroom include:

- **Writing tables**: enabling pupils to use a variety of writing tools (crayons, pencils, pens, pastels, chalks) on different shapes, sizes and types of paper (plain, coloured, graph).
- **Displays**: interest tables; displays of pupils' work and construction models; wall displays and posters to provide a stimulus for language and learning.
- **Sand and/or water trays plus other science and mathematics equipment**: to encourage exploration and conversation.
- **Pretend play areas**: home corner, shop, café, post office or space station to encourage language and communication skills through imaginative play.
- **Book displays and story corner**: to promote pupils' interest in books and to develop their literacy skills.
- **Computers**: to extend the pupils' range of literacy skills through word processing, referencing skills.

Areas for the secondary classroom include:

- **Suitable writing tables and writing materials for the curriculum area**: pens for writing activities; pens, pencils and plain or graph paper for recording results in Mathematics, Science and Geography.
- **Displays**: interest tables; wall displays including pupils' own work; posters to stimulate discussion and further learning.
- **Varied and interesting science or mathematics equipment/materials**: to stimulate exploration and discussion during experiments.

- **Books relevant to the curriculum area**: to promote interest in books, to develop literacy skills across the curriculum and to extend knowledge of the curriculum area.
- **Computers**: to extend literacy skills through word processing, researching and referencing; to extend knowledge in other areas such as graphs, statistics, etc.

Visual aids should play an essential part in the presentation and introduction of lessons or topics, for example: DVDs; maps; posters; pictures; interesting objects related to the topic or theme and computer graphics. Displays in the classroom and around the school should reflect linguistic and cultural diversity. Dual language textbooks should be available and in use where appropriate.

 Activity!

List the resources available in your school to support literacy development.

Figure 12.1: Pupil sharing a book with a teaching assistant

The teaching assistant's role in supporting literacy skills

The teaching assistant plays a key role in supporting the teacher and pupils during literacy activities. You need to find out from the teacher how the literacy activities are to be organised and your specific role in supporting various learning activities including class discussions, group activities and tasks for individuals. You must be able to: understand the intended learning outcomes for the pupils; agree the support strategies to be used for each pupil; obtain the resources required; implement the agreed strategies; provide feedback and encouragement during the activity; monitor the progress of the pupils and report any problems to the teacher.

Strategies to help pupils develop literacy skills

Support strategies to help pupils to develop their literacy skills include:

- Using targeted prompts and feedback to encourage independent reading and writing.
- Encouraging pupils to participate in shared reading and writing activities.
- Developing phonic knowledge and skills to help pupils read and spell accurately.
- Using specific reading or writing support strategies, such as paired reading or writing frames.
- Using specific reading or writing support programmes, such as graded reading books, Additional Literacy Support.
- Repeating instructions given by the teacher.
- Taking notes for a pupil while the teacher is talking.
- Explaining difficult words and phrases to a pupil.
- Promoting the use of dictionaries.
- Reading and clarifying textbook/worksheet activity for a pupil.
- Reading a story to an individual pupil or small group.
- Playing a word game with an individual pupil or small group.
- Directing computer-assisted learning programmes.
- Assisting pupils with special equipment such as a hearing aid or a Dictaphone.
- Encouraging shy or reticent pupils to participate in conversations and discussions.
- Providing any other appropriate assistance during an activity.
- Monitoring pupil progress during an activity.
- Reporting problems and successes to the teacher.

Figure 12.2: Pupils engaged in a literacy activity

Factors affecting support for literacy activities

Despite careful planning and organisation, you may have problems in providing support for pupils during literacy activities. You should know and understand the sorts of problems that might occur. For example: difficulties with the quantity, quality, suitability or availability of learning resources; issues relating to space, comfort, noise levels or disruptions within the learning environment; factors that may affect a pupil's ability to learn during literacy activities, such as social and cultural background, special educational needs such as learning difficulties or behaviour problems (see section below on supporting pupils with special literacy needs). You will need to be able to deal with any problems you may have in providing support for pupils as planned. For example: modifying or adapting an activity; providing additional activities to extend their learning; providing an alternative version of the activity; presenting the materials in different ways; offering a greater or lesser level of assistance; coping with insufficient materials or equipment breakdown and dealing with uncooperative or disruptive pupils.

 Key Task

Give a detailed account of an activity you have used to help pupils to develop their literacy skills. Include information on:

- the organisation of the activity including the resources used
- how you implemented the agreed strategies for each pupil
- how you provided feedback and encouragement during the activity
- how you monitored the progress of the pupils
- the learning outcomes achieved by the pupils
- how you reported any problems in providing support to the teacher.

NOS Links:

Level 3: STL18.1   STL20.2   STL8.2 (ICT)   STL23.2   STL23.3   STL24.2   STL25.1
STL25.2   STL25.3   STL27.2 (early years)   STL27.3 (early years)

Supporting pupils with special literacy needs

Some pupils may have special literacy needs due to additional language needs, for example, bilingual learners (see Chapter 11). Some pupils may have special literacy needs due to cognitive and learning difficulties, sensory impairment, physical disabilities or behavioural difficulties (see Chapter 13). The range of pupils with special educational needs (SEN) varies from school to school. Many pupils with SEN may not have special literacy needs and will not require extra or different literacy support. However, many classes will have one or more pupil with identified SEN who require a modified approach to the national literacy strategy.

There are two broad groups of pupils with special literacy needs:

1. A larger group of pupils who experience minor difficulties in learning, which is reflected in their attainment of levels of literacy which are below those expected for pupils of their age. The structure provided by the National Literacy Strategy can benefit these pupils. The pupils can usually overcome these difficulties through normal teaching strategies and will soon develop the essential literacy skills that will enable them to catch up and work at a comparable level to the rest of their year group.

2. The second smaller group includes pupils with severe and complex learning difficulties that require the use of different teaching strategies. These pupils may require different levels of work from the rest of their year group. They may need to be taught at a different pace for all or most of their school years. Some pupils with SEN will always need access to systems such as symbols, signing, Braille or electronic communicators.

(DfES, 1998)

Some pupils with identified SEN may work at earlier levels than those specified in the National Literacy Strategy Framework for their year group. Some pupils with SEN will need to work on one term's work for several terms. With structured, intensive teaching, some of these pupils will gradually progress through the levels in the Framework and will eventually be able to work at the levels appropriate to their age. Some pupils will require work on the development of particular literacy skills, or to work on some skills for longer than others, for example, pupils with speech and language difficulties may need to work on programmes devised by a speech therapist or specialist language teacher (see Chapter 13).

 ## Activity!

- Describe how you could provide support for a pupil with special literacy needs.
- Use examples from your own experience if applicable.

 ## Key Task

Design a booklet for new teaching assistants outlining your school's approach to supporting literacy. Include the following:

- a brief statement about the importance of literacy
- the school aims for literacy
- a brief outline of the curriculum requirements for English
- the key points of the literacy strategy
- a brief guide to how the school supports pupils with special literacy needs
- the role of the teaching assistant in supporting literacy skills.

NOS Links:

Level 3: STL 8.2 (ICT)   STL 18.1   STL20.2   STL 23.1   STL 23.2
STL 23.3   STL 24.1   STL 24.2   STL 25.1   STL 25.2
STL 25.3   STL 27.2 (early years)   STL 33.2   STL 35.2
STL 38.2 (SEN)   STL39.1   STL40.1   STL40.2   STL42.1

National frameworks and curriculum guidelines for mathematics

You should know the relevant national regulatory frameworks and curriculum guidelines for teaching mathematics relevant to the pupils you work with. (Information on curriculum frameworks is in Chapter 6.)

The Primary Framework for Mathematics

In October 2006 the Primary Framework for Mathematics replaced The National Numeracy Strategy – Framework for teaching mathematics from Reception to Y6 (1999) and applies to pupils aged 3 to 11 years. The renewed Framework builds on the learning that has taken place since the original Frameworks for teaching literacy and mathematics were introduced in 1998 and 1999.

The renewed Mathematics Framework is different from the 1999 Framework in the following ways: there is an electronic version and it has simplified learning objectives. The online version (Primary Framework for Literacy and Mathematics) can be accessed at **www.standards. dfes.gov.uk/primaryframeworks**. The electronic Framework provides a resource that will be added to and expanded with additional support and material as the Framework project develops. This will include any necessary revisions to the early years elements following the EYFS consultation (DfES, 2006).

Simplified learning objectives give a broad overview of the Mathematics Curriculum in the primary phase. The learning objectives are aligned to seven strands to demonstrate progression in each strand. These strands link directly to the Early Learning Goals and aspects of Mathematics in the National Curriculum. Covering the learning objectives will allow children to reach the Early Learning Goals for Mathematical Development and the appropriate National Curriculum levels for Key Stages 1 and 2. The learning objectives will be taught through the full range of texts described in the National Curriculum for Mathematics (DfES, 2006).

The seven strands are as follows.

1. Using and applying mathematics
2. Counting and understanding number
3. Knowing and using number facts
4. Calculating
5. Understanding shape
6. Measuring
7. Handling data

The daily mathematics lesson

Pupils have daily lessons for mathematics where they are taught the knowledge, skills and understanding set out in the National Curriculum for Mathematics. The guidance in the renewed Framework still places emphasis on carefully planned, purposeful, well-directed teaching and learning. When the numeracy framework was first published the context demanded that attention was given to the structure and organisation of the lesson. Now the challenge is about improving and refining what is in place. The daily mathematics lesson has been successful in structuring the pace of learning and planning for progression through Key

Stages 1 and 2. The daily mathematics lesson provides a structure for teaching in Key Stages 1 and 2, which can be adapted and revised to be sufficiently flexible to meet the learning needs of all pupils, and may sometimes be planned as individual lessons. The renewed Framework promotes planning across a sequence of lessons that offers pupils continuity with a blend of approaches that sustain the challenge and maintain an interest in learning (DfES, 2006).

The Framework for Secondary Mathematics

The ability to use mathematical thinking is essential for all members of modern society – in schools, the workplace, business and finance. Mathematics is fundamental to providing pupils with tools for understanding Science, Technology, Engineering and Economics. Pupils who have functional skills in mathematics can think independently in applied and abstract ways, as well as being able to reason, solve problems and assess risk (DCSF, 2010).

The renewed Framework builds on the original Framework for teaching mathematics produced in 2001. It is based on the programmes of study for the new secondary curriculum. The Framework is designed to increase pupils' access to excellent teaching and engaging, purposeful learning that will enable them to make good progress through Key Stages 3 and 4.

The Framework for Secondary Mathematics has yearly learning objectives that encourage ambition and provide challenge for all pupils, showing progression in the subject. The Framework for Mathematics' learning objectives set out in reasonable detail the knowledge, skills and understanding which need to be acquired in mathematics across a period of time. The objectives are organised across Key Stage 3 and Key Stage 4. These show strands of development in each subject which describe progression in learning, and set out a minimum expectation for the progression in learning of most pupils. The five strands of progression are as follows:

1. Mathematical processes and applications
2. Number
3. Algebra
4. Geometry and measures
5. Statistics

(DCSF, 2010)

Detailed information about the Framework for Secondary Mathematics can be accessed at: **http://nationalstrategies.standards.dcsf.gov.uk/node/16014?uc = force_uj.**

 **Activity!**

What are the national frameworks and curriculum guidelines for teaching mathematics relevant to your school?

National Curriculum targets for mathematics

During Key Stage 1 pupils learn to count and do basic number calculations, such as addition and subtraction. Pupils learn how to talk about mathematical problems and work out how to solve them through practical activities. Pupils demonstrate their thinking and problem-solving skills by using objects, pictures, diagrams, simple lists, tables, charts, words, numbers and symbols. They do mental calculations (work out sums in their heads) without relying on calculators. They handle and describe the various features of basic shapes. They learn to estimate and measure a range of everyday objects.

During Key Stage 2 pupils learn more about numbers and the number system including doing more difficult number calculations such as multiplication and division. Pupils talk about mathematical problems and decide on strategies to tackle them. Pupils demonstrate their thinking and problem-solving skills by using mathematical language, diagrams, words, numbers and symbols. Pupils learn how to use calculators to solve certain mathematical problems, but they are expected to solve most problems using mental calculations or writing them down on paper. They handle and describe the various features of more complex shapes. They learn to answer questions by selecting, organising and presenting appropriate data using tables, charts, and graphs.

During Key Stage 3 pupils learn more about numbers and the number system, more complex calculations, different ways of solving mathematical problems, and algebra. Pupils talk about mathematical problems and decide on strategies to tackle them. Pupils demonstrate their thinking and problem-solving skills by using more complex mathematical language, diagrams, words, numbers and symbols. Pupils learn to use scientific calculators to solve complex mathematical problems but they are still expected to solve most problems using mental calculations or writing them down on paper. They learn more about shapes and coordinates, constructing shapes (geometry), and measurement. They continue to answer questions by selecting, organising and presenting appropriate data using tables, charts, and graphs. Pupils learn to solve increasingly demanding mathematical problems, including problems that require a step-by-step approach to reach a solution.

In Key Stage 4 there are two programmes of study for Mathematics: foundation and higher. Pupils may be taught either the foundation or higher programme of study. The foundation programme of study is intended for those pupils who have not attained a secure Level 5 at the end of Key Stage 3. Pupils studying at the foundation level should: consolidate their understanding of basic mathematics, which will help them to tackle unfamiliar problems in the workplace and everyday life and develop the knowledge and skills they need in the future; become increasingly proficient in mathematical calculations; collect data, learn statistical techniques to analyse data and use ICT to present and interpret the results. The higher programme of study is intended for students who have attained a secure Level 5 at the end of Key Stage 3. Pupils studying at the higher level should: use short chains of deductive reasoning, develop their own proofs, and begin to understand the importance of proof in mathematics; see the importance of mathematics as an analytical tool for solving problems; refine their calculating skills to include powers, roots and numbers expressed in standard form; learn to handle data through practical activities, using a broader range of skills and techniques, including sampling; develop the confidence and flexibility to solve unfamiliar problems and to use ICT appropriately.

 **Key Task**

Observe a pupil during a mathematics activity in Key Stage 1, 2, 3 or 4. Then answer these questions:

- Did the pupil achieve the learning objectives set? If not, why not?
- If the pupil has achieved the learning objectives, what effect has it had (for example on the pupil's behaviour, learning, any special needs)?
- Were the learning objectives too easy or too hard for the pupil?
- How did any staff involvement affect the pupil's achievement?
- Was the lesson or activity plan successful? If not, why not?

NOS Links:
Level 3:   STL26.1   STL26.2   STL29.1

Developing numeracy skills

As a teaching assistant you may be involved in helping pupils to develop their numeracy skills. Working under the direction of the teacher you should provide support for pupils' numeracy development during whole class, group and individual learning activities including: discussing with the teacher how the learning activities will be organised and what your particular role will be; providing the agreed support as appropriate to the different learning needs of pupils; and giving feedback to the teacher about the progress of pupils in developing mathematical knowledge and skills.

Defining numeracy

The term 'numeracy' was introduced in about 1982 to describe what was previously called arithmetic. Individuals who are competent at arithmetic have always been described as 'numerate'; now this competency is called 'numeracy'. Numeracy is more than an ability to do basic arithmetic. Numeracy is a proficiency that involves confidence and competence with numbers and measures. It requires an understanding of the number system, a repertoire of computational skills and an inclination and ability to solve number problems in various contexts. Numeracy also demands practical understanding of the ways in which data is gathered, by counting and measuring, and is presented in graphs, diagrams and tables.

 **key words**

Numeracy: competency in arithmetic.

The importance of numeracy

Being able to do number calculations confidently is an essential life skill; it helps people function effectively in everyday life. It is also very important as a first step in learning mathematics. We use numeracy in everyday life including: shopping, when checking change, buying the right quantities, getting value for money; cooking, when weighing ingredients; decorating, when calculating the amount of wallpaper, paint, carpet or other materials needed for the required areas; sewing, when measuring materials; when plotting designs on graph paper; and when planning journeys and holidays, through understanding transport timetables, planning the best route, calculating the mileage or the time a journey will take or working out how much petrol is needed for a car journey.

Learning numeracy skills is the central part of mathematics, but children are also taught about geometry (space and shapes) and the beginnings of algebra (number patterns). Children need to develop numeracy skills that involve confidence and competence with numbers and measures including: knowledge and understanding of the number system; knowing by heart various number facts, such as multiplication tables; using a range of mathematical skills; making mental calculations; being able to solve number problems in a variety of contexts; and presenting information about counting and measuring using graphs, diagrams, charts and tables.

Developing mathematical skills

Pupils need to develop the following mathematical skills: using and applying mathematics; counting and understanding number; knowing and using number facts; calculating; understanding shape; measuring and handling data.

Using and applying mathematics

Pupils learn to select an appropriate mathematical skill to tackle or solve a problem. They learn to use words, symbols and basic diagrams to record and give details about how they solved a problem. Pupils develop problem-solving skills in order to work out the best approach to finding a mathematical solution. They learn which questions to ask as well as developing the appropriate skills to answer mathematical problems such as: What is the problem? Which mathematical skill needs to be used? Will a graph, chart or diagram help find the solution?

Counting and understanding number

Many children learn number names and how to count before they begin school. At home and/ or in early years settings (such as day nurseries or playgroups) they do counting activities and sing number songs and rhymes. During the primary school years pupils develop and extend their counting skills. Younger pupils begin with numbers 0 to 20 which are the most difficult to learn as each number name is different; numbers from 20 onwards have recognisable patterns which makes learning numbers up to 100 or more much easier. Pupils begin by counting forwards and then backwards from 20; once they are confident with this they learn to count forwards and backwards in sets of 2, 5 and 10 which helps with doing sums and the early stages of learning multiplication.

Knowing and using number facts

Primary pupils should learn to recognise and use: number symbols and words for whole numbers 1 (one) to 20 (twenty) by 4 to 5 years; all the whole numbers to 100 (hundred) plus halves and quarters by 6 to 7 years; numbers to 10,000 including more fractions and decimal places by 8 to 9 years; all whole numbers, fractions, decimals plus percentages by 10 to 11 years. During the primary school years, pupils also develop knowledge and understanding of the mathematical language relevant to numbers: smaller, bigger; more/less than; even and odd numbers; factors and prime numbers, etc.

From about 4 or 5 years old pupils begin to learn how to make mathematical calculations using real objects to add and subtract small whole numbers. Gradually they recognise number patterns which make doing calculations easier, for example being able to add 4 + 8 means they can also add 400 + 800. Memorising number facts also helps with calculations, such as learning multiplication tables by heart.

Calculating

By age 10 or 11 years pupils should have learned addition, subtraction, multiplication and division using whole numbers, fractions, decimals and negative numbers. As well as learning mental calculations pupils also learn the standard written methods for calculation operations.

Remember, the aim for older children is to calculate mentally and to become less reliant on fingers and apparatus. Older children should be encouraged to consider mental methods first through strategies such as: 'Think first, and try to work it out in your head. Now check on your number line' (DfES, 1999). Children with special needs may need particular equipment, books and materials for mathematics activities. (See section below on supporting pupils with special numeracy needs.)

Understanding shape

In addition to developing competency with numbers, pupils learn to recognise and name geometrical shapes; they also learn about the properties of shapes, such as that a triangle has three sides; a square has four right angles. Pupils learn about directions, angles and plotting points on a graph.

Measuring

Pupils learn to measure mass, distance, area and volume using appropriate units, such as kilogrammes, metres, centimetres or litres. Measuring also includes learning to tell the time in hours and minutes.

Handling data

Handling data is an essential skill in this technological age and using computers is an important aspect of mathematics today. Pupils learn to gather, arrange and convert data into useful information, for example, through working out the likelihood of rain so they know when to wear a raincoat or take an umbrella.

 Activity!

- How did you develop your mathematical skills? How did your own children (if any) develop their mathematical skills? (For example: singing number songs and rhymes; practical maths activities such as sorting shapes, measuring or shopping; playing number games; learning by rote such as reciting times tables; learning formal number operations such as addition, subtraction, multiplication and division.)
- What are the methods used to teach mathematics in your school?
- Consider the similarities and differences between these methods.

Ten ways to help pupils to develop their mathematical skills

You can help pupils to develop their mathematical skills by:

1. **Encouraging pupils to use and apply mathematics to tackle and solve everyday practical mathematical problems**, for example by giving change in shop play and real shopping trips (addition and subtraction); exploring volume and capacity during sand and water play filling various containers to encourage understanding of full, empty, half-full, half-empty, nearly full, nearly empty, more/less than, the same amount, then introduce idea of standard measures, such as litre of juice, pint of milk. Using weighing and measuring activities such as: shop play (using balance scales to compare toys and other items); real shopping (helping to weigh fruit and vegetables); sand play (heavy and light); cooking activities (weighing ingredients to show the importance of standard measures).

2. **Providing opportunities for pupils to use and apply mathematics in the school and wider environment**: orientation exercises, nature walks, Geography and Environmental Studies can develop numeracy skills; educational visits can also contribute to mathematics across the curriculum, for example through visits to science museums.

3. **Encouraging younger pupils to explore numbers** through playing games like dominoes, 'snakes and ladders' and other simple board games; looking for shapes/sizes and making comparisons, price tags and quantities in shop play and real shopping trips; number songs and rhymes like 'One, two, three, four, five, Once I caught a fish alive…'.

4. **Supporting pupils engaged in counting, calculating and solving mathematical problems**, for example addition and subtraction then multiplication and division. Supporting older pupils in employing standard methods to perform mental and written calculations including addition, subtraction, multiplication and division using whole numbers, fractions, decimals and percentages.

5. **Prompting pupils to communicate their reasoning about problems and explaining their solutions** using objects, pictures, diagrams, numbers, symbols and relevant mathematical language, for example using letter symbols in algebra, setting up and using simple equations to solve problems.

6. **Supporting pupils' use of calculator functions to complete complex calculations** and understand the answers calculators give in relation to the initial mathematical problem.

7. **Encouraging pupils to compare, estimate and measure a range of everyday objects**, for example through developing an understanding of length by comparing everyday objects/toys and using mathematical language, such as tall/taller/tallest, short/shorter/shortest, long/longer/longest, same height, same length; measuring objects using appropriate units such as centimetres, metres, kilogrammes or litres.

8. **Helping pupils to tell the time**: o'clock, half past and quarter past the hour; with older pupils telling the time in hours and minutes and solving problems relating to time using a 12-hour or 24-hour clock.

9. **Encouraging pupils to explore shape and space** through activities such as: games involving shape recognition; handling and describing the various features of basic shapes (for example using correct names for basic 2-D and 3-D shapes; knowing how many sides, corners or right angles a shape has); physical activities involving whole turns, half turns and quarter turns or right angles as well as spatial awareness, for example through PE, movement, dance. Helping older pupils to learn more about shapes and coordinates, constructing shapes (geometry), and measurement including using a ruler, protractor and compasses to create lines, angles and 2-D or 3-D shapes.

10. **Using ICT to encourage or extend pupils' knowledge, understanding and skills in mathematics**, for example through playing shape recognition games; writing instructions to create and change shapes on a computer; providing opportunities for pupils to select, collect, organise and present appropriate data using lists, charts, graphs, diagrams, tables, surveys, questionnaires and CD-ROMs.

 ## Key Task

Give examples of activities you have used to help pupils to develop their mathematical skills.

NOS Links:

Level 3: STL18.1 STL20.2 STL8.2 (ICT) STL23.2 STL25.3
STL27.2 (early years)

Resources to support numeracy development

A wide range of equipment and materials provide essential resources for supporting the development of pupils' mathematical skills both in and outside the classroom:

- **Boards and charts**: Large white board for whole class/group teaching and individual white boards for pupils with appropriate marker pens; flip chart and marker pens or chalkboard and chalk; overhead projector, transparencies and appropriate pens.

- **Number lines**: Large number line for teaching purposes at a suitable level for the pupils; a 'washing line' of numbers hung across the room that can be added to/altered; table top number lines, marked and unmarked, for individual use; for younger pupils, number tracks with the spaces numbered to 20, rather than number lines with the points numbered; by end of Key Stage 1 number lines should be to 100; for older pupils, number lines should include negative numbers; by the end of Key Stage 2 need marked and unmarked number lines on which decimals and fractions can be placed.

- **Number cards**: Pack of digit cards 0 to 9 for each pupil to hold up when answering questions in a whole-class setting, two-digit numbers can be formed from cards held side-by-side; place value cards with nine cards printed with multiples of 100 from 100 to 900, nine with multiples of 10 from 10 to 90, and ten with the numbers 0 to 9, two or three-digit numbers can be built up by overlapping cards of different widths; addition and subtraction cards for number bonds, first bonds to 5, then to 10, extending to 20; symbol cards for +, –, that can also be held up in response to questions about the operation needed to solve a problem; large 100 square, displayed where pupils can clearly see and touch it.

- **Mathematics equipment and materials**: small apparatus such as counters, interlocking cubes, wooden cubes, pegs and pegboards, straws, rulers, coins, dominoes, dice; variety of squared paper; selection of number games: range of measuring equipment; sets of shapes; various construction kits; pencils and pens for recording; calculators when required.

- **Books**: Interest books on mathematics and mathematical dictionaries suitable for the age of the pupils; mathematics schemes such as Cambridge Maths, Nuffield Maths and Letts Maths; other useful books for activities and practice exercises for class work and homework.

Remember, the aim is for pupils to calculate mentally and to become less reliant on fingers and apparatus. Pupils should be encouraged to consider mental methods first through strategies such as: 'Think first, and try to work it out in your head. Now check on your number line' (DfES, 1999). Pupils with special needs may need particular equipment, books and materials for mathematics activities.

 **Activity!**

List the resources available in your school to support numeracy development.

Figure 12.3: Pupils using mathematics resources

The teaching assistant's role in supporting numeracy skills

The teaching assistant has a key role in providing support for the teacher and pupils during numeracy activities. You need to find out from the teacher how the numeracy activities are to be organised and your specific role in supporting various learning activities, including whole class oral/mental maths activities, group work and tasks for individuals. You must be able to: understand the intended learning outcomes for the pupils; agree the support strategies to be used for each pupil; obtain the resources required; implement the agreed strategies; provide praise and encouragement during the activity (see page 63); monitor the progress of the pupils and report any problems in providing support to the teacher.

Strategies to help pupils develop numeracy skills

Support strategies to help pupils to develop their mathematical knowledge and skills include:

- Using questions and prompts to encourage mathematical skills.
- Repeating instructions given by the teacher.
- Taking notes for a pupil while the teacher is talking.
- Explaining and reinforcing correct mathematical vocabulary.
- Reading and clarifying textbook/worksheet activity for a pupil.
- Introducing follow-on tasks to reinforce and extend learning, such as problem-solving tasks and puzzles.
- Playing a mathematical game with an individual pupil or small group.
- Helping pupils to use computer software and learning programs.
- Helping pupils to select and use appropriate mathematical resources, such as number lines and measuring instruments.
- Assisting pupils with special equipment such as a hearing aid or Dictaphone.
- Encouraging shy or reticent pupils to participate in conversations and discussions.
- Providing any other appropriate assistance during an activity.
- Monitoring pupil progress during an activity.
- Reporting problems and successes to the teacher.

You must know and understand the sorts of problems that might occur when supporting pupils during learning activities and how to deal with these problems (see page 144). If a pupil is experiencing difficulties during a mathematics activity you should consider the following:

1. Does the pupil understand the task?
2. Has the pupil learned how to do the relevant technique (counting, adding, and learning times tables by repeating them)?
3. Does the pupil know which technique to use to solve the mathematical problem?

Figure 12.4: Pupils engaged in a numeracy activity

The pupil needs to understand the mathematical problem and decide which techniques are required to solve it. You can help the pupil develop problem-solving skills by encouraging them to: understand the problem, through explaining the task using visual aids or equipment; plan to solve the problem, through suggesting possible ways or drawing diagrams; attempt the solution, through trying a technique; review the problem and solution, through reconsidering the problem and checking the answer makes sense.

In practice

Paul (aged 8 years) finds it difficult to concentrate during some learning activities and can be easily distracted by his classmates. He likes practical activities and enjoys PE, particularly games involving climbing or ball skills. He requires some additional support for numeracy skills. Suggest ways to provide support for numeracy activities.

Factors affecting support for numeracy activities

Some pupils have difficulties with numeracy because the language used in mathematics may be too complex for them to understand the task. Poor memory skills can prevent some pupils from learning procedural techniques, such as times tables. Frequent experiences of failure during numeracy activities can make some pupils anxious, discouraged and lacking in confidence so that they fall behind in their numeracy development.

Mathematical skills involve a wide range of specific capabilities, any of which can prove difficult for particular pupils and affect their mathematical development. It is important to find out what the pupil knows and where the problem lies. It is important to make sure that the pupil's problem with numeracy is not in fact a problem with literacy. For example, some pupils may: not be able to understand the written question; have handwriting or directional problems resulting in inaccurate recording and errors or have poor motor skills causing miscalculations when using a calculator.

It is also important not to underestimate what pupils can do mathematically simply because they are learning English as an additional language (see below). They should be expected to make progress in their mathematical learning at the same rate as other pupils of the same age.

 **Key Task**

Give a detailed account of an activity you have used to help pupils to develop their mathematical knowledge and skills. Include information on the following:

- the organisation of the activity including the resources used
- how you implemented the agreed strategies for each pupil
- how you provided feedback and encouragement during the activity
- how you monitored the progress of the pupils
- the learning outcomes achieved by the pupils
- how you reported any problems in providing support to the teacher.

NOS Links:

Level 3:   **STL18.1   STL20.2   STL8.2 (ICT)   STL23.2   STL23.3   STL24.2   STL26.1 STL26.2   STL27.2 (early years)   STL27.3 (early years)**

Supporting pupils with special numeracy needs

Some pupils may have special numeracy needs due to special educational needs (SEN) such as cognitive and learning difficulties, behavioural difficulties, sensory impairment or physical disabilities (see Chapter 13). The range of pupils with SEN varies from school to school. Many pupils with SEN may not have special numeracy needs and will not require extra or different numeracy support. However, many classes will have one or more pupil with identified SEN who require a modified approach to the National Numeracy Strategy. There are two broad groups of pupils with special numeracy needs:

1. A larger group of pupils who experience minor difficulties in learning, which is reflected in their attainment of levels of numeracy which are below those expected for pupils of their age. The structure provided by the National Numeracy Strategy can benefit these pupils. The pupils can usually overcome these difficulties through normal teaching strategies and will soon develop the essential numeracy skills that will enable them to catch up and work at a comparable level to the rest of their year group.

2. The second smaller group includes pupils with severe and complex learning difficulties that require the use of different teaching strategies. These pupils may require different levels of work from the rest of their year group. They may need to be taught at a different pace for all or most of their school years. Some pupils with SEN will always need access to systems such as symbols, signing, Braille or electronic communicators.

(DfES, 1999)

Some pupils with identified special educational needs may work at earlier levels than those specified in the National Numeracy Strategy Framework for their year group. Some pupils with SEN will need to work on one term's work for several terms. With structured, intensive teaching, some of these pupils will gradually progress through the levels in the Framework and will eventually be able to work at the levels appropriate to their age.

Many pupils with special educational needs (for example pupils with physical disabilities or sensory impairment) will not require a separate learning programme for mathematics. For most of them access, materials, equipment and furniture may require adapting to meet their particular needs so that they can work alongside the rest of their class. They should work on the same objectives for their year group with emphasis on access and support. Adaptations that may be necessary include: sign language; Braille and symbols; tactile materials; technological aids; adapted measuring equipment.

Support staff (including specially trained teaching assistants) can provide assistance for pupils with special numeracy needs by: signing to support a pupil with hearing impairment during shared numeracy activities; supporting a pupil during group work to develop specific numeracy skills; asking questions aimed at the appropriate level; giving the pupil some extra help in a group and sitting next to the pupil to keep them on task.

Supporting pupils with learning difficulties

Pupils with learning difficulties will usually require constant repetition and revision of previous learning in mathematics. This is especially important in terms of language and mental operations. The understanding of language of mathematics and the ability to calculate mentally are essential to the development of numeracy skills. Pupils with learning difficulties may not have adequate language and mental strategies, which may have contributed to their problems with formal, standard methods of representing calculations. Some pupils with specific learning difficulties (such as dyscalculia) may not understand key concepts in numeracy. (See section on supporting pupils with specific learning difficulties in Chapter 13.)

Pupils with English as an additional language

Whole-class sessions can provide helpful adult models of spoken English and opportunities for careful listening, oral exchange and supportive, shared repetition. Group work provides opportunities for intensive, focused teaching input. You may need to repeat instructions for

Palmer, S. and Bayley, R. (2004) *Foundations of Literacy: A Balanced Approach to Language, Listening and Literacy Skills in the Early Years*. Network Educational Press Ltd.

Williams, S. and Goodman, S. (2000) *Helping Young Children with Maths*. Hodder & Stoughton.

Wright, R.J. et al. (2002) *Teaching Number: Advancing Children's Skills and Strategies*. Paul Chapman Publishing.

13. Meeting additional support needs

Supporting pupils with special educational needs

You must know, understand and follow the relevant legislation regarding pupils with disabilities and SEN. This includes supporting the school in carrying out its duties towards pupils with SEN and ensuring that parents are notified of any decision that SEN provision is to be made for their child.

Legislation relating to pupils with special educational needs

The Education Act 1993 defines children with special educational needs as:

(a) Having a significantly greater difficulty in learning than the majority of children of the same age

(b) Having a disability which either prevents or hinders the child from making use of educational facilities of a kind provided for children of the same age in schools within the area of the local education authority

(c) An under five who falls within the definition at (a) or (b) above or would do if special educational provision was not made for the child.

(HMSO, 1996, the Education Act 1996; Part IV, Chapter 1, Section 312)

The Special Educational Needs and Disability Act 2001 amends Part 4 of the Education Act 1996 to make further provision against discrimination, on the grounds of disability, in schools and other educational establishments. This Act strengthens the right of children with special educational needs (SEN) to be educated in mainstream schools where parents want this and the interests of other children can be protected. The Act also requires local education authorities (LEAs) to make arrangements for services to provide parents of children with SEN with advice and information. It also requires schools to inform parents where they are making special educational provision for their child and allows schools to request a statutory assessment of a pupil's SEN (**www.drc-gb.org**).

The Special Educational Needs Code of Practice 2001 gives practical advice to LEAs, maintained schools and others concerning their statutory duties to identify, assess and provide for children's special educational needs. This code came into effect on 1 January 2002 and re-enforces the right for children with SEN to receive education within a mainstream setting and advocates that schools and LEAs implement a graduated method for the organisation of SEN. The code provides a school-based model of intervention (Early Years Action or School Action, Early Years Action Plus or School Action and Statutory Assessment) for children with special educational needs to enable all children to have the opportunities available through inclusive education. Accompanying the code is the Special Educational Needs Toolkit which expands on the guidance contained in the code. This Toolkit is not law but does provide examples of good practice that LEAs and schools can follow.

Identification, assessment and provision for pupils with SEN

Some children may have been identified as having special educational needs prior to starting school, for example children with physical disabilities, sensory impairment or autism. Some children may not be making sufficient progress within the early learning goals/national curriculum targets or may have difficulties which require additional support within the school. Additional support for pupils with SEN in education settings may be provided through Early Years or School Action, Early Years or School Action Plus and Statutory Assessment.

Early Years or School Action

Pupils identified as having special educational needs may require support in addition to the usual provision of the school. The SENCO, in consultation with colleagues and the pupil's parents will decide what additional support is needed to help the pupil to make progress. Additional support at Early Years or School Action may include: the provision of different learning materials or special equipment; some individual or group support provided by support staff (such as early years practitioners/nursery nurses or teaching assistants); devising and implementing an Individual Education Plan (see below).

Early Years or School Action Plus

Pupils with special educational needs may require additional support which involves external support services. The SENCO, in consultation with colleagues, the pupil's parents and other professionals will decide what additional support is needed to help the pupil to make progress. Additional support at Early Years or School Action Plus may include: the provision of specialist strategies or materials; some individual or group support provided by specialist support staff (such as early years practitioners/nursery nurses or teaching assistants with additional training in SEN); some individual support provided by other professionals such as physiotherapists or speech and language therapists; access to LEA support services for regular advice on strategies or equipment, for example for an educational psychologist or autism outreach worker; devising and implementing an Individual Education Plan (see below).

Statutory Assessment

A few pupils with SEN in the school may still make insufficient progress through the additional support provided by Early Years or School Action Plus. When a pupil demonstrates significant cause for concern, the SENCO, in consultation with colleagues, the pupil's parents and other professionals already involved in the pupil's support, should consider whether to request a statutory assessment by the LEA. The LEA may decide that the nature of the provision necessary to meet the pupil's special educational needs requires the LEA to determine the pupil's special education provision through a Statement of Special Educational Need.

A Statement of SEN is set out in six parts:

- Part one: general information about the pupil and a list of the advice the authority received as part of the assessment.
- Part two: the description of the pupil's needs following the assessment.
- Part three: describes all the special help to be given for the pupil's needs.
- Part four: the type and name of the school the pupil should go to and how any arrangements will be made out of school hours or off school premises.
- Part five: describes any non-educational needs the pupil has.
- Part six: describes how the pupil will get help to meet any non-educational needs.

Individual Education Plans

All education settings should differentiate their approaches to learning activities to meet the needs of individual pupils. The strategies used to enable individual pupils with SEN to make progress during learning activities should be set out in an Individual Education Plan (IEP) whether they receive additional support in the school as part of Early Years Action, Early Years Action Plus or Statement of Special Educational Need.

A pupil's IEP should identify three or four individual targets in specific key areas, for example, communication, literacy, numeracy or behaviour and social skills. When supporting the teacher in developing individual educational plans, remember to have high expectations of pupils and a commitment to raising their achievement based on a realistic appraisal of children's abilities and what they can achieve. You may be involved in regular reviews of individual educational plans in consultation with the pupil's class teacher/form tutor, the SENCO, the pupil and their parents, perhaps at least three times a year.

A pupil's IEP should include the following information:

- pupil's strengths
- priority concerns
- any external agencies involved
- background information including assessment details and/or medical needs
- parental involvement/pupil participation
- the short-term targets for the pupil

- the provision to be put in place, for example resources, strategies, staff, allocated support time
- when the plan is to be reviewed
- the outcome of any action taken.

Documentation and information about the Special Educational Needs Code of Practice including Early Years or School Action, Early Years or School Action Plus and Statutory Assessment should be available from the school office or the SENCO.

 Key Task

Outline your school's procedures for ensuring that individual education plans for pupils are in place and regularly reviewed. Provide examples of the relevant forms, for example an Individual Education Plan; review sheets for pupil comments, parent comments and staff comments; record of review. Remember confidentiality.

NOS Links:

Level 3:   STL 38.1   STL 38.2   STL 38.3

Roles and responsibilities in supporting pupils with SEN

Supporting pupils with disabilities and/or special educational needs (SEN) in schools involves establishing the strengths and needs of pupils in partnership with their families and in collaboration with other agencies. It also involves the identification and provision of appropriate resources to enable inclusion and participation.

As a teaching assistant you should contribute to the inclusion of pupils with disabilities and special educational needs (SEN). You may be involved in supporting the teacher and the special educational needs coordinator in developing individual plans to meet each pupil's needs and requesting additional resources or a statutory assessment where appropriate.

The role of the special educational needs coordinator

All schools must have a special educational needs coordinator (SENCO) who is the Responsible Person as defined within The Special Educational Needs Code of Practice. Pupils with special educational needs require additional support in the school and usually have Individual Education Plans (IEPs). These plans will give information about the support being provided to help the pupil and will include details of the roles and responsibilities of staff members in providing appropriate learning and/or behaviour support. The SENCO is responsible for drawing up these plans, along with the teacher, support staff (for example the teaching assistant), the pupil and their parents or carers.

The SENCO also has the following responsibilities for managing pupil behaviour and learning:

- To provide support and guidance to all staff to help them manage pupil behaviour and learning effectively.
- To ensure that adequate training is provided to all staff to improve behaviour management strategies and the implementation of learning activities.

Individual Education Plan

Name	Fred Jones	**Stage**	Statutory Assessment
Area/s of Concern	Literacy, Maths, Behaviour	**Year Group/IEP No.**	Year 2, Class 7/IEP No 2
Class Teacher	Mrs J Smith	**Start Date**	April 2010
Supported by	Mr H Brown (TA)	**Review Date**	June 2010
Proposed Support	Twice a week	**Support Began**	October 2009

Targets to be Achieved:	Achieved:
1. To read/spell c-v-c words with vowel sounds 'a' and 'o'.	1.
2. To understand and use number bonds to 10.	2.
3. To sit still on the mat during class/group sessions.	3.
4. To give verbal answers of more than one word.	4.

Achievement Criteria:
1. Accurate when tested at random on three separate occasions.
2. Use number bonds to answer sums accurately on three separate occasions.
3. Achieved on 6 out of ten occasions over a period of a week.
4. Achieved on 4 occasions.

Possible Resources and Techniques:
1. Wooden/plastic letters. Phonic workbooks. Card games. Computer programs. Tracking. Dictation.
2. Additions games e.g. bingo, snap, dice game. Lists of number bonds for reference. Textbooks/worksheets.
3. Clear expectations of behaviour at story time/discussion time. Reward chart.
4. Open-ended questions.

Possible Strategies to use in Class:
1. Encourage Fred to write the sounds he hears in a spoken word and to read c-v-c words accurately.
2. Set verbal and written questions for practising using number bonds. Provide apparatus for support if needed.
3. Minimise the time spent sitting still at first, gradually build up. Seat Fred away from distractions.
4. Question and answer sessions. Encourage full sentence answers.

Ideas for Support Teacher or Teaching Assistant:
1. Use multi-sensory methods for teaching c-v-c words. Set rhyming activities.
2. Provide practical activities to practise number bonds e.g. find different ways of splitting ten objects.
3. Look at the reward chart with Fred. Praise achievement.
4. Use individual discussion.

Parents/Carers need to:
Make sure the words sent home are practised.
Use money to add to 10p.
Encourage Fred to speak in whole sentences.

Pupil needs to:
Try to apply spellings he has learnt to his own written work.
Try to sit still.
Try to speak in whole sentences.

Figure 13.1: Example of Individual Education Plan

- To ensure that (as far as is practical) all resources required are made available to facilitate appropriate learning experiences and effective behaviour management.
- To monitor the changing needs of pupils as they progress through the school.
- To liaise with external agencies.
- To ensure that there are programmes for identifying the needs of new pupils.

The role of the class teacher in supporting pupils with SEN

The class teacher should plan and organise an effective learning environment which: promotes equality, diversity and inclusion (see Chapter 8); promotes positive behaviour (see Chapter 7); and supports *individual* pupil development and learning (see Chapter 6). The class teacher should carefully monitor pupils' behaviour and learning in order to provide appropriate learning activities. When a pupil experiences difficulties with participating in learning activities and/or behaving appropriately, the class teacher should follow the relevant school strategies.

The class teacher has the following responsibilities for managing pupil behaviour and learning:

- To identify each pupil's needs and skill levels.
- To make the SENCO aware of any concerns about a pupil's behaviour and/or learning.
- To advise the child's parents of any concerns about behaviour and/or learning.
- To provide reports for external agencies.
- To monitor and assess learning/behaviour and maintain appropriate records.
- To fill in and maintain the Special Educational Needs Register.
- To fulfil all other duties required of the class teacher by the Code of Practice.
- To ensure the delivery of the curriculum enables all pupils, including those with special educational needs, to experience success.

The teaching assistant's role in supporting pupils with SEN

As a teaching assistant you should help pupils with special educational needs (SEN) to participate in the full range of activities and experiences (see section on promoting equality, diversity and inclusion in Chapter 8). You need to know and understand the details about particular disabilities or SEN as they affect the pupils in your school. Pupils with additional needs in your school may include pupils with: communication and interaction needs; cognition and learning needs; behavioural, emotional and social development needs; sensory impairment or physical disabilities. (See below for information about supporting specific special needs.)

Your role may involve supporting a child or young person with special educational needs or additional support needs to participate in activities and experiences offered by the setting in which you work. As well as providing care and encouragement to the child or young person, you will support the family according to your role and the procedures of the setting.

Ten ways to support pupils with special educational needs

You can help pupils with special educational needs to participate in all activities by:

1. Providing a stimulating language-rich learning environment which is visually attractive, tactile and interactive.

2. Maximising the use of space in the setting to allow freedom of movement for all children (including those who are physically disabled or visually impaired).

3. Ensuring accessibility of resources including any specialist equipment.

4. Providing opportunities for all children to explore different materials and activities.

5. Encouraging children to use the abilities they do have to their fullest extent.

6. Providing sufficient time for children to explore their environment and materials; some children may need extra time to complete tasks.

7. Encouraging independence through, for example, using computers, word processing, tape recorders.

8. Praising all children's efforts as well as achievements.

9. Supporting families to respond to their children's special needs.

10. Accessing specialist advice and support for children with special needs.

Figure 13.2: Teaching assistant supporting pupil with special needs

 **Activity!**

Describe your role and responsibilities for supporting children and/or young people with special educational needs in school.

Liaising with parents regarding their children with SEN

When liaising with parents about the special educational needs of their children you should consider the family's home background and the expressed wishes of the parents. You must also follow the setting's policies and procedures with regard to special educational needs, for example the inclusion strategies, policies, procedures and practice (see section on understanding children's needs and rights in Chapter 8). You may need to give parents positive reassurance about their children's care and education. Any concerns or worries expressed by a child's parents should be passed immediately to the appropriate person in the school, such as the class teacher and/or SENCO. If a parent makes a request to see a colleague or other professional, then you should follow the relevant school policy and procedures. (See section on sharing information with parents and carers in Chapter 3.)

 **Activity!**

Give examples of how your school exchanges information with parents with regard to their children with special educational needs, for example information packs, regular reviews, Individual Education Plans, home–school diaries.

Liaising with other professionals regarding pupils with SEN

The teaching assistant can make a valuable contribution to the school by providing effective support for colleagues and by liaising with parents. In addition, teaching assistants are involved in the network of relationships between staff at the school and other professionals from external agencies such as:

- **Local education authority**, for example the educational psychologists, special needs support teachers, special needs advisors, specialist teachers, education welfare officers.
- **Health services**, for example the paediatricians, health visitors, physiotherapists, occupational therapists, speech and language therapists, play therapists, school nurses, clinical psychologists.
- **Social services department**, for example the social workers; specialist social workers for sensory disabilities, physical disabilities, mental health or children and families.
- **Charities and voluntary organisations**, such as AFASIC, the British Dyslexia Association, the Council for Disabled Children, the National Autistic Society, RNIB, RNID, SCOPE.

Activity!

Find out which external agencies and other professionals are connected with the care and support of pupils with SEN at your school.

Pupils with special educational needs will often have support from external agencies. The teaching assistant is part of the educational support team, which also includes the teacher and the specialist. To provide the most effective care and support for the pupil, it is essential that the working relationships between the specialist, teacher and teaching assistant run smoothly and that there are no contradictions or missed opportunities due to lack of communication. With guidance from the teacher, teaching assistants can be involved with the work of the specialists in a number of ways: planning support for the pupil with the teacher; assisting pupils to perform tasks set by a specialist; and reporting the pupil's progress on such tasks to the teacher.

key words

Specialist: person with specific training/additional qualifications in a particular area of development, for example a physiotherapist, speech and language therapist, educational psychologist.

Any interactions with other professionals should be conducted in such a way as to promote trust and confidence in your working relationships. Your contributions towards the planning and implementation of joint actions must be consistent with your role and responsibilities as a teaching assistant in your school. You should supply other professionals with the relevant information, advice and support as appropriate to your own role and expertise. If requested, you should be willing to share information, knowledge or skills with other professionals. You should use any opportunities to contact or observe the practice of professionals from external agencies to increase your knowledge and understanding of their skills/expertise in order to improve your own work in supporting pupil's learning and development.

 Key Task

Compile an information booklet suitable for new teaching assistants which includes information on the following:

- The teaching assistant's role and responsibilities for supporting pupils with special educational needs in the school.
- Links with other professionals from external agencies established by your school.
- Liaising with parents and carers.
- Working with other professionals to support pupils.
- Sources of further information, for example special needs organisations, books, websites.

NOS Links:

Level 3:	STL 19.2	STL 20.1	STL 20.2	STL 20.3	STL 20.4	STL 34.1
	STL 37.1	STL 37.2	STL 37.3	STL 38.1	STL 38.2	STL 38.3
	STL 39.1	STL 39.2	STL 40.2	STL 41.2	STL 41.3	STL 50.1
	STL 50.2	STL 50.3	STL 50.4	STL 51.1	STL 51.2	STL 60.1
	STL 60.2	STL 62.1	STL 62.2			

Supporting pupils with communication and interaction needs

All pupils have *individual* language needs, but some may have *additional* or special needs that affect their ability to communicate and interact effectively with others. For example: autistic spectrum disorders; behavioural and/or emotional difficulties; cognition difficulties affecting the ability to process language; hearing impairment or physical disabilities affecting articulation of sounds. Depending on their individual language experiences, some pupils may not have reached the same level of language development as their peers or they may lack effective communication skills. Some pupils' language development may even be ahead of what is usually expected for their age. (See section on supporting communication and language development in Chapter 1.)

Here are some strategies you can use when supporting pupils with communication difficulties:

- Keep information short and to the point.
- Avoid complex instructions.
- Speak clearly and not too quickly.
- Be a good speech role model.
- Build up the child's confidence gradually (for example, through speaking one-to-one, then in a small group).
- Develop concentration skills by playing memory games, for example.
- Encourage reluctant children to speak, but do not insist they talk.
- Use stories and CDs to improve listening skills.
- Use rhythm to sound out name/phrases, music and songs.
- Use pictorial instructions and visual cues.
- Teach social skills as well as communication skills.
- Provide structured play opportunities and learning activities.
- Keep to set routines.
- Prepare for new situations carefully.
- Use the child's favourite activities as rewards.
- Get specialist advice and support, for example through AFASIC, the National Autism Society; health visitors; a Portage worker; the special needs advisor; specialist teacher or speech and language therapist.

Figure 13.3: Teaching assistant supporting pupil with additional communication needs

Key Task

Provide examples of how you have encouraged a pupil or pupils with additional communication and/or interaction needs to participate in the full range of activities and experiences in your school, for example through adapting learning activities or using specialist resources to enable the pupil's full participation.

NOS Links:

Level 3:   STL 38.1   STL 38.2   STL 39.1   STL 39.2

Supporting pupils with cognition and learning needs

All pupils have *individual* cognition and learning needs, but some may have *additional* or special needs that affect their ability to participate effectively in learning activities. For example, some pupils may not develop their intellectual processes in line with the expected pattern of development for their age for a variety of reasons: autistic spectrum disorders (see above); attention deficit disorders (see below); emotional difficulties (see below); cognitive and learning difficulties. Additional cognitive and learning needs can be divided into two main areas: general learning difficulties and specific learning difficulties (see below). (See also section on supporting intellectual development in Chapter 1 and information about supporting learning activities in Chapter 6.)

Supporting pupils with general learning difficulties

The term 'slow learners' is sometimes used to describe pupils with below average cognitive abilities across all areas of learning; the term general learning difficulties is preferable. The wide range of general learning difficulties is divided into three levels:

1. Mild learning difficulties: pupils whose learning needs can be met using resources within mainstream settings.

2. Moderate learning difficulties: pupils whose learning needs can be met using additional resources in designated classes/special units within mainstream settings or in special schools.

3. Severe or profound learning difficulties: pupils whose learning needs require the resources and staff usually available only in special schools.

 key words

General learning difficulties: cognitive difficulties across all areas of learning.

Pupils with general learning difficulties often have delayed development in other areas; they may be socially and emotionally immature and/or have problems with gross/fine motor skills. Pupils with general learning difficulties need carefully structured learning opportunities where new skills are introduced step-by step. Pupils with this type of cognitive difficulty may have problems processing information; they have difficulty linking their existing knowledge and past experiences to new learning situations, which makes it difficult to reach solutions or to develop ideas.

Identifying pupils with general learning difficulties

Pupils with general learning difficulties are usually identified by the adults working with them at an early stage. Here are some common signs to look out for: a delay in understanding new ideas/concepts; poor concentration/shorter than usual attention span; inability to remember new skills without constant repetition and reinforcement; poor listening skills; lack of imagination and creativity; difficulty following instructions in large group situations; difficulty comprehending abstract ideas; limited vocabulary; often giving one-word answers; problems with memory skills; poor coordination affecting hand–eye coordination and pencil control; needing lots of practical support and concrete materials; delayed reading skills, especially comprehension; and delayed understanding of mathematics and science concepts. Pupils with general learning difficulties (especially in mainstream settings) are often aware that their progress is behind that of their peers. This can be very damaging to their self-esteem. Some pupils may feel they are incapable of learning anything at all. Adults need to convince such pupils that they can and will learn as long as they keep trying and do not give up.

Praise and encouragement are essential to all children's learning. All pupils, regardless of ability, are motivated by achieving success. Make sure the learning activities provided are appropriate by using observations and assessments to plan activities (as appropriate to your setting) which are relevant to each pupil's abilities and interests. Praise and encouragement are especially important to raise the self-esteem of pupils who find learning difficult. (See the importance of praise and encouragement in Chapter 3.)

Strategies to support pupils with general learning difficulties

The following strategies may help to make learning activities more positive experiences for pupils with general learning difficulties:

- Build on what the pupils already know.
- Let the pupils work at their own pace.
- Provide activities that can be completed in the time available without the pupils feeling under pressure.
- Divide the learning into small steps in a logical sequence.
- Present the same concept or idea in various ways to reinforce learning and understanding.
- Use repetition frequently; short daily lessons are more memorable than one long weekly session.
- Demonstrate what to do as well as giving verbal instructions.
- Use real examples and practical experiences/equipment wherever possible.
- Keep activities short and gradually work towards increasing their concentration.
- Encourage active participation in discussion and group activities to extend language and communication skills.
- Provide more stimuli for learning activities rather than expecting the pupils to develop new ideas entirely by themselves.
- Help the pupils to develop skills in accessing information, for example use technology such as computers and internet; also libraries, reference books and museums.

- *Listen* to the pupils and take on board their points of view.
- Get specialist advice and support, for example through MENCAP; the educational psychologist; health visitor or Portage worker; the special needs advisor; specialist teacher or occupational therapist.

Supporting pupils with specific learning difficulties

Pupils with specific learning difficulties show problems in learning in one particular area of development. For example: a pupil with dyslexia has difficulties in acquiring literacy skills; a pupil with dyscalculia has difficulties in acquiring numeracy skills; a pupil with dyspraxia has difficulties with the way the brain processes information, which affects the coordination of movement.

 **key words**

Dyslexia: difficulties in acquiring literacy skills.
Dyscalculia: difficulties in acquiring numeracy skills.
Dyspraxia: difficulties with the way the brain processes information which affects the coordination of movement.

Identifying pupils with dyslexia

Pupils with dyslexia have difficulties in acquiring literacy skills and consequently other aspects of learning may be affected. It is estimated that 4 per cent of pupils are affected by dyslexia. Look out for these signs of possible specific learning difficulties in the under-5s: a delay or difficulty in speech development; a persistent tendency to mix-up words and phrases; persistent difficulty with tasks such as dressing; unusual clumsiness and lack of coordination; poor concentration and a family history of similar difficulties. However, many young children make similar mistakes; specific learning difficulties are only indicated where the difficulties are severe and persistent or grouped together (BDA, 1997).

Look out for these possible signs of specific learning difficulties in 5 to 9 year olds: particular difficulties in learning to read, write and spell; persistent and continued reversing of letters and numerals (e.g. 'b' for 'd', 51 for 15); difficulty telling left from right; difficulty learning the alphabet and multiplication tables; difficulty remembering sequences such as days of the week/months of the year; difficulty with tying shoelaces, ball-catching and other coordination skills; poor concentration; frustration, possibly leading to behavioural difficulties and difficulty following verbal and/or written instructions (BDA, 1997).

Look out for these possible signs of specific learning difficulties in 9 to 12 year olds: difficulties with reading including poor comprehension skills; difficulties with writing and spelling including letters missing or in wrong order; problems with completing tasks in the required time; being disorganised at school (and at home); difficulties with copying from chalk board, white board or textbook; difficulties with following verbal and/or written instructions and lack of self-confidence and frustration (BDA, 1997).

Look out for these possible signs of specific learning difficulties in 12 to 16 year olds: reads inaccurately and/or lacks comprehension skills; inconsistency with spelling; difficulties with taking notes, planning and writing essays; confusion of telephone numbers and addresses; difficulties with following verbal instructions; severe problems when learning a foreign language and frustration and low self-esteem (BDA, 1997).

Strategies to support pupils with dsylexia

The following strategies may help when working with pupils with specific learning difficulties:

- Ensure the pupil is near you or at the front of the class/group.
- Check unobtrusively that copy-writing, note-taking, etc. is done efficiently.
- Use a 'buddy' system, where another pupil copies for this one.
- Give positive feedback and encouragement, without drawing undue attention to the pupil.
- Use computers to help the pupil (such as a word-processing program with spell check facility).
- Help the pupil to develop effective strategies and study skills which may differ from those used by other pupils.
- Get specialist advice and support, for example, from the British Dyslexia Association; educational psychologist; health visitor; special needs advisor; specialist teacher or occupational therapist.

(BDA, 1997)

In practice

Axel (aged 8 years) is a hard working pupil most of the time but he can lack concentration at times due to difficulties with reading and writing tasks. He is currently being monitored for SEN at School Action due to possible dyslexia. Suggest ways in which you could support this pupil's learning needs.

Identifying pupils with dyscalculia

The term dyscalculia, meaning difficulty in performing mathematical calculations, is given to a specific disorder in the ability to do or learn mathematics. Pupils with dyscalculia will experience difficulty with understanding number concepts and the relationships of numbers as well as using application procedures. Pupils with dyscalculia may have difficulties with:

- Distinguishing between mathematics signs and symbols (1, 2, £, etc.).
- Distinguishing between digits that are similar in shape (6 and 9, 7 and 1, 2 and 5) when reading and writing numbers.
- Sequencing, for example saying times tables, predicting the next number in a series, use of number line, following a sequence of instructions (such as when doing a two-stage calculation).
- Remembering the range of alternative words and phrases for number operations (such as the fact that *add*, *plus*, and *sum* are all addition terms).
- The correct use of place value and the direction of number operations (for example that subtraction starts with smallest place value, division starts with highest place value).
- Mathematics word problems including reading and language processing difficulties or losing track of number operation mid-process, especially if this is being done mentally.
- Organising and setting out calculations in writing.
- Memorising and recalling maths facts (such as recalling tables, mental arithmetic).

(DfES, 2003d)

Strategies to support pupils with dyscalculia

- Concrete materials (real objects) are important for all pupils but especially for pupils with learning difficulties. Pupils need real objects and experiences to help them develop an understanding of the abstract concepts used in mathematics.
- Use flash cards and illustrated wall displays to demonstrate the specific mathematical vocabulary for a particular task.
- Keep written instructions and explanations on worksheets to a minimum.
- Mathematics has a strong visual element so make frequent use of a number line, 100 square, number apparatus, pictures, diagrams, graphs and computer programs.
- Use games and puzzles where pupils can quickly pick up the rules after watching a demonstration.

(DfES, 2003d)

Identifying pupils with dyspraxia

Pupils with dyspraxia have a difficulty in the way the brain processes information, which results in messages not being properly or fully transmitted so that the coordination of movement, perception and thought are affected. Dyspraxia is a difficulty in formulating the plan rather than a primary problem of motor execution.

Dyspraxia may be shown by marked delays in achieving motor milestones (such as crawling or walking), dropping things, difficulties with balance, 'clumsiness', or poor performance in sports or handwriting. Pupils with dyspraxia may have problems using knives and forks, tying shoelaces or holding a pencil. When writing, they may also show difficulties with directionality and pressure on the page. Visual and perceptual difficulties (such as copying from the board or following sequential instructions) can also be symptoms of dyspraxia.

Strategies to support pupils with dyspraxia

- Give clear and unambiguous instructions.
- Break down activities into small steps.
- Arrange a 'buddy system'.
- Allow extra time for completing work.
- Teach the pupil strategies for remembering things.
- Use activities and strategies to encourage development and limit the impact of difficulties in school as suggested by the pupil's occupational therapist.
- Get specialist advice and support from The Dyspraxia Foundation.

In practice

Rose (aged 7 years) is a very quiet and hesitant pupil. She is currently receiving additional support for SEN at School Action Plus due to coordination difficulties (dyspraxia). She requires extra support for writing activities and during physical activities such as PE. Suggest ways in which you could support this pupil's learning needs.

 **Key Task**

Provide examples of how you have encouraged gifted or talented pupils to extend their learning, for example through providing additional challenges and/or access to advanced resources.

NOS Links:

Level 3:   **STL 34.1**   **STL 34.2**

Supporting pupils with behavioural, social and emotional development needs

All pupils have *individual* behavioural, social and emotional needs, but some may have *additional* or special needs that affect their ability to interact appropriately with others and/or participate effectively during routines and activities. For example, some pupils may have behavioural, social and/or emotional difficulties which hinder their ability to: follow specific routines or instructions for activities; interact positively with other pupils or adults; participate in play and learning opportunities; or express their feelings appropriately.

Identifying pupils with behavioural, social and emotional difficulties

The adult's response to a pupil's behaviour is as important as the behaviour itself. Different people have different attitudes to what is or is not acceptable behaviour. The social context also affects adult attitudes towards children's behaviour (see Chapter 8). All adults should consider certain types of behaviour unacceptable; these include behaviour which causes: physical harm to others; self-harm; emotional/psychological harm to others and destruction to property.

Pupils whose unwanted behaviour is demonstrated through aggressive or disruptive behaviour are usually the ones to attract the most adult attention, as they are easily identified and hard to ignore. Pupils who demonstrate unwanted behaviour in a withdrawn manner may be overlooked, especially by inexperienced adults or in very busy settings. (See sections on recognising behaviour patterns and other influences on pupil behaviour in Chapter 7).

Most pupils with behavioural, social and emotional development needs respond favourably to a positive approach. However, some pupils may have been identified and assessed as having particular emotional and behavioural difficulties:

- Pupils with emotional difficulties: can be difficult to include and may have learning difficulties (see below).
- Disruptive pupils: disrupt the teaching and learning process; they can be a nuisance; have a short concentration span; and display attention-seeking behaviour (see Chapter 7).
- Disaffected pupils: can be lacking in motivation; cannot see the point of learning; appear totally uninterested and don't want to be in school; can be difficult to re-engage; difficult to motivate; do not seem to appreciate any efforts the teacher might make (see below).
- Pupils with Attention Deficit Disorders: pupils with ADD have short concentration span; divergent mind; can be difficult to engage/motivate; pupils with ADHD can have similar difficulties as pupils with ADD, but more complex and difficult to manage; can ignore 'classroom rules'.

Pupils with emotional difficulties

Pupils may experience emotional difficulties for a variety of reasons. Some emotional difficulties are part of the usual pattern of children's emotional development and are only temporary. For example: emotional outbursts (see Chapter 3); common childhood fears; reactions to family or friend's accident/illness, child's own accident/illness or pet illness/death; adjusting to transitions such as starting nursery/school or the arrival of new baby or step-sibling; pressures at home or school; concerns about tests or exams; worries about local, national or international crises witnessed in the media.

Some pupils may experience emotional difficulties of a more lasting nature. For example, emotional difficulties as a result of traumatic experiences such as: child abuse and bullying (see Chapter 2); parental separation and divorce (especially when there are disputes about child support and/or residency); terminal illness or bereavement in a child's family; domestic violence; armed conflict; or witnessing a violent or catastrophic event such as a shooting, stabbing, car crash or natural disaster.

Disaffected pupils

Indicators of disaffection in school range from disruptive behaviour to unauthorised absence and persistent truancy. Schools should regularly review the progress of pupils to identify any pupils at risk of failure at school, in partnership with the Education Welfare Service and other agencies. Where there are signs of disaffection, early intervention by the school may prevent problems from worsening. It is important that schools closely monitor attendance so that any patterns of non-attendance are identified and dealt with, for example by tackling and preventing pupil absenteeism before it reaches the point where the pupil is referred to the Education Welfare Service. Pupils who do not respond to school actions to combat disaffection may be at serious risk of permanent exclusion or criminal activity.

A whole school approach to attendance and absence is essential to handling signs of disaffection and should include: a strong school attendance ethos; clear absence policies; effective systems to monitor attendance; promoting the importance and legal requirements of good attendance to pupils and their parents; early intervention when pupil absences give cause for concern; support systems for vulnerable pupils; and rewards for good and improved attendance.

Pupils with Attention Deficit Disorders

Attention Deficit Disorder can occur with or without hyperactivity. If hyperactivity is not present then disorder is usually called just Attention Deficit Disorder (ADD). Attention Deficit Disorder (ADD) or Attention Deficit Hyperactivity Disorder (ADHD) affects about 5 per cent of school-aged children and it is possible that about 10 per cent of children have a milder form of the disorder. Some children with ADD or ADHD may also have other difficulties, such as specific learning difficulties like dyslexia. Boys are more likely to be affected than girls. ADD and ADHD are rarely diagnosed before the age of 6 years because many young children demonstrate the behaviours characteristic of this disorder as part of the usual sequence of development. From about 6 years old it is easier to assess whether the child's behaviour is *significantly* different from the expected norm. Most children with ADD or ADHD are formally identified between 5 and 9 years old.

Pupils with ADD are usually:

- Inattentive with a short attention span; unable to concentrate on tasks, easily distracted; they forget instructions due to poor short-term memory; they may seem distant or be prone to 'day dreaming'.
- Lacking in coordination skills and may have poor hand–eye coordination resulting in untidy written work; they may be accident prone.
- Disorganised and unable to structure their own time; unable to motivate themselves unless directed on a one-to-one basis; they may be very untidy.

In addition pupils with ADHD are usually:

- Over-active with high levels of activity and movement; restless and fiddle with objects.
- Extremely impulsive, which may lead to accidents as they have no sense of danger; they often speak and act without thinking.
- Lacking in social skills as they do not know how to behave with others; very bossy and domineering; unable to make or keep friends; they may demonstrate inappropriate behaviour or misread social cues, for example treating complete strangers as close friends.
- Changeable and unpredictable with severe, unexplained mood swings; short-tempered with frequent emotional or extremely aggressive outbursts.

The National Institute for Clinical Excellence recommends that 1 per cent of children with severe ADHD (around 100,000) should receive medication such as methylphenidate (Ritalin). Methylphenidate is a stimulant which enhances brain function and it has been very effective in children with severe ADHD. Such medication helps focus the child's attention, keeps them on task and allows the child to think before they act. Once the child's concentration and behaviour improves the dose can be decreased. With or without medication, it is important to have a consistent system for managing the child's behaviour within the childcare setting and at home.

In schools, staff need to provide the following for pupils with ADD or ADHD: a quiet group/ class with one or two adults who are firm but fair and can provide consistent care and education throughout the year; calmness and a clear routine; seating near a known adult away from distracting pupils; step-by-step instructions and constant feedback, praise and encouragement.

Strategies to support pupils with behavioural, social and emotional difficulties

Providing support for pupils with behavioural, social and emotional difficulties is one of the most challenging roles that teaching assistants may have to undertake. When supporting pupils with such difficulties you may sometimes feel hopeless, annoyed or helpless. However, working with pupils with additional behavioural, social and emotional needs can also be very rewarding, as by providing appropriate support, you are helping them to develop the life skills and coping strategies they need.

You can provide effective support through positive strategies and inclusion by:

- enhancing the pupil's self-esteem
- assisting the pupil to recognise the effect of the behaviour
- being constructive
- clearly explaining what constitutes unacceptable behaviour
- fostering and encouraging parental support where possible

- early identification of possible difficulties
- using rewards and sanctions that are fair, and consistently applied
- liaising with colleagues and other professionals.

Pupils with behavioural, social and emotional difficulties usually have an Individual Education Plan (IEP) and/or an Individual Behaviour Support Plan (BSP) or a Pastoral Support Plan (PSP) if they are at risk of being excluded from school. These plans will give you information about the support being provided to help the pupil and will often include details of your role and responsibilities in providing behaviour support. You may sometimes be involved in drawing up these plans, along with the teacher, the pupil and their parents or carers. (For detailed information, see sections on promoting positive behaviour and managing pupils' challenging behaviour in Chapter 7. See also sections on encouraging positive social interactions in Chapter 3 and supporting social development in Chapter 1.)

In practice

Michael (aged 6 years) is very physically active and can be disruptive during group and class learning activities. He is currently being assessed for SEN at School Action Plus due to possible ADHD. Suggest ways in which you could support this pupil's behaviour needs.

 Key Task

Provide examples of how you have encouraged a pupil with behavioural, social and emotional difficulties to participate in the full range of activities and experiences in your school. For example:

- Encouraging the pupil to participate effectively in learning activities.
- Encouraging the pupil to behave in more acceptable ways by using appropriate rewards and sanctions.
- Improving school attendance.
- Helping the pupil to develop a positive self-image and self-esteem.
- Providing opportunities for the pupil to express their feelings more appropriately such as discussion, story time and play activities.

NOS Links:

Level 3:	STL 19.1	STL 19.2	STL 20.3	STL 37.1	STL 37.2	STL 37.3
	STL 38.1	STL 38.2	STL 40.1	STL 40.2	STL 41.1	STL 41.2
	STL 41.3	STL 45.1	STL 45.4	STL 50.1	STL 50.2	STL 50.3
	STL 50.4	STL 51.1	STL 51.2			

Supporting pupils with sensory and/or physical needs

Some pupils may require additional support in school due to sensory and/or physical needs such as hearing, visual and/or physical impairment. As pupils with sensory or physical impairments may be dependent on others for some of their needs, it is essential to provide opportunities for them to be as independent as possible. Give them every chance to join in, to express opinions and to interact with their peer group. Remember to focus on each child as a unique person with individual strengths rather than focusing on the child's particular disabilities, look at what they *can* do rather than what they cannot.

Supporting pupils with hearing impairment

Hearing loss may range from a slight impairment to profound deafness. One in four children under the age of 7 experiences a hearing loss of some degree at some time. The loss may affect one or both ears at different levels. There are two types of hearing impairment:

1. Conductive hearing loss – involving the interference of the transmission of sound from the outer to the inner ear. This may be due to congestion or damage to the inner ear. The loss may be temporary or permanent; it makes sounds seem like the volume has been turned down. Hearing aids can be useful to amplify speech sounds, but unfortunately background noise is also increased. The most common form of conductive hearing loss in younger children is 'glue ear'. This temporary condition is caused by the collection of fluid behind the ear drum triggered by congestion during an ear, nose or throat infection. Sometimes 'glue ear' can cause language delay as it interferes with a young child's hearing at an important stage of speech development. Persistent or repetitive cases of glue ear may require a minor operation to drain the fluid and to insert a grommet or small tube into the ear drum to prevent further fluid build up.

2. Sensori-neural loss is a rarer condition that is more likely to result in permanent hearing impairment. The damage to the inner ear results in distorted sounds where some sounds are heard but not others. High frequency loss affects the child's ability to hear consonants; low frequency loss is a less common condition. Hearing aids are not as effective with this type of hearing impairment as the child will still be unable to hear the missing sounds. Children with sensori-neural loss therefore find it more difficult to develop speech and have a more significant language delay.

Identifying pupils with hearing impairment

Pupils with hearing impairment, especially those with conductive hearing loss, may be difficult to identify. However, even a slight hearing loss may affect a pupil's language development. Look out for these signs of possible hearing loss in pupils: slow reactions; delay in following instructions; constantly checking what to do; apparently day-dreaming or inattentive; over-anxiety; watching faces closely; turning head to one side to listen; asking to repeat what was said; difficulty regulating voice; poor language development; finding spoken work more difficult to do than written work; may have emotional or aggressive outbursts due to frustration and problems with social interaction.

Pupils with hearing loss will use lip-reading and non-verbal clues such as gesture and body language to work out what is being said. Some pupils will wear hearing aids to improve their hearing abilities. Some schools may encourage the use of signing systems such as British Sign Language or Makaton and have specially trained staff to facilitate the use of sign language throughout the school. Cochlear implants are relatively new but are being used with more and more children. A prosthesis is worn partly inside the body and partly outside, and is used to aid hearing.

- **Supporting pupils with communication and interaction needs** including: identifying pupils with additional communication and/or interaction needs; common language difficulties such as lisping and stammering; autistic spectrum disorders; strategies to support pupils with additional communication and/or interaction needs.

- **Supporting pupils with cognition and learning needs** including: supporting pupils with general learning difficulties; identifying pupils with general learning difficulties; strategies to support pupils with general learning difficulties; supporting pupils with specific learning difficulties; identifying pupils with dyslexia; strategies to support pupils with dyslexia; identifying pupils with dyscalculia; strategies to support pupils with dyscalculia; identifying pupils with dyspraxia; strategies to support pupils with dyspraxia; supporting gifted and talented pupils; identifying gifted and talented pupils; strategies to support gifted and talented pupils.

- **Supporting pupils with behavioural, social and emotional development needs** including: identifying pupils with behavioural, social and emotional difficulties; pupils with emotional difficulties; disaffected pupils; pupils with attention deficit disorders; strategies to support pupils with behavioural, social and emotional difficulties.

- **Supporting pupils with sensory and/or physical needs** including: supporting pupils with hearing impairment; identifying pupils with hearing impairment; strategies to support pupils with hearing impairment; supporting pupils with visual impairment; identifying pupils with visual impairment; strategies to support pupils with visual impairment; supporting pupils with physical disabilities; identifying pupils with physical disabilities; strategies for supporting pupils with physical disabilities.

Further reading

Alcott, M. (2002) *An Introduction to Children with Special Needs*. Hodder & Stoughton.

ATL (2002) *Achievement for All: Working with Children with Special Educational Needs in Mainstream Schools and Colleges*. Association of Teachers and Lecturers. (Available free from: **www.atl.org.uk**)

Autism Working Group (2002) *Autistic Spectrum Disorders: Good Practice Guidance*. DfES. DfES (2001) Inclusive Schooling. DfES. (Available free online from: **http://www.teachernet.gov.uk/_doc/4621/InclusiveSchooling.pdf**.)

Brookes, G. (2007) *The Teaching Assistant's Guide to Dyspraxia*. Continuum International Publishing.

Cartwright, A. and Morgan, J. (2008) *The Teaching Assistant's Guide to Autistic Spectrum Disorders*. Continuum International Publishing.

Davis, P. (2003) *Including Children with Visual Impairment in Mainstream Schools: A Practical Guide*. David Fulton Publishers.

DfES (2001) *The Special Educational Needs Code of Practice 2001*. DfES.

(Available free at: **http://www.teachernet.gov.uk/_doc/3724/SENCodeOfPractice.pdf**.)

Diaz, L. (2008) *The Teaching Assistant's Guide to Speech, Language and Communication Needs*. Continuum International Publishing.

Distin, K. (ed) (2006) *Gifted Children: A Guide for Parents and Professionals*. Jessica Kingsley Publishers.

Halliwell, M. (2003) *Supporting Special Educational Needs: A Guide for Assistants in Schools and Pre-schools*. David Fulton Publishers.

Lee, C. (2007) *Resolving Behaviour Problems in Your School: A Practical Guide for Teachers and Support Staff*. Paul Chapman Educational Publishing.

Lovey, S. (2002) *Supporting Special Educational Needs in Secondary School Classrooms*. David Fulton Publishers.

Reid, G. and Reid, S. (2007) *The Teaching Assistant's Guide to Dyslexia*. Continuum International Publishing.

Spohrer, K. (2007) *The Teaching Assistant's Guide to ADHD*. Continuum International Publishing.

Spooner, W. (2006) *The SEN Handbook for Trainee Teachers, NQTs and Teaching Assistants*. Routledge.

Watson, L. et al. (2006) *Deaf and Hearing Impaired Pupils in Mainstream Schools*. David Fulton Publishers.

14. Providing pastoral support

This chapter relates to QCF units:

TDA 3.24 Support children and young people during transitions in their lives

CYPOP 44 Facilitate the learning and development of children and young people through mentoring

SCMP 2 Promote the well being and resilience of children and young people

Identifying transitions

Transitions are central to children's experiences and well-being. Transitions can be defined as '… key events and/or processes occurring at specific periods or turning points during the life course' (Vogler et al., 2008; p.1). Transitions are generally linked to changes in a person's appearance, activity, status, roles and relationships as well as changes of setting (Vogler et al., 2008).

The process of adjusting to a new situation is known as a **transition**. Transitions involve the experiences of change, separation and loss. A transition may involve the transfer from one setting to another or changes within the same setting. For example: home to childminder's home, nursery, playgroup or school; one year group or key stage to another, for example Reception to Year 1, Key Stage 1 to 2; mainstream to or from special school; secondary school to college or work; staff changes due to illness, maternity leave, promotion, retirement, etc.

Common transitions

The progression from childhood through adolescence to adulthood necessarily involves change. All children and young people will experience some changes in their daily lives as part of growing up. Some changes can be foreseen, or even planned. These changes involve common transitions such as: progressing from one level of development to another, for example puberty, entering adulthood; starting nursery or school; moving schools, for example primary to secondary; moving class; starting college or training; entering voluntary or paid work; and first sexual experiences.

 **Activity!**

- Identify the common transitions that you have experienced in childhood and adolescence.
- Predict transitions which you are likely to or have experienced in adulthood.

Personal transitions

Transitions may also involve other significant changes in the child's life which may be unforeseen or only happen to some individuals. These changes involve personal or particular transitions such as: death or serious illness of a family member or close friend; parental separation or divorce; moving house; going into hospital; living with disability; death of a favourite pet; arrival of a new baby or step-brothers and sisters; changes in main carer such as adoption, fostering, entering / leaving care system; and the process of asylum.

 Activity!

- Identify your own personal transitions, for example moving house.
- Describe your emotions and the challenges you faced.
- How did you manage the change?

Family circumstances

There are a number of family circumstances that may lead to particular or personal transition including: birth of sibling; moving house; poverty; environment; employment status; family break-up or divorce; parent's new partner/relationships; terminal illness or death in the family; child abuse and neglect; mental health needs; substance abuse or consequences of crime, such as a parent in prison.

 Activity!

Discuss family circumstances which may lead to transition. For example, discuss transition issues from the 'soap operas' or 'real life' shows on television, such as family break-up or divorce.

How transitions may affect children's behaviour and development

When change unsettles children, their feelings will emerge one way or another. Different patterns of behaviour show how children are trying to cope with change. Children's responses to change are not always negative and some children will go to tremendous lengths to hide their true feelings about certain changes.

Change is not always disruptive or distressing. A lot depends on the emotional competence of the adults and their willingness to find out from the children how they feel about the change instead of assuming everything is okay or expecting turmoil. When facing change, everyone experiences some feelings of confusion and uncertainty. The prospective change may be anticipated with a mixture of emotions, such as excitement at a new opportunity, regret for what is being left behind, or elation at leaving an unhappy setting. Change is more likely to cause emotional distress when someone's life has been turned upside down, especially by events that could not be anticipated by anyone. The emotions experienced are still unpredictable, for example, anger, sadness, grief, numbness or a combination of these. High levels of distress and disrupted patterns of behaviour or development are more likely when children are not kept informed, feel out of control or cannot access emotional support. Children can feel overwhelmed when more than one significant change occurs during the same period, or when changes keep piling up and there is no prospect of stability (Lindon, 2007; p.89). For example, children may feel particularly distressed if they are starting school at the same time as moving house and dealing with the arrival of a new baby.

Children may react to change in the following ways:

- They may behave differently from the child you have come to know well. Some children may become quieter and withdraw. Some may show obvious distress or a lowered ability to deal with the usual ups and downs of life in the setting. Depending on your relationship with a child, they may need no more than a friendly or relatively private, 'Is something bothering you?' and body language that says clearly that you are ready to listen.
- Some children may struggle with emotional distress which then emerges as anger directed at peers or adults who 'deserve' a verbal or physical attack. You need to deal fairly with the outburst and any consequences, but also give the child the chance to talk about what happened soon after the incident. For example, 'I know you shouted at Damian because of the offside business but you were really angry. It looked to me like there's something else weighing you down. What's up?'.
- Sometimes children will temporarily regress in their development and self-help skills. It may be that a usually competent child, struck by anxiety, really wants to be cosseted or is keen to say, 'I can't do that'. Children who were dry at night may start to wet the bed, and their distress at this situation can lead them to feel even more emotionally fragile.
- Some children really want to talk – perhaps to a trusted adult. Perhaps you even hear from the child about their dad being made redundant before the parents tell you.
- Depending on the family situation, some children find it harder to say goodbye to their parent when being left at the setting and they may worry about their well-being while they are apart.
- Sometimes children demonstrate their concerns through play or they may be unwilling to play as usual. For some children the issues emerge through their drawings or written stories and poems.

(Lindon, 2007; pp.90/91)

The positive and negative effects of transitions

Transition is a natural process and there are often positive effects. For example: increased levels of motivation; promoting development; educational progress; confidence; good health; improved self-esteem; increased independence and ability to form relationships. Successful transitions can lead to a positive self-image (including gender, sexuality and cultural identity) and result in emotionally healthy and resilient children, young people and adults (Turnbull, 2006).

Most transitions that children make are successful, but for a few children they are not. For example, they may experience: decreased levels of motivation; developmental delay; educational delay; depression; ill health; poor self-esteem; sleep disruption; self-harm; eating disorders; bullied or bullying; dependence; inability to form or sustain relationships or use of illegal substances. Unsuccessful transitions have negative implications for children's future well-being and their ability to enjoy and achieve in their childhood and adolescence (Turnbull, 2006).

Starting nursery or primary school

Many children (especially young children) experience anxiety and stress when they first attend a new setting or have a new child carer due to:

- Separation from their parent or previous child carer.
- Encountering unfamiliar children who may have already established friendships.
- The length of time spent in the setting, for example 8.00 am to 6.00 pm in a day nursery or 9.00 am to 3.30 pm in school.
- Differences in the culture and language of the setting to child's previous experiences.
- Unfamiliar routines and rules.
- Worry about doing the wrong thing.
- Unfamiliar activities such as sports/PE, playtime, lunchtime or even storytime.
- The unfamiliar physical environment, which may seem overwhelming and scary.
- Difficulties in following more structured activities and adult directions.
- Concentrating on activities for longer than previously used to.

Moving from primary to secondary school

Children face a wide range of new experiences when making the transition from primary to secondary school. For example: going from being the oldest to the youngest in their school; moving around for lessons far more; having several subject teachers instead of one class teacher; starting to learn new subjects; being given increased amounts of homework and facing the developmental changes of puberty at the same time. For most children the transition is a smooth one, but some children find it difficult and problematic (Turnbull, 2006; p.9).

The transition from primary to secondary may cause additional concerns due to:

- Lack of sufficient information about individual children on transfer.
- Discontinuity of Years 6 and 7 curriculum, despite the National Curriculum.
- Decrease in pupil performance after transfer.

Changing schools

If a family moves home, children can change to a new school at any age. These non-compulsory school moves may have important implications for the life chances of the children involved. A study found that: pupils, at all stages of schooling, from lower social backgrounds are more likely to switch schools than other pupils; pupils who change schools are more likely to have a low previous academic attainment record than pupils who do not change schools; pupils placed in schools with high key stage performance levels move less than pupils from lower performance schools; pupils who move school and home simultaneously are typically more socially disadvantaged than otherwise. This suggests that for many in this group of children there is a potential negative impact on future academic attainment and therefore on these young people's future contribution to society (Turnbull, 2006; p. 17).

 **Activity!**

- Investigate the effects of starting primary/secondary school or changing schools.
- Consider why some children start primary/secondary school or change schools with apparently no effects or with a positive response whilst others become distressed.

Support transitions

The *Common Core of Skills and Knowledge for the Children's Workforce* includes children's transitions as a key area of work. In the chapter 'Supporting transitions', it notes:

'As recognised in effective communication and child development, it is important to understand a child or young person in the context of their life, to recognise and understand the impact of any transitions they may be going through. It is also vital to recognise the role of parents and carers in supporting children at points of transition and to understand the need for reassurance, advice and support that parents and carers may express at these points'. (DfES, 2005a; p.16)

To alleviate some of this anxiety and stress, preparation is now seen as an essential part of successful transfers and transitions including nurseries, schools, foster care and hospitals. Most settings have established procedures for preparing children for transfers and transitions.

Ten principles to support children's transitions

The National Children's Bureau has developed ten principles to help workers support children and young people's transitions at all ages and whatever the transitions they are facing. These are:

1. Identify key changes, critical moments and transition points for children and young people.
2. Ensure mainstream work with children and young people builds life skills including emotional resilience and empathy, and emphasises the importance of asking for help and support when they are needed.
3. Develop curriculum and project work that focuses on transitions.
4. Prepare children and young people for leaving school or leaving care well in advance, providing an opportunity to reflect on successes and challenges and celebrate their work together.
5. Identify individuals who may need particular support through transitions. Identify the support mechanisms and agencies that are available for the child and their family. Work in partnership to provide this support, where possible.
6. Involve children and young people in providing support to their peers as part of everyday friendships and relationships.
7. Involve and support parents and carers in transitions work.
8. Encourage optimism and work with the excitement and opportunities, as well as the fears and anxieties.
9. If the behaviour of a child or young person changes, encourage them to acknowledge it and talk about it.
10. Provide consistent responses to critical moments and events in children and young people's lives, such as when they are bullied, bereaved or experiencing parental divorce or separation. Ensure the child is at the heart of deciding what support and help they need.

(Worthy, 2005 as quoted in Turnbull, 2006; p.30.)

Transitions and children aged 3 to 11 years

The move to nursery or primary school is still a big step, even though many young children have already spent time in other early years group settings, such as day nurseries and pre-school playgroups. The first days and weeks are much easier when children have already met their new (next) teacher, who has ideally already visited the children in their current setting as well as welcoming them to the new setting (Lindon, 2007).

You can help prepare children aged 3 to 11 years for transitions by:

- Talking to the children and explaining what is going to happen.
- Listening to the children and reassuring them that it will be fine.
- Reading relevant books, stories and poems about transitions, such as starting nursery or primary school; moving to secondary school; visiting the dentist; going into hospital.
- Watching appropriate videos or television programmes which demonstrate the positive features of the new setting or situation.
- Providing opportunities for imaginative play to let children express their feelings and fears about the transition.
- Visiting the children's current setting or going on home visits to meet the children in a familiar setting, particularly if working with children with special needs.
- Organising introductory visits for the children and their parents/carers so that the children can become familiar with the setting and the adults who will care for and support them.
- Providing information appropriate to both children and parents, for example an information pack or brochure plus an activity pack for each child.
- Obtaining relevant information from parents about their child, such as their correct name and address, contact details, medical information, dietary requirements and food preferences.
- Planning activities for an induction programme (children's first week in new setting).

Figure 14.1: A pupil's first day at school

Transitions from 11 to 16 years and beyond

Children and young people need the opportunity to visit the next setting (for example the secondary school, sixth form or further education college) more than once so that they can become familiar with the layout. Open evenings to meet their new teachers or tutors are also useful, especially if they can meet them on more than one occasion. Being involved in activities at what will be their next school (or college) is also helpful, such as a learning festival, summer school or taster days (Lindon, 2007).

You can help prepare children and young people aged 11 to 16 years for transitions by:

- Encouraging children and parents to attend open days and evenings at the setting.
- Visiting the children's current setting to meet the children in a familiar environment, particularly if working with children with special needs.
- Arranging taster days for children to experience the layout and routine of the setting, for example, in secondary schools moving to different classrooms for lessons with different subject teachers through fun activities in science, IT and sport.
- Discussing individual children's performance with relevant members of staff.
- Exchanging relevant documentation, such as child observations and assessments, test results, any special educational needs information including Individual Education Plans, Behaviour Support Plans, Statements, etc.
- Looking at children's records of achievement including their interests and hobbies.
- Encouraging children with challenging behaviour to look at this as a fresh start.
- Providing the setting's information pack or brochure for children and parents, including information on bullying as this is often a key area of concern.
- Obtaining relevant information from parents about their child, such as their correct name and address, contact details, medical information, dietary requirements and food preferences.
- Providing opportunities for work experience to help children with the transition from the learning environment to the world of work.
- Providing opportunities for careers advice and information on further education or training, for example through using the Connexions service for 13 to 19 year olds.
- Encouraging children and parents to attend open days/evenings for local colleges.

Key Task

Make a leaflet which includes the following:

- The transitions that are experienced by most children, such as starting school.
- The transitions that are experienced by some children, such as bereavement.
- Examples of how transitions may affect child behaviour and development.
- The role of the adult in supporting transitions.

NOS Links:

Level 3:   STL 2.1   STL 2.2   STL 2.3   STL 2.4   STL 4.1   STL 4.2   STL 4.3
STL 4.4

Learning mentors

Learning mentors work with school pupils and college students to help them overcome barriers to learning and so have a better chance of achieving to their potential. Learning mentors play a key role in supporting children and young people with special needs, working closely with teachers and a range of support agencies. Learning mentors use regular one-to-one and group sessions with the pupils/students, to agree targets and strategies (for example to improve academic work, attendance, behaviour and relationships). They help pupils/students develop coping strategies, enhance their motivation, raise their aspirations and encourage them to re-engage in learning. Learning mentors should take into account the range of complex issues that are often behind problems with learning and achievement, such as bereavement, lack of confidence/low self-esteem, low aspirations, mental health issues, relationship difficulties, bullying, peer pressure and family issues/concerns.

The role of the learning mentor

A learning mentor's role involves initiating and maintaining professional helping relationships with the children and young people who have been referred to them. This includes a range of responsibilities such as:

- Establishing and developing effective one-to-one mentoring and other supportive relationships with children and young people.
- Developing, agreeing and implementing a time-bound action plan with groups, with individual children and young people and with those involved with them, based on a comprehensive assessment of strengths and needs.
- Facilitating access to specialist support services for children and young people facing barriers to learning.
- Assisting in identifying early signs of disengagement and contributing to specific interventions to encourage re-engagement.
- Operating within agreed legal, ethical and professional boundaries when working with children and young people and those involved with them.

(CWDC, 2007)

A structured approach to learner mentoring

A structured approach to learner mentoring helps to keep practice intentional and focused on outcomes as well as maintaining boundaries so that learning mentors do not become overwhelmed with requests for support. The section on learning mentors on the Children's Workforce Development Council website provides an overview of a structured approach to one-to-one mentoring, and shows the types of records that learning mentors will need to keep. Children and young people referred to a learning mentor will be experiencing barriers to learning and participation. Procedures for referral to a learning mentor should therefore be robust and accountable. Many schools and other settings use a referral form (CWDC, 2007). (For information see: **http://www.cwdcouncil.org.uk/learning-mentors/**.)

 Key Task

Give a reflective account of how you have supported learners through mentoring.

Include detailed information on:

- Identifying the learning and development needs of the children or young people.
- Planning with the children or young people how learning and development needs will be addressed through mentoring.
- Mentoring the children or young people to achieve the identified outcomes.
- Reviewing the effectiveness of mentoring with the children or young people.

NOS Links:

Level 3: **STL 50.1** **STL 50.2** **STL 50.3** **STL 50.4**

Enabling pupils to relate to others

Promoting children's well-being and resilience involves helping children to: develop and sustain healthy lifestyles; keep safe and maintain the safety of others; develop and maintain positive self-esteem; take responsibility for their own actions; have confidence in themselves and their own abilities; make and keep meaningful and rewarding relationships; be aware of their own feelings and those of others; consider and respect the differences of other people and be active participants as citizens of a democratic society. Promoting children's health and well-being can be particularly helpful for children who are experiencing negative social or environmental factors. For example, actively promoting children's well-being may help to reduce the numbers of young people involved in teenage pregnancies, alcohol/drug misuse, truancy and crime (Goleman, 1996).

Encouraging positive social interactions

Having at least one secure and personal relationship with a parent or carer enables children to form other relationships. Consistent, loving care from parent/carer who is sensitive to the child's particular needs enables children to feel secure and to develop self-worth. Observing the behaviour of parents and other significant adults (child carers, play workers, teachers, and teaching assistants) affects children's own behaviour including how they relate to others. A child's ability to relate to others may also be affected by: special needs, such as communication and/or social interaction difficulties; family circumstances such as separation or divorce; death, abandonment or other permanent separation from parent or main carer. All children need affection, security, acceptance, encouragement, patience and a stimulating environment. Children deprived of these in the first 5 to 6 years of life may find it difficult to relate to other people throughout childhood (and even adulthood). However, children are amazingly resilient and subsequent sustained relationships with caring adults in a supportive environment can help children overcome early parental separation, rejection or neglect.

Adults who provide inconsistent or inappropriate care may unwittingly encourage difficult behaviour in children. This can lead to adults spending less time interacting with the child, resulting in the child having poor communication skills as well as difficulties in establishing and maintaining positive relationships with other people. In contrast, positive social interactions with adults (and other children) in various settings will lead to children being able to demonstrate positive ways of relating to others and using appropriate social skills.

Group dynamics

As a teaching assistant, you should understand how group dynamics affect the various stages of group development; that is, pupil interaction and their behaviour within social groups. As well as coping with the demands of the curriculum, pupils are dealing with their peers and the social world of other pupils. Friendship and membership of a peer group seem especially important. Each individual has different personal characteristics that affect their ability to communicate effectively and work comfortably alongside others. From your experiences of working with pupils you may have identified their differing characteristics that influence their willingness or reluctance to interact within a group.

 **Activity!**

Think about the personal characteristics of the pupil or pupils you work with. How do they interact in group situations?
- Do they take turns at speaking and listening?
- Do they work cooperatively?
- Do they try to impose their own ideas on the group?

Where the group size is appropriate to the task and the group dynamics are right, the contribution levels from pupils will be fairly even. Pupils usually know when it is their turn to speak and are aware if anyone has not had an opportunity to contribute and will try to involve that member of the group. Most pupils understand that to effectively work together it is important to utilise the offerings of all members of the group – even when this means considering different viewpoints and conflicting ideas. To achieve this level of positive social interaction and effective learning experience, the composition of any group is very important. Pupils may not work well with certain others; they may ask to work with pupils they know well in order to make better progress.

Opportunities for learning should be flexible and available in a variety of groupings: one-to-one; pairs/small groups; large groups; and whole class. This allows for individual differences within the class and gives every pupil opportunities to develop many different learning skills in a variety of meaningful ways. Group work allows pupils to: identify and solve problems; select relevant information; collaborate socially to increase own knowledge; structure effective discussions; evaluate conflicting ideas and develop communication skills (Prisk in Pollard, 1987; p. 97).

You also need to be aware of the stages in the development of groups and how these affect group dynamics. Research suggests that groups and teams grow and develop through a four-stage cycle – see the section on stages in team development in Chapter 9. When working with a group of children and/or young people, you can take on the role of the 'team leader' to help the group get to know each other and learn how to work well together.

Encouraging pupils to share and cooperate

Encouraging children to take turns is also an essential element of helping them to interact positively with other children. From about the age of 3 young children begin to cooperate with other children in play activities. By about 5 years they should be quite adept at playing cooperatively with other children. Gradually children should be able to participate in more complex cooperative play, including games with rules, as their understanding of abstract ideas increases.

We live in a highly competitive society; we all want to be the best, fastest, strongest or cleverest. The media (television, magazines and newspapers) focuses our attention on being the best. Most sports and games have only one *winner* that means all the other participants are *losers*. To win is the aim of all contestants. *Winning* makes the individual feel good, confident and successful; *losing* makes the individual feel bad, inadequate and unsuccessful. Competitive games can prepare children for the competitiveness of real life. However, competition can also contribute to children's: negative self-image and low self-esteem; aggressive behaviour; lack of compassion for others and overwhelming desire to win at *any* cost.

Competitive sports and games can be beneficial to children's social development as long as they emphasise: cooperation and working as a team; mutual respect; agreeing on rules and following them; that participation and the pleasure of taking part are more important than winning and doing their *personal* best.

As well as being competitive, people can also be sociable and cooperative; we like to be part of a group or groups. Cooperative activities encourage children to: be self-confident; have high self-esteem; relate positively to others; work together and help others; make joint decisions; participate fully (no one is left out or eliminated); have a sense of belonging.

Ten ways to enable pupils to relate positively to others

You can enable pupils to relate positively to others by encouraging pupils to:

1. Celebrate our individual differences. We are all important, valued and unique individuals.
2. Listen and be attentive to what others have to communicate.
3. Regard and value the needs and rights of others.
4. Recognise and respect the culture and beliefs of others.
5. Be considerate and courteous towards others.
6. Help and care for each other as much as we are able.
7. Cooperate and work together to reach the best solutions.
8. Share and take turns; remember compromise equals wise.
9. Praise and encourage others to raise their self-esteem.
10. Inspire respect in others through our own kindness, fairness and honesty.

 Key Task

Plan and implement an activity that encourages pupils to relate to others, for example through working cooperatively during group activities.

NOS Links:

Level 3:   STL 3.4   STL 4.1   STL 4.3   STL 20.1   STL 20.2   STL 20.3   STL 41.2
           STL 45.1

Encouraging children's self-reliance, self-esteem and self-image

As a teaching assistant, you should encourage children's self-reliance, self-esteem and self-image by: engaging with and providing focused attention to individual pupils; treating pupils with respect and consideration as individual people in their own right; and showing empathy to pupils by demonstrating understanding of their feelings and points of view. You should encourage pupils to take decisions and make choices (see section below on involving pupils in decision-making). You should communicate with pupils openly and honestly in ways that are not judgemental. You should help pupils to choose realistic goals that are challenging but achievable (see section on setting goals and boundaries in Chapter 7). You should praise specific behaviour that you wish to encourage as well as directing any comments, whether positive or negative, towards the demonstrated behaviour not the pupil (see sections on rewards and sanctions in Chapter 7).

You should work with colleagues and other professionals, as required, to encourage children's self-esteem and resilience, for example by providing opportunities to encourage children's self-reliance, positive self-esteem and self-image (see below). You may need to work with other professionals (counsellors, psychologists or social workers) to promote the well-being and resilience of pupils with additional support needs (see Chapter 13).

Encouraging children's self-reliance

Encouraging children's self-reliance is an important part of helping them to develop their independence and resilience, which will enable them to face life's demands and challenges in preparation for their adult lives. Encouraging self-reliance involves helping children to develop: independence (or autonomy) the ability to think and act for oneself; dependence on own capabilities and personal resources; competence in looking after self; trust in their own judgement and actions; and confidence in their own abilities and actions.

Eight ways to encourage children's self-reliance

You can encourage children's self-reliance in the following ways:

1. Provide freedom for pupils to become more independent.

2. Be patient and provide time for pupils to do things for themselves, for example let younger pupils dress themselves (for PE); although it takes longer, it is an essential self-help skill. Pupils with physical disabilities may need sensitive support in this area.

3. Praise and encourage their efforts at becoming more independent.

4. Be aware of individual needs for independence; every pupil is different and will require encouragement relevant to their particular level of development. Do not insist pupils be more independent in a particular area until they are ready.

5. Be sensitive to changing needs for independence. Remember a pupil who is tired, distressed or unwell may require more adult assistance than usual.

6. Offer choices to help pupils feel more in control. As they develop and mature, increase the scope of choices. Involve the pupils in *decision-making* within the school. (See below)

7. Provide play opportunities that encourage independence, for example dressing-up is a fun way to help younger pupils learn to dress independently.

8. Use technology to encourage independence, such as specialist play equipment; voice-activated word-processing; motorised wheelchairs.

Figure 14.2: Pupil demonstrating self-help skills

 Key Task

- Observe a pupil demonstrating self-help skills such as: washing hands; getting dressed/undressed (for example, for PE); tidying up.
- Assess the pupil's ability to perform the skill independently. Outline the adult's role in developing the pupil's self-reliance in this area.

NOS Links:

Level 3:   **STL 45.2**   **STL 45.4**

Involving children and young people in decision-making

As a teaching assistant, you should know and understand the importance of encouraging pupils to make choices and involving pupils in decision-making. This includes encouraging pupils to take responsibility for everyday tasks within the school. Younger pupils are quite capable of making their own decisions and this helps to develop their independence and extends their own communication skills even further. For example, pupils as young as 4 years old can: be responsible for tidying up their own activities, getting equipment out (under adult supervision for safety reasons, of course); choose their own activities; and select and follow written and/or pictorial instructions for tasks/activities to be done that session.

Children have the right to be consulted and involved in decision-making about matters that affect them (UN Convention on the Rights of the Child, Article 12 – see page 171). Children should have opportunities to be involved in the planning, implementation and evaluation of policies that affect them or the services they use (Children and Young People's Unit, 2001). Involving pupils in decision-making within your school will help you to support the teachers in providing better educational provision based on the children's real needs rather than adult assumptions about children's needs. It will also help the school to promote social inclusion by encouraging the pupils to participate as active citizens in their local community.

You could involve pupils in decision-making in the following ways:

1. A suggestion box for their comments and complaints about the provision including play opportunities.
2. Questionnaires and surveys to find out their opinions about the setting's policies and procedures including any gaps in the provision.
3. Consultation exercises such as discussion groups; drama and role play activities, music and games to provide opportunities for children to express ideas.
4. Direct involvement, for example taking part in staff development and recruitment activities, assessing new initiatives, mentoring other children, providing information via leaflets, posters and IT for other children.

(CYPU, 2001)

 Key Task

- How does your school involve children and young people in decision-making?
- What opportunities are provided to enable young people to be active citizens?

NOS Links:

Level 3:   **STL 20.1**   **STL 20.2**   **STL 45.2**   **STL 45.4**   **STL 47.1**   **STL 47.2**

Encouraging children's positive self-esteem

A person's self-esteem is changeable; sometimes we feel more positive about ourselves than at other times. Even if we have had past experiences that resulted in negative or poor self-esteem, we can overcome this and learn to feel more positive about ourselves. Self-esteem involves: feelings and thoughts about oneself (positive or negative); respect or regard for self (or lack of it); consideration of self; self-worth (value of self); self-image (perception of self). How we feel about ourselves depends on a number of factors: who we are with at the time; the social context – where we are; current and past relationships; and past experiences (especially in early childhood).

We cannot see self-esteem, but we can assess children's (and adults') levels of self-esteem by their emotional responses, attitudes and actions. People with positive or high self-esteem are usually: calm and relaxed; energetic, enthusiastic and well-motivated; open and expressive; positive and optimistic; self-reliant and self-confident; assertive; reflective (aware of own strengths and weaknesses); sociable, cooperative, friendly and trusting. People with negative or low self-esteem tend to be: anxious and tense; lacking in enthusiasm, poorly motivated and easily frustrated; secretive and/or pretentious; negative and pessimistic; over-dependent, lacking in confidence and constantly seeking the approval of others or over-confident, arrogant and attention seeking; aggressive or passive; self-destructive or abusive towards others; resentful and distrustful of others.

Possible reasons for low self-esteem

All children begin with the *potential* for high self-esteem, but their interactions with others contribute to whether positive self-esteem is encouraged or diminished. Experiences in early childhood have the most significant effect on children's self-esteem; sometimes these effects may not become apparent until adolescence or adulthood when serious psychological and social problems may result due to very low self-esteem. Children (and adults) are very resilient and can learn to have greater self-esteem even if their earlier experiences were detrimental. Factors which lead to low self-esteem include: being deprived of basic needs or having these needs inadequately met; having feelings denied or ignored; being put-down, ridiculed or humiliated; participating in inappropriate activities; feeling that their ideas and opinions are unimportant; being over-protected, under-disciplined or excessively disciplined; and being physically or sexually abused (Lindenfield, 1995).

✎ Activity!

- Think of as many *positive* words to describe yourself using the same initial as your first name, for example *caring, creative,* Carlton; *magnificent, marvellous,* Miriam; *sensitive, sharing,* Shazia; *terrific, tremendous* Tom.
- You could also try this with friends, colleagues or a group of pupils.

Factors affecting self-image and identity

The development of self-image is strongly linked to self-esteem. Self-image can be defined as the individual's view of their own personality and abilities including the individual's *perception* of how other people view them and their abilities. This involves recognising ourselves as separate and unique individuals with characteristics which make us different from others. Self-image also involves a number of factors which influence how we *identify* with other people. For example: gender, culture, race, nationality, religion, language, social status/occupation, disability/special needs, early childhood experiences and relationships.

Children develop their self-image through interactions with others starting with family members and gradually including child carers, teachers, teaching assistants, friends and classmates. Through positive interactions, children learn to value themselves and their abilities *if* they receive approval, respect and empathy. Early childhood experiences and relationships may have positive or negative influences on children's self-image.

Research shows that intelligence or physical attractiveness are *not* factors in children's self-image or self-esteem; very intelligent or attractive children may still have poor self-esteem and self-image. The main reason for poor self-image and low self-esteem is the treatment that children receive from their parents (Fontana, 1984). Children with positive self-image: tend to come from homes where they are regarded as significant and interesting people; have their views invited and listened to; have parents with high, but reasonable and consistent expectations; receive firm discipline based on rewards and sanctions *not* physical punishment. Children with negative self-image: tend to come from homes where no one takes any real interest in them; have parents with limited, negative or unreasonable expectations; are given little consistent guidance and/or care; receive too little discipline or overly strict discipline or a confusing mixture of the two.

However, it is not just parents who influence children's self-image and self-esteem. Adults working with children (such as child carers, play workers, teachers and teaching assistants) also influence children's self-image and self-esteem through their attitudes, words and actions. In schools pupils soon become aware that certain levels of performance are expected by adults and begin to compare their own achievements with that of other pupils. If pupils regularly feel that their achievements do not compare favourably with those of other pupils, then they begin to experience a sense of failure and inferiority. Pupils may react to this feeling by either passively accepting that they are a failure and being reluctant to attempt new learning activities or rebelling against and rejecting all learning activities that remind them of failure.

Adults have important roles to play in children's development of self-image and identity. Children are able to see and feel not only the way adults interact with them personally, but also the way adults interact with other children and adults at home, in the child care setting or at school. Young children are very capable and accurate at assessing what the adult expectations of them are and behaving accordingly! The constraints of class size, time and resources mean that many classrooms do group pupils according to ability. Nursery and primary education are now more curriculum and assessment orientated due to early learning goals, baseline assessment, the National Curriculum, including the literacy and numeracy hours, and Standard Assessment Tasks (SATs).

Some children may experience particular difficulties in developing a positive self-image. For example: children with special needs; children from ethnic minorities; and children who are/ have been abused. These children may be experiencing prejudice and/or discrimination on a regular basis which affects their ability to maintain a positive self-image.

As a teaching assistant you need to be aware of your own self-image and the importance of having positive self-esteem. This may mean that you need to deal with issues regarding your own self-image and to raise your own self-esteem before you can encourage a child's positive self-image.

 Activity!

- Think about the factors which influence your own self-image (male or female; full or part-time student; employment status; nationality and race; any special needs; early experiences and relationships).
- How do you think these factors influence your self-image and the ways you think other people see you? (For example, some people may consider a female studying for a teaching assistant qualification is appropriate for a woman, but a male studying the same course may be regarded differently.)

Encouraging children's positive self-esteem and self-image

By praising *all* children and encouraging them to feel good about themselves and their achievements, adults can help *all* children to establish and maintain a positive self-image. Developing and implementing inclusive policies, procedures and strategies will also help (see section on promoting equality, diversity and inclusion in Chapter 8).

Ten ways to encourage positive self-esteem and self-image

You can encourage pupils to develop positive self-esteem and self-image by:

1. Treating every pupil as an individual; every pupil has unique abilities and needs.

2. Being positive by using praise and encouragement to help pupils to focus on what they are good at.

3. Helping pupils to maximise their individual potential.

4. Encouraging pupils to measure their achievements by comparing them to their own efforts.

5. Having high but realistic expectations of all pupils.

6. Taking an interest in each pupil's efforts as well as achievements.

7. Encouraging positive participation during learning activities, e.g. sharing resources, helping others and contributing ideas.

8. Giving pupils opportunities to make decisions and choices.

9. Promoting equality of opportunity by providing positive images of children, young people and adults through books, stories and songs.

10. Remembering to label the behaviour not the pupil as this is less damaging to their self-esteem: 'That was an unkind thing to say' rather than 'You are unkind'.

Figure 14.3: Example of child's personal flag

 **Activity!**

- Design your own 'personal flag'. Use words and pictures to describe the following: my happiest memory; my best qualities; my significant achievements; my current goal.
- If possible, try this activity with a pupil or small group of pupils.

Encouraging children's resilience

The pressures of modern living in the twenty-first century affect the emotional well-being and resilience of both children and adults. For example:

1. Parents in the UK work longer hours than in any other country in Europe; consequently working parents have less time to spend with their children.
2. National Curriculum demands have led to a return to more formal methods of teaching with increased emphasis on academic achievement for all children, for example literacy and numeracy hours, end of key stage tests.
3. Technological advances and concerns about personal safety mean many children and young people spend more time in front of televisions, computers and games consoles then playing out with friends.

Academic intelligence or achievement has very little to do with emotional well-being. According to research, intelligence quotient (IQ) contributes 20 per cent to the factors that lead to success in life, while other factors contribute the other 80 per cent. These other factors include: environmental and social factors (see section below on factors that affect resilience); luck, e.g. being in the right place at the right time or wrong place at the wrong time and emotional intelligence or competence (Goleman, 1996).

 key words

Intelligence quotient: a person's mental age in comparison to their chronological age.

Emotional intelligence: a person's ability to deal with life's highs and lows.

In Britain we tend to place great importance on people's qualifications and job status. We need to put more emphasis on people's emotional intelligence or well-being as this would lead to people having better life skills, for example making better use of leisure time, maintaining positive relationships, being able to pass exams, getting satisfying and challenging jobs, and being better parents.

Emotional intelligence or emotional well-being involves developing: positive self-esteem and self-image; emotional strength to deal with life's highs and lows; confidence to face the world with optimism; and an awareness of our own feelings and those of other people.

We all need to feel valued – that who we are and where we come from are respected; that our ideas and abilities are important. On this solid emotional platform the building blocks for a stimulating and fulfilling life can be successfully constructed. Even if these building blocks are damaged by life experiences, personal difficulties, tragedy or trauma they can be rebuilt in childhood, adolescence and even adulthood.

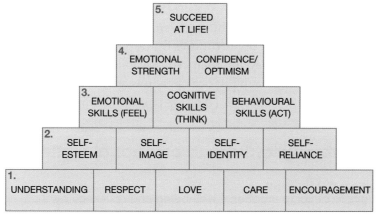

Key:

1. These **foundation stones** are established by parents, grandparents and carers in childhood; as adults we can regain them through partners/spouses, close friends, etc.
2. These **self-building blocks** are influenced by others including family, carers, teachers, teaching assistants, playworkers, friends, peers, colleagues, etc. throughout life.
3. These **skills** can be developed as a child and/or as an adult.
4. These **qualities** can be demonstrated as a child and/or as an adult.
5. **Individual achievements** in different areas of life as a child and as an adult.

Figure 14.4: Emotional building blocks

Factors that affect resilience

Children vary in their responses to a set of circumstances. Some children may do well even in extremely adverse circumstances while others may not be able to cope with small amounts of stress. Rutter describes resilience as 'the phenomenon of overcoming stress or adversity' (DH, 2000). Resilience (or protective) factors cushion children from the worst effects of adversity and may help a 'child or young person to cope, survive and even thrive in the face of great hurt and disadvantage' (Bostock, 2004).

Resilience factors are things which help children and young people withstand adversity and to cope in unfavourable circumstances or times of difficulty. Resilience factors include:

- Positive attachment experiences, for example caring relationship with parents and/or carers.
- Positive relationships with caring, concerned and sincere adults (such as child carers, teachers, teaching assistants) can also increase self-esteem.
- Positive early years/school experiences, including participation in activities they enjoy build positive self-esteem.
- Recognition, respect and rewards for special skills and talents that everyone has as unique individuals, for example nurturing academic, artistic, musical, sporting and vocational abilities through activities both in the setting and in spare time.
- Opportunities to take responsibility or contribute to decisions which affect one's life, such as involvement in discussions/reviews to develop services for children/young people.
- A sense of direction that provides stability and control by building up a picture of what the future might hold, for example helping to develop goals and understanding how to reach these goals.

(Bostock, 2004)

Promoting children's emotional well-being and resilience

As a teaching assistant you can promote children's emotional well-being and resilience by working with the teacher to provide opportunities for pupils to: learn about their feelings; understand the feelings of others; develop their creative abilities, for example in art and craft, drama, musical activities; participate in physical activities, games and sport; interact with other pupils. make friends and play together; and develop emotional intelligence.

Five ways to promote children's emotional well-being and resilience

You can help pupils to develop emotional well-being and resilience by:

1. **Developing their self-awareness** including helping pupils to establish a positive self-image and to recognise their own feelings.

2. **Helping them to handle and express feelings** in appropriate ways, such as through creative, imaginative and physical play.

3. **Encouraging their self-motivation** by helping pupils to establish personal goals, through developing self-control and self-reliance.

4. **Developing their empathy for other people** by encouraging pupils to recognise the feelings, needs and rights of others.

5. **Encouraging positive social interaction** by helping pupils to develop effective interpersonal skills through play and other cooperative group activities in the school and in the local community.

 Key Task

Describe how you have helped pupils to develop emotional well-being and resilience.

NOS Links:

Level 3:	STL 20.1	STL 20.2	STL 20.3	STL 41.3	STL 45.1	STL 45.2	
	STL 45.3	STL 45.4	STL 47.1	STL 47.2	STL 48.1	STL 48.2	STL 48.3

Summary of key points in this chapter:

- **Identifying transitions** including: common transitions; personal transitions; family circumstances.

- **How transitions may affect children's behaviour and development** including: the positive and negative effects of transitions; starting nursery or primary school; moving from primary to secondary school; changing schools.

- **Supporting transitions** including: ten principles to support children's transitions; transitions and children aged 3 to 11 years; transitions from 11 to 16 years and beyond.

- **Learning mentors** including: the role of the learning mentor; a structured approach to learner mentoring.

- **Enabling pupils to relate to others** including: encouraging positive social interactions; group dynamics; encouraging pupils to share and cooperate.
- **Encouraging children's self-reliance, self-esteem and self-image** including: encouraging children's self-reliance; involving children and young people in decision-making; encouraging children's positive self-esteem; possible reasons for low self-esteem; factors affecting self-image and identity; encouraging children's positive self-esteem and self-image.
- **Encouraging children's resilience** including: factors that affect resilience; promoting children's emotional well-being and resilience.

Further reading

Burns, D.M. (2010) *When Kids are Grieving: Addressing Grief and Loss in School*. Corwin Press.

Cefai, C. and Cooper, P. (2008) *Promoting Resilience in the Classroom: A Guide to Developing Students' Emotional and Cognitive Skills*. Jessica Kingsley Publishers.

CWDC (2007) *Learning Mentors Practice Guide. Children's Workforce Development Council*. Available free at: **www.cwdcouncil.org.uk**.

Cowie, H. et al. (2004) *Emotional Health and Well-Being: A Practical Guide for Schools*. Sage Publications.

Evangelou, M. (2008) *What Makes a Successful Transition from Primary to Secondary School?* DCSF. **http://www.standards.dfes.gov.uk/research/themes/transition/successfultransition/**

Fabian, H. (2002) *Children Starting School: A Guide to Successful Transitions and Transfers for Teachers and Assistants*. David Fulton Publishers.

Roberts, M. and Constable, D. (2003) *Handbook for Learning Mentors in Primary and Secondary Schools*. David Fulton Publishers.

15. Supporting the wider work of the school

This chapter relates to QCF units:

TDA 3.25 Lead an extra-curricular activity

TDA 3.27 Monitor and maintain curriculum resources

TDA 3.28 Organise travel for children and young people

TDA 3.29 Supervise children and young people on journeys, visits and activities outside of the setting

Leading extra-curricular activities

You may be involved in providing support for extra-curricular activities for children and/ or young people to develop their skills and talents, for example through sporting, musical, artistic, creative, intellectual or linguistic activities. Extra-curricular activities include clubs, sports teams, recreational activities or performing arts groups which are under the direction of the school but with limited supervision. When supporting extra-curricular activities you will need to help with preparing children and/or young people for the activity and supporting the children and/or young people during the activity.

Preparing children and young people for an extra-curricular activity

When preparing children and young people for an extra-curricular activity, you will be involved in:

- Helping the children/young people to feel welcome and at ease.
- Following your school's procedures for checking the children/young people present.
- Ensuring the children/young people's dress and equipment are safe and appropriate.
- Organising the children/young people so that you can communicate effectively with them.
- Explaining the aims and content of the session to the children/young people.
- Finding out if the children/young people have any relevant experience you could build on.
- Ensuring the children/young people are mentally and physically prepared for the planned activities.

(TDA, 2007)

Introducing children and young people to an extra-curricular activity

When introducing children and young people to an extra-curricular activity, you will be involved in:

- Explaining and demonstrating key points to the children/young people, using methods appropriate to their age, stage of development and needs.
- Emphasising the importance of, and reasons for, these key points to the children/young people.
- Encouraging the children/young people to ask questions.
- Answering the children/young people's questions helpfully and clearly.
- Checking that the children/young people understand what you want them to do.
- Motivating the children/young people to take part without putting them under undue stress.

(TDA, 2007)

Figure 15.1: Adult leading an extra-curricular activity

Leading an extra-curricular activity

When leading an extra-curricular activity, you will be involved in the following:

- Ensuring the children/young people are following your instructions throughout the activity.
- Developing the activity at a pace suited to the children/young people and in a way that meets its aims.
- Giving the children/young people clear and supportive feedback at appropriate points.
- Providing the children/young people with additional explanations and demonstrations when necessary.
- Encouraging the children/young people to say how they feel about the activity and respond to their feelings appropriately.

- Varying the activity to meet new needs and opportunities.
- Encouraging and supporting the children/young people to identify what learning they can transfer to areas of their school curriculum and/or other areas of their life.

(TDA, 2007)

Encouraging effective working relationships during an extra-curricular activity

When maintaining and encouraging an extra-curricular activity, you will be involved in:

- Communicating and interacting with the children/young people in a way that is appropriate to their age, stage of development and needs.
- Establishing and maintaining a relationship with the children/young people consistent with the situation and ethical requirements.
- Giving adequate attention to each child/young person in the group, according to their needs.
- Encouraging effective communication and inter-personal skills between the children/young people.
- Encouraging and supporting the children/young people to consider the impact of their behaviour on others, themselves and their environment.
- Highlighting and praising types of behaviour that have a positive effect on the group as a whole.
- Identifying and challenging inappropriate behaviour in a way that maintains the emotional welfare of the children/young people and follows agreed procedures.

 Key Task

Describe how you have been involved in leading an extra-curricular activity. Include information on:

- preparing the children or young people for the activity
- introducing the activity to the children or young people
- leading the activity
- maintaining and encouraging effective relationships during the activity.

NOS Links:

Level 3:   **STL 20.1**   **STL 20.2**   **STL 53.1**   **STL 53.2**   **STL 53.3**   **STL 53.4**

Helping to organise the learning environment

Central to creating an appropriate learning environment for all pupils in school is providing space, time and resources relevant to the needs of the pupils and the requirements of the curriculum for your home country. As well as provision for the curriculum subjects, there should be regular times for routines such as playtimes/breaks, lunchtime, lunchtime clubs and after school activities. A daily routine provides stability and security for pupils. The class timetable should be clearly displayed in a manner appropriate to the ages of the pupils; older pupils should have their own copy of their weekly timetable. Flexibility is also important to allow for special events such as educational visits, swimming lessons or visitors to the school.

The precise way the learning environment is organised depends on: specific curriculum requirements; the resources for particular subject areas; the learning objectives for the pupils; individual teaching and learning styles; behaviour management strategies; and the inclusion of pupils with special educational needs. Effective organisation is also influenced by the general quality of the learning environment. The learning environment should have:

- **Adequate floor space for the age, size and needs of the pupils**. This means teaching space including space for teaching assistants to work with individuals or groups of pupils as needed. Pupils with physical disabilities may require additional floor space for wheelchairs and other specialised equipment or furniture. Pupils with emotional and/or behavioural difficulties may also benefit from adequate personal classroom space.

- **Appropriate sources of heating, lighting and ventilation**. Pupils need to work in an environment that is neither too hot nor too cold as these can affect concentration levels. The heating source must be safe and fitted/maintained to the required legal standards. There should be good sources of both natural and artificial light.

- **Appropriate acoustic conditions** to enable pupils to listen during essential discussions and to help reduce noise levels. Carpeted floor areas, sound absorbent screens, displays, drapes and curtains all help to absorb reverberation.

- **Adequate storage space** for the materials and equipment needed to meet the demands of the National Curriculum. There should also be space for computer workstations with access to mains power.

The classroom layout should be free from clutter and easily accessible to all pupils including those with physical disabilities or sensory impairment. The learning environment should also be welcoming and user-friendly. This includes taking account of cultural differences by providing displays and notices which reflect the cultural diversity of the school and local community.

 Key Task

With the class teacher's permission, take a photograph of the classroom and comment on how the learning environment provides:

- adequate floor space for the age, size and needs of the children
- appropriate sources of heating, lighting and ventilation
- appropriate acoustic conditions
- adequate storage space for materials and equipment
- access for all pupils including those with physical disabilities or sensory impairment.

NOS Links:
Level 3:   STL 3.1   STL 31.1   STL 31.2   STL 31.3

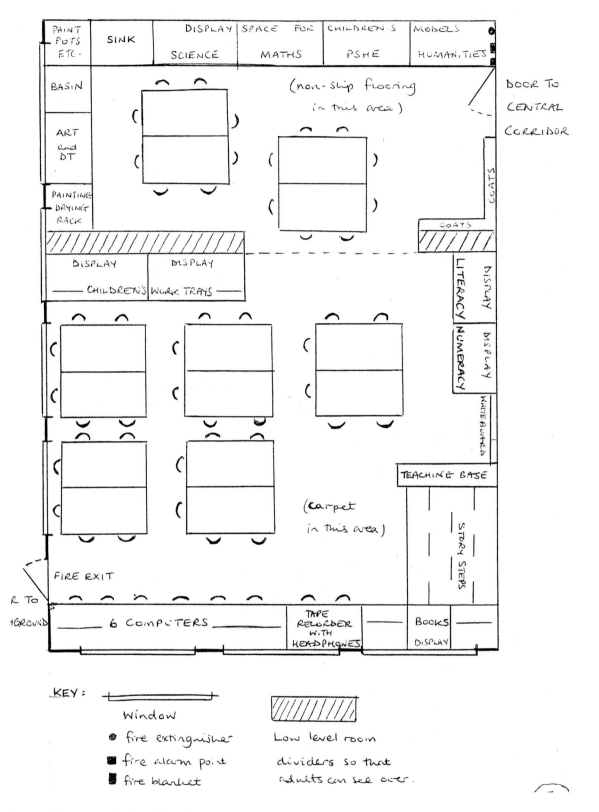

Figure 15.2: An example of an effective learning environment

As part of your role of assisting the teacher with the organisation of the learning environment, you may be responsible for:

- **A group of pupils** and be involved in setting out materials or helping the pupils to access them, explaining a task, maintaining their concentration and interest, asking and/or answering questions, helping pupils to clear away afterwards before moving on to support them with their next activity.
- **A specific activity** with different groups of pupils throughout the day or week (for example supporting literacy, numeracy, science or ICT).
- **A pupil with special educational needs** and ensuring that they have the necessary materials and equipment to participate in the lesson including any specialist equipment.

In addition to knowing the timetable for the pupil and/or class you work with, you should have your own timetable showing where, what and with whom you are working throughout the school day. (Detailed information about your role and responsibilities is in Chapter 5.)

 **Activity!**

- Outline the daily/weekly routine for the pupil and/or class whose learning you support.
- Provide a copy of your own personal timetable.

Organising classroom resources

Every classroom is equipped with a basic set of resources and books appropriate to the age range. Care is taken to ensure that resources reflect the cultural and linguistic diversity of our society, and that all pupils have equality of access. Examples of general classroom resources include:

- Visual aids: wall displays including pupils' work, maps, pictures and posters; interest tables with interesting objects related to topic work; 3-D displays of pupils' work including construction models; videos; computer graphics and books. Displays in the classroom reflect the linguistic and cultural diversity of the school.
- Groups of tables for whole class and group work, including literacy and numeracy activities.
- Groups of tables for 'messy' practical activities (for example art and design, design technology) including storage for art/design materials and equipment such as paint, paint pots, drying rack; sink for washing paint pots and brushes; basin for washing hands.
- Some computers and a printer with selection of appropriate software (see below).
- Tape recorder/compact disc player with headphones with a selection of audiotapes/CDs.
- Book/story corner with appropriate range of fiction and non-fiction books including some dual language books.
- Storage units for specific curriculum areas.
- White board, over-head projector and teaching base including marker pens, transparencies, textbooks, teaching manuals and other resources needed by the teacher or teaching assistant on a regular basis.
- Writing and drawing materials including a variety of writing tools (crayons, pencils, pens, pastels, chalks); different shapes, sizes and types of paper (plain, coloured, graph).

- Children's work trays to store individual exercise books for literacy, numeracy and science; individual folders for topic work; individual reading books and reading logs; personal named pencils; individual crayon tins.
- Area with individual coat pegs for coats and PE bags.

The learning environment will also have <u>specialist resources</u> to support specific curriculum areas: English; Mathematics; Science; Information and Communication Technology (ICT); Art and Design; Design Technology; Food Technology; Physical Education (PE); Music; PSHE, Citizenship, Religious Studies, Geography and History. Specialist resources include: videos, maps, posters, pictures, artefacts, story and information books related to class topics or themes. Specialist resources should be stored in the appropriate curriculum resource cupboard or area, and be regularly audited by the curriculum subject co-ordinator. Staff may contact curriculum subject coordinators with suggestions for specialist materials that may need ordering. If you support pupils' learning in any of these areas then you need to be aware of the specific resources and any particular safety requirements.

key words

General classroom resources: equipment and materials that support all areas of the curriculum, for example pictures, posters and 3-D displays, books, computers, white board, writing and drawing materials.

Specialist resources: to support specific curriculum areas, for example mathematical and scientific equipment, art and design materials, maps, books and DVDs relating to specific subjects.

Consumable resources: materials that get used up such as stationery items (paper, cardboard, glue, pens, pencils, exercise books), cleaning materials and ingredients for cooking activities.

Non-consumable resources: equipment and materials that do not get used up such as furniture, computers, books, teaching packs, posters and play equipment.

 **Activity!**

- What are general classroom resources?
- What are specialist resources for specific curriculum areas? If possible, give examples from the resources you use on a regular basis.

Here are some general guidelines about organising resources and materials in the classroom:

- Fire exits must not be obstructed, locked or hidden from view.
- Chairs and tables need to be the correct size and height for the age and level of development of the children.
- Books, jigsaws, art/design materials and computers need to be used in areas with a good source of light, if possible near a source of natural light.
- Water, sand, art and design technology activities need to be provided in an area with an appropriate floor surface with washing facilities nearby.
- Ensure that activities requiring maximum concentration, such as literacy or numeracy activities, are not on the direct route to the hand-washing area or too close to messy/noisy activities or doorways.
- Any large or heavy equipment that has to be moved for use should be close to where it is stored.

Checking classroom resources

As part of your role you may need to make regular checks to ensure that essential materials or equipment are not running out. Clearing away equipment and materials provides you with a regular opportunity to check whether classroom supplies are running low. You may need to keep a weekly check on <u>consumable resources</u> such as art and craft materials, paper, cardboard and other stationery items. Items such as soap, paper towels and so on may need to be checked everyday. When the class teacher or teaching assistant requires resources, a stock requisition form should be completed and given to the person responsible for the storage area. Non-consumable resources are things like teaching packs, flash cards, posters and books. When you need to borrow non-consumable resources, it is necessary to sign them out. There should be a logbook in each storage area for this purpose. There will be an inventory or stock list for classroom resources that is checked on a regular basis. Larger items such as classroom furniture may be included on an inventory checked annually. There will be a school procedure for doing this.

 Key Task

- Outline your main role and responsibilities for helping to organise the learning environment.
- What are the school's procedures for monitoring and maintaining the supply of classroom resources?
- What is your role and responsibility in relation to these procedures? Include examples of different records you have used to monitor and maintain the supply of classroom resources, such as copies of stock requisition forms, inventory or stock lists.

NOS Links:

Level 3:	STL 3.1	STL 18.1	STL 18.2	STL 23.1	STL 24.1	STL 28.2
	STL 31.1	STL 31.2	STL 31.3	STL 38.1	STL 45.1	STL 45.2
	STL 45.3	STL 47.1	STL 52.1	STL 52.2	STL 56.1	STL 56.2

Encouraging pupils to help maintain their learning environment

The routine of getting out and putting away equipment is part of the learning experience for pupils. This routine helps younger pupils to develop mathematical concepts such as sorting and matching sets of objects and judging space, capacity and volume. It helps all pupils to develop a sense of responsibility for caring for their own learning environment. Pupils of all ages can also gain confidence and independence when involved in setting out and clearing away learning materials as appropriate to their age/level of development and any safety requirements. Materials and equipment should be stored and/or displayed in ways that will enable pupils to choose, use and return them easily. You must ensure that pupils only help in ways that are in line with the school's health and safety policy. Pupils must never have access to dangerous materials, such as bleach, or use very hot water for cleaning, and they should not carry large, heavy or awkward objects due to the potential risks of serious injury. (Detailed information about health and safety is in Chapter 5.)

Organising travel for children and young people

Part of your role may include supporting travel out of setting involving children and young people with adult supervision, for example for home-to-school travel, educational visits, field studies or sports fixtures. This may involve organising and supervising travel for children, young people and adults. Travel may be 'self-powered', for example on foot or by bicycle, in an owned or hired vehicle, or by public transport (TDA, 2007).

To ensure pupil safety you must follow the school's policy and procedures for supporting travel out of setting including:

- Collecting the relevant information for the pupils to be escorted.
- Ensuring the staff/pupil ratio meets organisational and legal requirements.
- Ensuring that everyone involved is aware of the travel arrangements.
- Ensuring that staff are at the meeting point at the agreed time.
- Escorting the pupils in a safe manner using the agreed route and mode of transport.
- Ensuring the pupils enter the setting in a safe manner.
- Carrying out the agreed procedures for pupils who are not at the meeting point.

 Key Task

Describe the policy and procedures for organising and supervising travel.

NOS Links:

Level 3:   STL 3. 1   STL 3.2   STL 58.1   STL 58.2   STL 59.1   STL 59.2

Helping to supervise pupils on educational trips and out-of-school activities

The health and safety of pupils on educational visits is part of the school's overall health and safety policy. The most senior member of staff on the educational visit will usually have overall responsibility and act as the group leader. Any other teachers present will also have responsibility for pupils on educational visits at all times. Teaching assistants on educational visits should be clear about their exact roles and responsibilities during any visit.

Teaching assistants helping to supervise pupils on educational visits must:

- Follow the instructions of the group leader and teacher supervisors.
- Not have sole charge of pupils (unless previously agreed as part of the risk assessment for the visit).
- Help to maintain the health and safety of everyone on the visit.
- Help with the control and discipline of pupils to avoid potential dangers/accidents.
- Never be alone with a pupil wherever possible (this is for the protection of both the adult and the pupil).
- Report any concerns about the health or safety of pupils to the group leader or teacher supervisors immediately.

(DfEE, 1998)

Teaching assistants should be aware of pupils who might require closer supervision during educational visits (such as pupils with special educational needs or behavioural difficulties). Additional safety procedures to those used in school may be necessary to support pupils with medical needs during educational visits (for example arrangements for taking medication). Sometimes it might be appropriate to ask the parent or a care assistant to accompany the pupil to provide extra help and support during the visit.

Organising emergency procedures is a fundamental part of planning an educational visit. All participants, including staff, pupils and parents, should know who will take charge in an emergency during the educational visit and what their individual responsibilities are in the event of an emergency. The group leader would usually take charge in an emergency and must ensure that emergency procedures, including back up cover have been arranged. (See section on dealing with accidents and injuries in Chapter 5.)

Ten Golden Rules for maintaining pupil safety during educational visits

All outings with pupils should be both safe and enjoyable, so to make this possible you should work with the teacher and follow these ten Golden Rules:

1. Check the educational visit is suitable for the ages and levels of development of the pupils participating.

2. Obtain written permission from the children's parents.

3. Ensure the destination, leaving time and expected return times are written down.

4. Know how to get there, the location, route and mode of transport.

5. Check the seasonal conditions, weather and time available.

6. Assess any potential dangers or risks, such as activities near water, suitability and safety of playground equipment.

7. Carry essential information/equipment such as identification, emergency contact numbers, mobile phone, first aid, spare clothing, food, money, and any essential medication.

8. Make sure you and the pupils are suitably dressed for the occasion, for example sensible shoes or boots for walks; waterproof clothing for wet weather; sunhat and sun screen in hot weather; clean, tidy clothes for cinema, theatre, museum visits, etc.

9. Ensure the correct number of children is accountable throughout the outing.

10. All participants, including staff, children and parents, should know who will take charge in an emergency during the outing and what their individual responsibilities are in the event of an emergency (see Chapter 5.)

Figure 15.3: Teaching assistant with pupils on educational visit

 Key Task

- Outline your role and responsibilities with regard to maintaining pupil safety during educational visits and out-of-school activities.
- Give a reflective account of your involvement on an educational visit.

NOS Links:

Level 3:   **STL 3. 1   STL 3.2   STL 31.1   STL 31.2   STL 32.1   STL 32.2   STL 58.1   STL 58.2**

Summary of key points in this chapter:

- **Leading extra-curricular activities** including: preparing children and young people for an extra-curricular activity; introducing children and young people to an extra-curricular activity; leading an extra-curricular activity; encouraging effective working relationships during an extra-curricular activity.

- **Helping to organise the learning environment** including: adequate floor space for the age, size and needs of the pupils; appropriate sources of heating, lighting and ventilation; appropriate acoustic conditions; adequate storage space; organising classroom resources; checking classroom resources; encouraging pupils to help maintain their learning environment.

- **Organising travel for children and young people** including: helping to supervise pupils on educational trips and out-of-school activities; maintaining pupil safety during educational visits.

Further reading

Cheminais, R. (2007) *Extended Schools & Children's Centres: A Practical Guide*. David Fulton Publishers.

Constable, D. (2005) *The Teaching Assistant's Pocketbook*. Teachers' Pocketbook. (Includes section on extra-curricular activities.)

Dean, J. (2001) *Organising Learning in the Primary School* Classroom. Routledge.

DfEE (1998) *Health and Safety of Pupils on Educational Visits: A Good Practice Guide*. DfEE.

DfES (2006) *Learning Outside the Classroom*. DfES.

Gordon, L. (2002) *52 After School Activities*. Chronicle Books.

Holmes, E. (2007) *FAQs for TAs: Practical Advice and Working Solutions for Teaching Assistants*. Routledge.

Miller, F.P. et al. (2010) *After-school Activity*. VDM Publishing House.

Preston, A. (2003) *Yards of Playground Fun*. Educational Printing Services Ltd.

Bibliography

Alexander, R. et al. (2009) *Introducing the Cambridge Primary Review*. Cambridge: University of Cambridge.

ATL (2000) 'ATL guide to children's attitudes' in *Report*. June/July issue. London: Association of Teachers and Lecturers.

ATL (2002) *Achievement For All: Working with Children with Special Educational Needs in Mainstream Schools and Colleges*. London: Association of Teachers and Lecturers.

ATL (2007) *Statutory Rights: Support Staff in the Maintained Sector*. London: Association of Teachers and Lecturers.

Ball, C. (1994) *Start Right: The Importance of Early Learning*. London: RSA.

Balshaw, M. and **Farrell**, P. (2002) *Teaching Assistants: Practical Strategies for Effective Classroom Support*. London: David Fulton Publishers.

Bartholomew, L. and **Bruce**, T. (1993) *Getting To Know You: A Guide to Record-Keeping in Early Childhood Education and Care*. London: Hodder & Stoughton.

BDA (1997) *Dyslexia: An Introduction for Parents, Teachers and Others with an Interest in Dyslexia*. London: British Dyslexia Association.

Becta (2004) *Data Protection and Security: A Summary for Schools*. Coventry: British Educational Communications and Technology Agency.

Becta (2006) British Educational Communications and Technology Agency website: **www.becta.org.uk**

Booth, T. and **Swann**, W. (eds) (1987) *Including Pupils with Disabilities*. Milton Keynes: Open University Press.

Bostock, L. (2004) *Promoting Resilience in Fostered Children and Young People*. London: Social Care Institute for Excellence.

Brennan, W.K. (1987) *Changing Special Education Now*. Milton Keynes: Open University Press.

Bruce, T. and **Meggitt**, C. (2002) *Child Care and Education*. Third revised edition. London: Hodder Arnold.

Burton, G. and **Dimbleby**, R. (1995) *Between Ourselves: An Introduction to Interpersonal Communication*. Revised edition. London: Hodder Arnold.

CAPT (2002) *Taking Chances: The Lifestyles and Leisure Risks of Young People*. London: Child Accident Prevention Trust.

CAPT (2004a) *Factsheet: Children and Accidents*. London: Child Accident Prevention Trust.

CAPT (2004b) *Factsheet: Playground Accidents*. London: Child Accident Prevention Trust.

CRE (1989) *From Cradle to School: Practical Guide to Race Equality and Childcare*. London: Commission for Racial Equality.

CWDC (2007) *Learning Mentor Practice Guide*. Leeds: Children's Workforce Development Council.

CYPU (2001) *Learning to Listen: Core Principles for the Involvement of Children and Young People*. Children and Young People's Unit. London: DfES.

Cunningham, B. (1993) *Child Development*. London: HarperCollins.

Davies, R. (1984) 'Social development and social behaviour' (see **Fontana**, D.)

DCMS (2004) *Getting Serious about Play: A Review of Children's Play*. London: Department for Culture Media & Sport.

DCSF (2007) *The Early Years Foundation Stage – Effective Practice: Play and Exploration*. London: DCSF.

DCSF (2008a) *Information Sharing: Guidance for Practitioners and Managers*. London: DCSF & Communities and Local Government.

DCSF (2008b) *Practice Guidance for the Early Years Foundation Stage*. Revised edition. London: DCSF.

DCSF (2008c) *Statutory Framework for the Early Years Foundation Stage*. Revised edition. London: DCSF.

DCSF (2009) *Promoting and Supporting Positive Behaviour in Primary Schools: Developing Social and Emotional Aspects of Learning (SEAL)*. London: DCSF.

DCSF (2010a) *The Use of Force to Control or Restrain Pupils: Guidance for Schools in England*. London: DCSF.

DCSF (2010b) *Working Together to Safeguard Children: A Guide to Inter-Agency Working to Safeguard and Promote the Welfare of Children*. London: DCSF.

DfEE (1998) *Health and Safety of Pupils on Educational Visits: A Good Practice Guide*. London: DfEE.

DfEE (2000a) *Learning Journey* [3–7 and 7–11]. London: DfEE.

DfEE (2000b) *Learning Journey* [11–16]. London: DfEE.

DfEE (2000c) *Guidance – Roles of Governing Bodies and Head Teachers*. London: DfEE.

DfES (1998) *The National Literacy Strategy – Framework for Teaching YR to Y6*. London: DfES.

DfES (1999) *The National Numeracy Strategy – Framework for Teaching Mathematics from Reception to Y6*. London: DfES.

DfES (2000) *Bullying: Don't Suffer in Silence – An Anti-Bullying Pack For Schools*. London: DfES.

DfES (2001) *The Special Educational Needs Code of Practice 2001*. London: HMSO.

DfES (2003a) *Electronic Adult Numeracy Core Curriculum with Access for All*. London: DfES.

DfES (2003b) *Key Stage 3 National Strategy Advice on Whole School Behaviour and Attendance Policy*. London: DfES.

DfES (2003c) *Primary National Strategy – Speaking, Listening, Learning: Working With Children in Key Stages 1 and 2 Handbook*. London: DfES.

DfES (2004) *Every Child Matters: Change for Children*. London: DfES.

DfES (2005a) *Common Core of Skills and Knowledge for the Children's Workforce*. London: DfES.

DfES (2005b) *Primary National Strategy: KEEP – Key Elements of Effective Practice*. London: DfES.

DfES (2005c) *Ethnicity and Education: The Evidence on Minority Ethnic Pupils*. London: DfES.

DfES (2006a) *Primary Framework for Literacy and Mathematics*. London: DfES.

DfES (2006b) *What To Do If You're Worried a Child is Being Abused*. London: DfES.

DfES/DH (2005) *Managing Medicines in Schools and Early Years Settings*. London: DfES/Department of Health.

DH (1991) *The Children Act 1989 Guidance and Regulations N Volume 2: Family Support, Day Care and Educational Provision for Young Children*. London: HMSO.

DH (2000) *Assessing Children in Need and their Families: Practice Guidance*. London: The Stationery Office.

DH (2009) *Birth to Five: 2009 Edition*. London: Department of Health.

Donaldson, M. (1978) *Children's Minds*. London: Fontana.

Douch, P. (2004) 'What does inclusive play actually look like?' in *Playtoday*. Issue 42, May/June.

Drummond, M. et al. (1984) *Making Assessment Work*. Swindon: NFER Nelson.

Dunn, K. et al (2003) *Developing Accessible Play Space: A Good Practice Guide*. London: ODPM.

Elliott, M. (2002) *Bullying: A Practical Guide to Coping for Schools*. Third edition. Harlow: Pearson Education in association with Kidscape.

Fontana, D. (1994) 'Personality and personal development' in D. Fontana (ed.) *The Education of the Young Child*. Oxford: Blackwell.

Foster-Cohen, S. (1999) *Introduction to Child Language Development*. Harlow: Longman.

Fox, G. (1998) *A Handbook for Learning Support Assistants*. London: David Fulton Publishers.

Griffin, S. (2008) *Inclusion, Equality and Diversity in Working with Children*. London: Heinemann.

Goleman, D. (1996) *Emotional intelligence*. London: Bloomsbury.

Harding, J. and **Meldon-Smith**, L. (2001) *How to Make Observations and Assessments*. Second Edition. London: Hodder & Stoughton.

HSE (2004) *Getting to Grips with Manual Handling: A Short Guide*. Leaflet INDG143 (rev2) London: Health and Safety Executive Books.

HSE (2006) *Health and Safety Law: What You Should Know*. London: Health and Safety Executive Books.

HPA (2001) *Nutrition Matters for the Early Years: Guidance for Feeding Under Fives in the Childcare Setting*. Belfast: Health Promotion Agency.

Houghton, D. and **McColgan**, M. (1995) *Working With Children*. London: Collins Educational.

Hutchcroft, D. (1981) *Making Language Work*. London: McGraw-Hill.

ILAM (1999) *Indoor Play Areas: Guidance on Safe Practice*. Reading: Institute of Leisure and Amenity Management.

Johnstone, D. (2001) *An Introduction to Disability Studies*. London: David Fulton Publishers.

Kamen, T. (2000) *Psychology for Childhood Studies*. London: Hodder & Stoughton.

Kamen, T. (2005) *The Playworker's Handbook*. London: Hodder Arnold.

Kamen, T. (2008) *Teaching Assistant's Handbook Second edition*. London: Hodder Arnold.

Kay, J. (2002) *Teaching Assistant's Handbook*. London: Continuum.

Kirby, P. et al. (2003) *Building a Culture of Participation: Involving Children and Young People in Policy, Service Planning, Delivery and Evaluation – Handbook*. London: DfES.

Knowles, G. (2009) *Ensuring Every Child Matters*. London: Sage Publications.

Laing, A. and **Chazan**, M. (1994) 'Young children with special needs' (see **Fontana**, D. 1994).

Leach, P (1994) *Children First*. London: Penguin.

Lee, V. and **Das Gupta**, P. (eds) (1995) *Children's Cognitive and Language Development*. Oxford: Blackwell.

Light, P. et al. (eds) (1991) *Learning to Think*. London: Routledge.

Lindenfield, G. (1995) *Self Esteem*. London: Thorsons.

Lindon, J. (1999) *Too Safe for Their own Good? Helping Children Learn about Risk and Lifeskills*. London: National Early Years Network.

Lindon (2002) *What is Play? Children's Play Information Service Factsheet*. London: National Children's Bureau.

Lindon, J. (2007) *Understanding Children and Young People: Development from 5–18 years*. London: Hodder Arnold.

Lindon, J. (2008) *Safeguarding Children and Young People: Child Protection 0–18 years*. 3rd Edition. London: Hodder Education.

Matterson, E. (1989) *Play with a Purpose for the Under Sevens*. London: Penguin.

Meadows, S. (1993) *Child as Thinker: The Development of Cognition in Childhood*. London: Routledge.

Miller, L. (2002) *Observation Observed: An Outline of the Nature and Practice of Infant Observation*. London: Tavistock Clinic Foundation.

Moon, A. (1992) 'Take care of yourself' in *Child Education*, February issue. Leamington Spa: Scholastic.

Morris, J. and **Mort**, J. (1997) *Bright Ideas for the Early Years: Learning Through Play*. Leamington Spa: Scholastic.

Moyle, D. (1976) *The Teaching of Reading*. London: Ward Lock Educational.

Mulvaney, A. (1995) *Talking with Kids*. Sydney: Simon & Schuster.

Munn, P. et al (1992) *Effective Discipline in Secondary Schools and Classrooms*. London: Paul Chapman Publishing Ltd.

NAGC (2007) *Fact Sheet: Able Children's Needs*. Milton Keynes: National Association for Gifted Children.

National Commission on Education (1993) *Learning to Succeed*. London: Heinemann.

NDNA (2004) *National Occupational Standards in Children's Care, Learning and Development*. Brighouse: National Day Nurseries Association.

NPFA et al (2000) *Best Play: What Play Provision Should do for Children*. London: National Playing Fields Association.

O'Hagan, M. and **Smith**, M. (1994) *Special Issues in Child Care*. London: Bailliere Tindall.

Parsloe, E. (1999) *The Manager as Coach and Mentor*. London: Chartered Institute of Personnel & Development.

Petrie, P. (1997) *Communication with Children and Adults: Interpersonal Skills for Early Years and Play Work*. Second edition. London: Arnold.

Play Wales and PlayEducation (2001) *The First Claim: A Framework for Playwork Quality Assessment*. Cardiff: Play Wales.

Prisk, T. (1987) 'Letting them get on with it: a study of unsupervised group talk in an infant school' in A. Pollard (ed.) *Children and their Primary Schools*. London: Falmer Press.

QCA (2001) *Planning for Learning in the Foundation Stage*. London: Qualifications and Curriculum Authority.

QCA (2005) *ICT in the Foundation Stage*. London: Qualifications and Curriculum Authority.

RoSPA (2004a) *Play Safety Information Sheet: Information Sheet Number 16 – Legal Aspects of Safety on Children's Play Areas*. Birmingham: Royal Society for the Prevention of Accidents.

RoSPA (2004b) *Play Safety Information Sheet: Information Sheet Number 25 – Risk assessment of Children's Play Areas*. Birmingham: Royal Society for the Prevention of Accidents.

Sameroff, A. (1991) 'The social context of development' in M. Woodhead et al. (eds) *Becoming a Person*. London: Routledge.

Scottish Executive (2006) *Nutritional Guidance for Early Years: Food Choices for Children Aged 1 – 5 Years in Early Education and Childcare Settings*. Scottish Executive.

Sirjai-Blatchford, I. (1994) *The Early Years: Laying the Foundations for Racial Equality*. Stoke-on-Trent: Trentham Books.

SkillsActive (2004) *National Occupational Standards NVQ/SVQ Level 3 in Playwork*. London: SkillsActive.

Smart, C. (2001) *Special Educational Needs Policy*. Abbots Bromley: Special Educational Needs Press.

Steiner, B. et al. (1993) *Profiling, Recording and Observing – A Resource Pack for the Early Years*. London: Routledge.

Street, C. (2002) *The Benefits of Play*. Highlight No.195. London: National Children's Bureau.

Taylor, J. (1973) *Reading and Writing in the First School*. London: George Allen and Unwin.

TDA (2006) *Primary Induction: Role and Context – For Teaching Assistant Trainers*. London: Training and Development Agency for Schools.

TDA (2007) *National Occupational Standards for Supporting Teaching and Learning in Schools*. London: Training and Development Agency for Schools.

Tharp and **Gallimore** (1991) 'A theory of teaching as assisted performance' (see **Light**, P. 1991).

Tobias, C. (1996) *The Way They Learn*. Colorado Springs: Focus on the Family Publishing.

Tough, J. (1976) *Listening to Children Talking*. London: Ward Lock Educational.

Tough, J. (1994) 'How young children develop and use language' (see **Fontana**, D. 1994).

Turnbull, A. (2006) *Children's Transitions: A Literature Review*. Cambridge: Cambridgeshire Children's Fund.

Vogler, P. et al. (2008) *Early Childhood Transitions Research: A Review of Concepts, Theory and Practice*. The Hague: Bernard van Leer Foundation.

Watkinson, A. (2003) *The Essential Guide for Competent Teaching Assistants*. London: David Fulton Publishers.

Whitehead, M. (1996) *The Development of Language and Literacy*. London: Hodder & Stoughton.

Wood, D. (1991) 'Aspects of teaching and learning' (see **Light**, P. 1991).

Wood, D. (1998) *How Children Think and Learn*. Second edition. Oxford: Blackwell Publishing.

Woodhead, M. (1991) 'Psychology and the cultural construction of children's needs' in M. Woodhead et al. (ed) (1991) *Growing Up in a Changing Society*. London: Routledge.

Woolfson, R. (1991) *Children with Special Needs: A Guide for Parents and Carers*. London: Faber & Faber.

Yardley, A. (1994) 'Understanding and encouraging children's play' (see **Fontana**, D. 1994).

Index

Note: page numbers in **bold** refer to keyword definitions.